PENGUIN BOOKS

UNHOLY PILGRIMS

Tom Trumble has lived his whole life in Melbourne, and has made a range of poor career choices involving hospitality, journalism, policy development, data entry, envelope stuffing and book retailing. He has studied music and journalism. He is looking for a real job.

UNHOLY PILGRIMS

HOW ONE MAN THOUGHT WALKING 800 KILOMETRES ACROSS SPAIN WOULD SORT OUT HIS LIFE

TOM TRUMBLE

PENGUIN BOOKS

PENGUIN BOOKS

Published by the Penguin Group
Penguin Group (Australia)
250 Camberwell Road, Camberwell, Victoria 3124, Australia
(a division of Pearson Australia Group Pty Ltd)
Penguin Group (USA) Inc.
375 Hudson Street, New York, New York 10014, USA
Penguin Group (Canada)
90 Eglinton Avenue East, Suite 700, Toronto, Canada ON M4P 2Y3
(a division of Pearson Penguin Canada Inc.)
Penguin Books Ltd
80 Strand, London WC2R 0RL England
Penguin Ireland
25 St Stephen's Green, Dublin 2, Ireland
(a division of Penguin Books Ltd)
Penguin Books India Pvt Ltd
11 Community Centre, Panchsheel Park, New Delhi – 110 017, India
Penguin Group (NZ)
67 Apollo Drive, Rosedale, North Shore 0632, New Zealand
(a division of Pearson New Zealand Ltd)
Penguin Books (South Africa) (Pty) Ltd
24 Sturdee Avenue, Rosebank, Johannesburg 2196, South Africa

Penguin Books Ltd, Registered Offices: 80 Strand, London WC2R 0RL, England

First published by Penguin Group (Australia), 2011

10 9 8 7 6 5 4 3 2 1

Cover and text design by Adam Laszczuk © Penguin Group (Australia)
Front cover photograph by Andrea Pistolesi / Photolibrary (town) and
    Antonio Molero / Photolibrary (statue)
Back cover photograph Mikhail Zahranichny / Shutterstock
Typeset in Fairfield Light by Sunset Publishing Services, Brisbane, Queensland
Printed and bound in Australia by McPherson's Printing Group, Maryborough, Victoria

National Library of Australia
Cataloguing-in-Publication data:

    Trumble, Tom.
    Unholy pilgrims / Tom Trumble.
    9780143205852 (pbk.)
    Christian pilgrims and pilgrimages – Spain – Santiago de Compostela.
    Santiago de Compostela (Spain) – Description and travel, Northern – Description and travel.

    946.11

penguin.com.au

TO MUM AND DAD,
WITH LOVE AND GRATITUDE

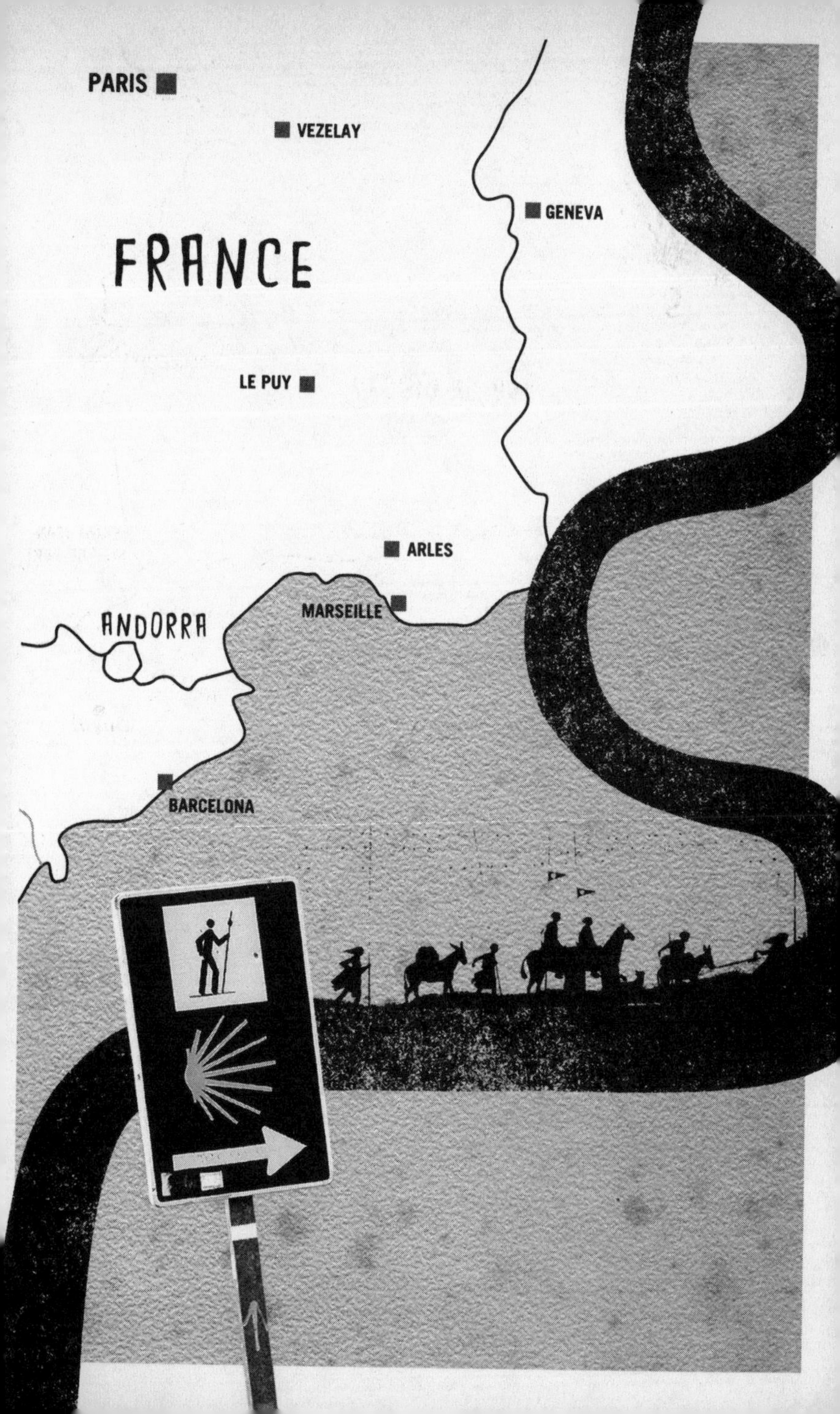

PARIS
VEZELAY
GENEVA
FRANCE
LE PUY
ARLES
MARSEILLE
ANDORRA
BARCELONA

PROLOGUE

The idea to walk 800 kilometres across northern Spain was not my own. My good friend Dave had convinced me. This is a statement of fact rather than an attempt to apportion blame. That said, he knew from the beginning that in spirit and physique I'm not exactly what you'd describe as the 'pilgrim type'. As a man with a taste for tobacco and saturated fats, I am not amenable to long walks. And yet I can't dismiss the whole exercise as born of misplaced exuberance; it wasn't a commitment made in a fit of drunken stupidity. This was a calculated, well-thought-out decision that began with a pledge.

Dave and I would leave Saint-Jean-Pied-de-Port in the French Pyrenees on the first day of October and arrive in Santiago de Compostela on the last day of the month. We would conclude our journey with pilgrim mass the next day – All Saints' Day. Neither of us was devoutly religious, but we knew this to be a significant enough date in the Christian calendar for the clergy to roll out the *botafumeiro*, Santiago Cathedral's giant thurible. Some form of celebration would be appropriate to mark our journey's completion. Inhaling plumes of incense billowing out of a 60-kilogram censer swung from transept to transept would do just fine.

Sticking to the timeline was no less important than adhering to the two conditions of the pledge. Firstly, we had to lodge the entire way in the albergue (pronounced ul-ber-gay) network, the accommodation dedicated to pilgrims. Secondly, under no circumstances were we to receive vehicular assistance. The pledge gave us boundaries, presented a challenge. But I'd invested more in this pilgrimage than just honouring a pact with an old mate.

In quitting my job I had knowingly created a break in the routine of things. For the moment, I would stay the inexorable march towards thirty and the decade of mortgage, marriage and kids. To be honest, chucking in work wasn't a big deal. I was not exactly holding down the sort of high-powered position that would catapult me into the corporate stratosphere. I was working as a data-entry operator for an energy retailer. My closest work colleague was a man who had changed his name by deed poll to 'John Citizen' and walked around the office carrying a four-foot cactus. John's competence in punching gas-meter reads into a computer was matched by his skill in stealing cutlery and condiments from the office kitchen.

These were dark times indeed. I needed to get out of the country to clear my head and work things out. I wasn't asking for much, just an idea that could be parlayed into a career. Somewhere along those 800 kilometres of ancient path a moment of clarity was just waiting to be experienced. So I accepted Dave's offer. He would meet me in the French village at the foot of a Pyrenean mountain pass on the last day of September. After a night's rest, we would walk the Camino Francés, the Way from France, the most popular and historic of the many routes that comprise the Camino de Santiago de Compostela.

Beforehand, Dave would travel through Europe with his wife from their home in Granada, leaving me three months to get in shape. My physical training didn't require whole-sale life changes. I walked twenty minutes to and from work and cut down on my smoking. The real regime was all about educating myself on the pilgrimage's history. From monastic orders and military orders and the lives of saints and ancient pilgrim rites, to dynastic wars and Moorish skirmishes and vile despots and chivalrous knights, I read it all. I even managed to download a translation of the French priest Aimery Picaud's twelfth-century travelogue. The multi-volume *Codex Calixtinus* (named in honour of Pope Calixtus II) described every detail of Picaud's experience on the Camino Francés. Nine centuries on, I would be walking the same path.

Perhaps it was the built-in romance of my pilgrimage that snared me, that marriage of ancient history and personal quest. Not once did the possibility that I'd encounter hardship on the Camino ever enter my mind. I was thinking about cloudless blue days, snow-capped peaks, leaves carried on the autumnal breeze and deer scampering across the path. I was thinking about San Miguel beer and sangria and tapas and sultry flamenco dancers igniting a room to the sound of a strident guitar. And I was thinking about me – a bronzed Aussie carrying the pilgrim accessories of staff and gourd and carling felt cap – sending one of those passionate black-haired women of the Iberian Peninsula into a weak-kneed stupor with a manfully deployed wink.

Thoughts like these got me through those final two months of work. Before I knew it, I was sitting at Bayonne Station in the south of France, waiting to board the train for Saint-Jean-Pied-de-Port. I hoped it wouldn't be late. I had an appointment to keep with an old friend.

The moment I alighted the train at Saint-Jean-Pied-de-Port marked my transition from tourist to pilgrim. I shared this moment with a dozen or so others who had taken the train from Bayonne. As we ambled towards the centre of Saint-Jean, I pondered whether our long-dead pilgrim kin were looking down on us with pride from their place in Paradise. After more closely surveying our party, I suspected they were wondering whether the circus had just come to town.

A portly man of a Mediterranean hue led the group while chastising his pilgrim companion in vitriolic Spanish. He looked ridiculous. He wore a disastrous ensemble of tattered old garb and new-fangled pieces of hiking gear, no doubt purchased at great expense on the insistence of some website. His faded football shirt and extremely tight running shorts struggled to meet the demands of a frame that was looking desperately for a way out. They were clothes that harked back to more athletic days, which, judging from his new hiking boots, he was hoping to recapture while on pilgrimage.

Bouncing alongside him was an immaculately turned out young lady with her blonde hair in a bun. She wore sparkling white runners, fluorescent pink leggings and a singlet top that seemed inadequate for the crisp breeze of the Pyrenees. Had it not been for the cockleshell strung around her neck, I would have written her off as a Parisian touring the south of France.

Walking laboriously at the side of the pack was a slim man with closely cropped salt-and-pepper hair and silver-rimmed glasses. The audible wheeze that rode on the bow of each breath told of a life dedicated to cigarettes. He smoked one now, pulling out every milligram of tar as greedily as a leech draws blood. I thought about asking whether he'd packed a defibrillator for the journey ahead, but then I was in no position to judge.

My blue jeans drooped over six-year-old hiking boots that each had a small but ominous-looking hole around the bridge of the toe. Sweat marks had already formed along the straps of my dusty old backpack and the stitching of my baseball cap looked ready to evaporate into thin air. But for my top-of-the-line retractable walking pole, my worn-out gear might have lent an air of mountaineering experience. The pole did not complete the whole outfit, however, so much as contradict it. It was an eleventh-hour purchase made in the hope that such an accessory might magically make up for my being out of shape.

There were others: a gangly man in chinos and a beret; four older women looking like they were off to a game of bridge; a nervous-looking fellow leafing through a guidebook, trying to identify his whereabouts. This was a party that looked ready for a stiff drink and a lie-down rather than an 800-kilometre haul across Spain.

We began to disperse as we entered the town proper. Some checked into hotels while others – including the smoker, whose cough had developed a jagged edge – slid off into an appealing bar placed at the base of an unappealing rise.

Those of us who were left headed further into the old town. I paused for a moment where two winding cobblestone paths met and looked about. The day was yawning to a close and the city of Saint-Jean was nearly at rest in the mountain's shade. Tasteful sandstone buildings fashioned with wooden shutters and sharply elongated roofs sat on either side of me. Abstract shadows cast by street lamps decorated a Volkswagen parked treasonously between a Peugeot and a Renault. I closed my eyes and allowed myself a smile. I was in the south of France and at the dawn of something magnificent.

'Don't tell me it has happened already,' came a familiar voice.

'What are you talking about?' I said, spinning around to greet my old friend.

'If I didn't know better,' said Dave, 'I'd say you'd become a spiritualist before we've even set foot on the Camino.'

'That's got to be better than a born-again Christian.'

'In that case, I'll give you some privacy to meditate. You can find me in the bar drinking San Miguel.'

This went on for a while before we shook hands and made for the pilgrim's office up the hill. We fell into a conversation that covered the events of the months since last we'd met. Here we were at last, breathing alpine air in the shadow of the Pyrenees, having a tête-à-tête on a cobblestoned road in a French village. The real world and chest-tightening thoughts of responsibility, finding a job and paying off credit cards seemed to collapse away until they were as distant and remote as my homeland.

'Are youse blokes Aussie?' emerged a voice behind us, its drawn-out accent causing us both to halt sharply and look around.

Seated on the gutter was a shaven-headed man in his mid twenties, a cigarette jutting out the corner of his mouth. He mistook our temporary loss of speech for a hardness of hearing and repeated his question, louder than before. 'Are *youse* fuckin' blokes Aussie?'

'Ah . . . yeah, mate,' said Dave, recovering his poise. 'I'm Dave and this is Tom. How's it going?'

'How are ya, boys?' said the young man, accepting Dave's hand and nearly shaking it off. 'I'm Warren. This is Jack and Steve.' He waggled a crooked finger in the direction of an unassuming-looking pair of identical twins sitting on the other side of the road.

'It's good to hear some Aussie accents,' said Warren, glancing about. 'Not that this place is too bad, I suppose.'

Warren spent the next few minutes outlining their aspirations while on pilgrimage. Reading between his sharp-tongued lines it was clear they were preparing for five weeks of sex and booze. These were boys with wallets crammed with freshly minted credit cards and loins swollen on the promise of exotic women with a weakness for Australian accents. This was their chance to continue their days of teenage intemperance. They were Aussies on tour. I was not judging them. In travelling across the planet to sort out my life, I felt I had forfeited any right to be critical of other people's motivations for walking the Camino.

We farewelled the boys and then made for the pilgrim's office. The pilgrims spilling out the front door of a building below a giant cockleshell, the symbol of the Camino, suggested we had arrived at our first destination. The square-shaped registration lobby inside was converted into a kind of pilgrim war room. Its walls were covered in large maps of every kind – topographical, topological, satellite. There were weather charts, too, as well as lists of *refugios* and albergues and diagrams tracking pilgrim movements along the trail. These people were not preparing us for a hike. They were preparing us for battle.

Dave and I sat down in front of a French woman who apologised at the end of each sentence for not knowing a syllable of English. *'Je suis désolé!'* Dave's fluent Spanish was no help and neither was my schoolboy French; it was a subject I'd abandoned, having repeatedly failed to conjugate the bloody verb. We communicated instead through a series of gestures. She issued us both our *credencial del peregrino* – the pilgrim passport, which would permit entry into the albergue network along the Way – and a topographical map of the Camino Francés.

After we'd paid our two-euro donation, she pushed a dusty book the size of a photo album in front of us. The columns on each page marked a space for our name, date of birth, nationality, occupation and a small message. I looked at the occupations of my pilgrim brethren expecting to find priests, prophets, mediums and oracles. With mild disappointment, I saw lawyers, doctors, teachers, public servants, accountants and bankers. Apart from the odd student, the modern Camino de Santiago would seem to be the preserve of the bourgeoisie. My pen loitered above the page while I contemplated what to write. I scribbled something down and handed the book to Dave, who copied my job description: unemployed.

We walked to our accommodation in darkness, the sun having retired early behind the giant mountains that surrounded us. A cool gust cut through. It was a westerly wind sent from somewhere along the Camino that carried the promise of a new season. We found a bar for a drink and then headed to the albergue.

And on the next day we went to walk to Santiago de Compostela.

PART ONE

FILLING UP ON SPIRIT

OCTOBER 1
SHATTERED CHAKRAS

Dave and I stood before the archway of the Porte Saint Jacques in Saint-Jean-Pied-de-Port, the gateway to the Camino Francés. We were set to follow in the footsteps of the millions whose shoes had polished the stones of the road to Santiago. Our motives for walking might not have been those of traditional pilgrims – piety and veneration – but Dave at least had something of the pilgrim's physical hardiness. He had powerful legs and toned arms. But for his short hair and fair complexion, Dave could have been a Sherpa poised to tackle a Himalayan ascent. The sight of him prompted me to loosen a notch on my belt.

I'd read that a pilgrim sheds 10 per cent of their body weight walking the Camino. During the Australian winter just past, I had seen this as an invitation to bulk up. Any suggestion of corpulence I waved off: I was carbo-loading before the big walk. Now, at the start of an 800-kilometre hike, I was experiencing the unwelcome sensation of top-heaviness. No matter, I thought, picturing the motley crew I'd met yesterday, pilgrims come in all shapes and sizes.

13

From Saint-Jean there are two paths leading into Spain. The Ibañeta Pass is the route that has carried the armies of Charlemagne and Napoleon over the Pyrenees. The other is a modern road slickly asphalted, recommended in poor weather or for those with bad hearts. Dave and I would take the route of the emperors.

We'd mapped out a twenty-nine-stage itinerary that allowed for two rest days. The stages averaged out at about 27 kilometres of walking each day and would have us in Santiago on the last day of October. We had accounted for fluctuations in our speed, depending on the steepness of the terrain, and other variables such as the availability of accommodation, injuries, wet weather and hangovers. On the whole it was more a rough guide than a fixed schedule.

Stage one stretched 25 kilometres, mostly uphill followed by a plunge into Roncesvalles, the Valley of Thorns. This stage was one of the most challenging along the Camino. For bodies not yet acclimatised to the Pyrenean altitude and untested by day-long hikes it was an utter stinker. Standing in the gateway, I was hit in the face with a freezing gust of wind. It heralded a stark realisation: I was not prepared for what lay ahead.

Dave was away, his walking pole setting a metronomic beat on the cobblestones. The Madonna and Child carved into the archway seemed to be looking down at me, stifling a laugh. I gave my guts one more notch of relief and then stumbled after my friend.

The cobblestone path descended through Saint-Jean.

Across the River Nive we came to our first Camino way-marker, a yellow cockleshell and arrow depicted on a blue background. The arrow pointed us up a bitumen road that would become grass as we climbed through the wooded hills. Eventually the path would crest Col de Lepoeder, the second highest point of the Camino Francés.

Not yet halfway up the slope, I catalogued my ills. My pack was bullying my shoulders into a hunch, and I was struggling to keep pace with Dave. There was a chill in the air but still rivulets of sweat had formed a lagoon between my collarbones. My old shorts were beginning to give me chafe. To accommodate this last ailment I took to a cowboy swagger, which, along with my hunch, gave me the appearance of an oversized Quasimodo in running gear.

I was able to admire the Pyrenees only thanks to Dave, who stopped intermittently to allow me to catch my breath. Clouds scuttled over snow-capped peaks. Ponies in neck halters negotiated the terrain and griffon vultures soared on updrafts. It was a scene of epic tranquillity. Then Warren arrived.

'Already stopped for a breather, ya big pooftas?'

We swivelled around to see bounding up the hill the boy from Manly, every bit the drill sergeant on bivouac. He was dressed in the same tight army singlet he'd worn when we first met him, with khaki shorts and wraparound sunglasses. Like privates, the twins laboured in his wake, their heads bowed and chests heaving.

'You've taken your time today, fellas,' ventured Dave.

'Horseshit!' shouted Warren. 'We just wanted to give you ladies a head start. My map says there's a place called Orisson not much further up. I reckon we'll stop there for food. See you up there. C'mon, boys, let's give these princesses some peace and quiet.'

One of the twins mumbled something in agreement as Warren brushed past us. I caught the other's eye. I couldn't tell whether his silence was from exhaustion or fear of reprisal. This was an exacting stage, all the more so when General Patton was wielding the cane. I proffered a weak smile in solidarity, hoping it might spirit him over the pass.

Not long after Warren and the boys had stalked off ahead, a two-storey hostel came into view. According to my map, we were a measly halfway up the slope, certainly not far enough to justify a lengthy break. Even so, I welcomed the chance to eat. Out the front of the hostel pilgrims were slumped over tables in various attitudes of exhaustion, cradling cigarettes, bottles of beer and *bocadillos* (baguettes). I wasn't alone in my fatigue. We walked inside. Warren and his subordinates had already positioned themselves at the bar.

'*HOLA*,' Warren was shouting at the barmaid. '*UNA BOCA*-DILDO, *POR FAVOR*.'

'I think that's bo-kah-dee-oh, Waz,' said one twin, flicking through the pages of his *Beginner's Guide to Spanish*.

'Righto,' said Warren impatiently. '*Una bocadillo* and *una cerveza*. Hear that, boys? I know beer in any language.'

Warren threw back the brew in one go and ordered another, the barmaid looking on in wonder.

'C'mon, love,' he barked, rapping his fingers on the bar. 'This man's not a camel.' He then laughed uproariously, throwing an absurd wink in our direction. He bought another four *bocadillos* and instructed the twins to get back on the road: 'Let's put some space between us and these bloody tailgaters.'

Dave and I found a table outside and got started on our San Miguel beers and cured-ham *bocadillos* and took in the view. The sun shone brightly enough for us to pull out our caps. Only in this happy mood, with beer and *bocadillo* in hand, can one truly appreciate the Pyrenees. But given the option of casting an eye across a spectacular landscape or admiring a willowy blonde in pink leggings, the male pilgrim's choice is clear. The pious entertained unholy thoughts and smokers let their cigarettes ember out, each of us held by the sight of the small cockleshell, strung on a necklace, trampolining off the girl's chest.

Hers was a figure most likely moulded by Pilates and strict dieting. Astonishingly, she was walking towards Dave and me. I recognised her from the previous day; her hair still in a bun, her runners still spotless, her leggings as pink as ever. I was wrong about her being Parisian. Her accent was Australian.

'We haven't met but I've been watching you.' She looked to be in her early thirties but I couldn't say for sure. Those sorts of details were less engrossing than her vivid green eyes. Dave raised his eyebrows and made as if to leave the two of us alone.

'Oh! Not like that,' she laughed. 'I've been watching you, too.'

Dave, his eyebrows raised even higher, began pointedly fiddling with the ring on his left hand. Ignoring Dave, the woman continued staring at me. There was something in her gaze that prompted stirrings within. I put down my food and stood up. For the first time that day my breath was short for reasons other than my being stuffed. I hadn't come to Spain for serious romance, but I hadn't ruled it out either. I smiled warmly before she said, 'I just thought you should know that your fourth and fifth chakras are shattered.'

'Excuse me?' I said, taken aback.

'Yep, shattered – as in *completely* fucked.'

At that moment walking an ancient pilgrimage across Spain in the hope of figuring out what to do with my life seemed idiotic. It had not been the sort of thing I was comfortable about announcing at farewell dinners, but I needed some sort of excuse to satisfy curious friends and worried relatives. I guess I was hoping that my reasoning could be explained through the prism of some elaborate social theory – as part of a generational phenomenon rather than simply embarrassing naivety. How else could I justify my willingness to use the phrases 'journey of self-discovery' and 'spiritual quest' and spend the little money I had left to walk across a foreign country? Frankly, it wasn't that far-fetched. I had been, after all, born in the boom time of the self-help book, an era in which achievement was predicated not on hard work, but on meditation, yoga and soggy cliché. Indeed, for twenty-five dollars and a night of very light reading I discovered that thinking happy thoughts was the secret to success, adulation, love and untold riches. With this in mind, my journey might be seen as the consequence of living in a world where second-rate gurus converted hapless punters to kooky spiritualism. 'He was but a victim of cod philosophy,' they would say, 'a man who not only bought the books but flew to the other side of the globe to live the dream.' But when I pared back all those fatuous excuses for throwing in my job, the truth was decidedly uglier. I was running away.

Maybe it was fate that had put me on a path where oddly dressed women were on the lookout for shattered chakras. I don't usually go in for all that predetermination stuff, but if walking to Santiago was part of some master plan, then meeting this woman at the beginning made perfect sense.

'I'm sorry, who *are* you?' I asked.

'I've never seen anything like it before,' she muttered, ignoring my question. 'You have some serious issues to work out. Who knows, by the time you've finished the pilgrimage, your chakras might have even begun to heal. My name's Sally.'

'What the hell are chakras?' The tension in my voice caught the attention of a few nearby pilgrims, who were now staring in my direction. Not for the first time that day did the reality of this pilgrimage seem a long way removed from what I'd imagined. The women of the Camino weren't sexy raven-haired Spaniards as I'd hoped, but blonde nutjobs from my own country.

'They're focal points in your fourth dimension that

govern the reception and transmission of energy. There are six chakras stacked in a column from the base of the spine to the middle of the forehead. The seventh chakra is, of course, beyond the physical realm. Anyway, two of yours are broken.'

'The fourth and fifth,' said Dave matter-of-factly. 'How are my chakras?' He was really enjoying this.

'Completely intact. You are incredibly centred. Your energy is vibrant and creative.'

Dave slapped my shoulder. 'Bad luck, mate.' She told us that she would love to talk some more about her specialisation in enlightenment and rebirthing clinics back in Sydney, but she had to keep walking to harness all the energy out there. With that, she turned on her heel and set off at a fearsome clip.

'Wait,' I shouted after her, 'how do I fix my bloody chakras?'

'Just keep walking,' she said over her shoulder, the cockleshell now dancing cheerily on her backpack.

'What a weirdo, huh?' I said to Dave after Sally had slipped out of sight.

'I wouldn't say that,' he said, standing up alongside me and putting on his backpack. 'I wonder if she does tarot readings, too? From the sound of things, I'm barrelling towards a sparkling future.'

'From the sound of things, my life is going to the shithouse.'

'C'mon, mate,' he said, helping me with my backpack, 'let's get to work on those buggered chakras of yours.'

We climbed upwards to where the road became a grassy

path, passing pilgrims who were struggling even more than I was. One poor man was kneeling before a statue of the Virgin placed at the path's shoulder on a particularly steep incline. Our Lady was probably put here to boost morale. With a pilgrim gasping at her feet, she cut a mournful figure.

Shortly before midday, a full five hours after setting off, we passed a crucifix that marked the summit. Nine centuries after Aimery Picaud had walked the Camino Francés, his description of the Ibañeta Pass still holds true: 'He who makes the ascent believes that, with his own hand, he can touch the sky.' After a brief look over the rooftop of France, we turned our feet for Spain.

The Camino was now mud and pebbles that skirted precipices and squeezed through steep-sided gorges. It was terrain that demanded our undivided attention. A loss in concentration along this passage might result in a twisted ankle or a nasty spill. I was lucky that the sight of Warren leading the twins in prayer caused me nothing worse than a stubbed toe. All three had their heads bowed in the direction of an unprepossessing fountain carved into a small rise at the side of the path. As we neared them, I heard Warren reciting a familiar lament.

'. . . At the going down of the sun and in the morning, we will remember them.' Warren paused. 'Lest we forget.'

Dave and I quickly removed our hats out of respect. My first reaction was one of shame. How could I have overlooked the fact that this pilgrimage took us past a memorial to my country's fallen soldiers? I recalled foggy memories of history classes at school, straining to remember which conflict brought our boys to this part of Europe. We had sustained heavy losses along the Western Front in World War One, but we were well south of any of those places.

'Warren,' I began softly, 'I don't mean to interrupt, but —'

'*Shhh!* We're observing a minute's silence.'

I turned to Dave, who shrugged his shoulders. As quietly as possible, I reached into my pack and retrieved my guidebook, opening it to the pages featuring the Ibañeta Pass. The fountain *was* a memorial to a soldier. But one who fell in a campaign earlier than the Great War. Much earlier.

'Warren,' I said after at least a minute had elapsed. 'Do you realise —'

'Are you fucking serious, mate? I thought you blokes were Aussies. Haven't you heard of the Last Post?' Warren puffed out his cheeks and hummed from the back of his throat, producing a sound more like that of a strangled possum than a bugle. Reluctantly, the twins joined in. I could see Dave biting down on his lip. He looked like he was about to draw blood. When they had finished, Warren picked up his bag, saluted the fountain and then gave me a disapproving shake of the head.

'According to my book, the soldier you just honoured was a knight called Roland. He was killed in the Battle of Roncesvalles. In 778,' I said.

'Your point being?'

'Since when was the "Ode of Remembrance" read for classical knights?'

'In *my* book it says he was a great warrior who fought for a just cause. That makes him worthy as one of our own.' Whether Charlemagne's military push into Spain in the eighth century amounted to a 'just cause' is a matter of historical conjecture. Warren was echoing the sentiment expressed in the chivalric romances glorifying the first Holy Roman Emperor. Roland, the Emperor's first knight, features prominently in these tales. We would have more brushes with the history of Roland and Charlemagne the further we walked. If Warren intended on commemorating each site, those twins would be in for a hell of a long pilgrimage. 'Don't worry about it, mate,' Warren said to me. 'You're not a digger.'

'But neither was Roland!'

'Let's leave these blokes to it,' he said to the twins. 'I thought they were patriots, but I guess I was wrong.'

'Roland was a Breton for Christ's sake!' I turned to Dave for support. 'C'mon,' he chuckled, 'let's go pay our respects to this eighth-century digger.'

Roland's fountain was metres from a sign marking the French–Spanish border. Dave and I performed our own rituals commemorating the historic site. We drank greedily from the fountain, toasting Roland, and took photos of each other, annoying tourist–style: legs astride the border, thumbs pointed upwards, grins idiotic. Then we began our descent into the valley. After spending the afternoon negotiating our way down a path lined thickly with beech trees, we arrived at Roncesvalles, the first village inside the Spanish border along the Camino Francés.

We made for the town's albergue, a converted medieval hospital with bunks arranged in infirmary-style rows. Albergues serve a crucial purpose in the modern Camino beyond just accommodating pilgrims. Each albergue has a unique insignia that is stamped and dated on the pilgrim's *credencial* or pilgrim passport. The coveted *compostela*, the document each pilgrim is entitled to at the end of walking the Camino, will only be given out after officials have examined the *credencial*. So, no stamps on your *credencial*, no *compostela* in Santiago.

The albergue network along the Camino is vast. There is at least one in every town or village no matter how small. They each fall into one of six different categories. Albergues *municipal* are owned and maintained by the local authority; albergues *privado* are privately run hostels; confraternity hostels are owned and operated by international confraternities of the Camino de Santiago; *monasterio* and *convento* albergues are run by monks and nuns respectively; and albergues *parroquia* are run by the local diocese and maintained by the parish priest. The entire network is bound by a single principle: only pilgrims bearing the *credencial*, the pilgrim passport, will be admitted.

We would discover that the rules of albergues varied according to their type. They all, however, were intended to foster a collegial spirit among pilgrims, offering physical respite and spiritual rejuvenation. The gothic severity of this albergue, with its crucifixes on grey walls, Gregorian chant music humming from the stereo and smattering of Christians showing insufferable cheer, gave us the impression that we'd be better served by a San Miguel.

After claiming our beds, we went searching for a bar. We found one that doubled as a restaurant. After knocking back a couple of rounds, we ordered our first pilgrim's menu – a prescribed three-course meal of pasta with a tomato-based sauce and plenty of cheese, a piece of mountain trout and crème brûlée.

By the time we had polished off our mains, scores of pilgrims had dribbled past the bar. They came from over the Pyrenees as we had or by bus from Pamplona and Zaragoza. We watched the parade as we tucked into dessert.

After dinner we followed the crowd to a pilgrim mass held in the Iglesia de Santa María, a church at the town's centre. It was my first church appearance for some years. I hadn't suddenly been refilled with the spirit of the Lord; there just weren't a lot of competing options. Roncesvalles, it would seem, does not possess a robust night-life. But I didn't regret going along.

The priest blessed us in eight different languages, accommodating the various nationalities represented. Many of these pilgrims I would never see again. They would fall behind or surge ahead. But at that moment, being among them, I felt a pang of significance, a sense of shared purpose. Perhaps this was the collegial spirit I'd been told about.

After the mass had finished, I shared a cigarette with a couple of Russians as we wandered back to the albergue. The first stage was behind us, one of the toughest the Camino had to offer. I took stock of my condition. I could feel welts forming around my groin, the result of chafing, my cartilage-less left knee was beginning to ache, I had been accused of being unpatriotic and someone in pink leggings had diagnosed turmoil in my fourth dimension. Things looked worrying, but I was certain that after a few more uncomfortable days, our bodies would adjust and we would be doing this on the bit. We arrived back at the albergue. This pilgrimage would be a cinch. Little did I realise that a night on the Camino is no less exacting than a day's hike over the Pyrenees.

LIKE JESUS IN THE DESERT

Dave had been holidaying in Hungary with his wife Rachel before we rendezvoused in Saint-Jean-Pied-de-Port. His flight from Budapest to Zaragoza in northern Spain had gone off without a hitch. The trip over the mountains to Saint-Jean, however, had been a harrowing affair.

Dave was among twelve pilgrims taking the bus from Zaragoza Airport to Saint-Jean. From the sound of things, the local authority should upgrade the popular bus service that carries pilgrims over the hills from Spain to their starting destination. Dave said the minibus looked to have been in service since the Spanish Civil War. Shortly after the bus had left the airport, an olive-skinned Spanish man clambered aboard in clothes that smelt as if they'd been rinsed in a vat of San Miguel and then dried above smouldering cigarettes. Once the bus had started the climb up into the mountains, he stood up and declared himself an Islamic extremist with plans to commandeer the vehicle and drive it off a cliff. It seemed unlikely that al-Qaeda was now recruiting in the public bars of northern Spain, but in the wake of the Madrid bombings and considering the region itself was no stranger to Basque separatists, such a comment was taken seriously. The bus fell silent as people searched his expression to determine whether he was for real.

After his pronouncement, the man fell back on his seat, laughing in a way that suggested serious inebriation, before passing out. The passengers were just starting to breathe normally again when the engine's shrieks through the lacerated muffler roused the would-be terrorist. He leapt into the vacant front-passenger seat, and began hurling abuse at the driver and his shitty bus. This driver was no shrinking violet and could match his aggressor's sharp tongue, but the passengers were sure he should have been focusing on the hairpin turn up ahead.

When the drunk attempted to push the driver out the bus's missing side window, Dave decided to intervene in the best fashion he knew how: a singalong. I quite enjoyed the thought of Dave on ukulele leading a dozen ashen-faced pilgrims in a rendition of 'Imagine', while the bus negotiated the road's shoulders by hitting the barriers – the only thing between the passengers and a 400-foot plunge into a Pyrenean ravine.

The night before we left Saint-Jean, Dave and I had seen the drunk Spaniard wildly waving his hiking staff around and insulting bemused bystanders. 'Surely he's not intending to walk the Camino?' I had asked.

'I think he'll have enough trouble finding his way back to the hotel,' Dave said.

You can imagine our amazement when we saw him staggering into the Roncesvalles albergue moments before lights out. He slouched towards the bed adjoining Dave's and collapsed fully clothed, staff in hand, snoring obnoxiously before he'd hit the mattress.

His snore was the stuff of a Warner Bros cartoon. Each inhale seemed to draw the drapes across the windows, each blustering exhale to rattle the metal frame of every bunk. Eventually a heavy-set German with the bearing of a Luftwaffe Kommandant strode over to the Spaniard's bunk and thundered, 'STOP ZIS SNORINK!' To no avail. Had the planet slipped into a black hole, the Spaniard would have simply snored his way to oblivion.

The following morning I found Dave sleep-deprived and irritable out the front of the albergue. He'd awoken early, preferring the bitter mountain air to the shards of tobacco-flecked snot he'd copped in the face throughout the night. We departed in silence, passing a sign built where the ancient path converged with a highway out of Roncesvalles. Santiago de Compostela was 790 kilometres away.

'Don't worry, pal,' I said. 'That's a highway sign. According to my book, on our route we have less than 775 kilometres to go.'

'Careful there, mate, or you'll be nursing more than just busted chakras.'

We walked briskly out of the town and into woodland, bound for Larrasoaña. Drizzle made my spirits as frosty as Dave's until we stumbled into a cosy café at the township of Burguete. With the help of a *tortilla* (omelette) and *café Americana* (the Spanish long black coffee), our moods were just beginning to thaw when the snoring Spaniard made his way through the café, sober and looking refreshed after a dazzling night's sleep. A number of pairs of eyes with murderous intent followed him through that café. Whoever it was who had told me about albergues cultivating a collegial spirit had clearly never slept in one.

Wearing the same red-and-black checked shirt he had slept in, the Spaniard sipped on his *Americana* and laughed with the barman; he was nothing like the razor-tongued tippler or self-proclaimed terrorist we knew him to be. He was a man of warmth and good cheer. 'I'm going to kill him,' I said to Dave, stubbing out my cigarette and pushing back my chair with my foot as I stood up.

'Relax, mate,' chided Dave, dragging me back down. 'I'll have a chat to him.'

Dave wandered over, and propped himself up on a bar stool alongside the Spaniard. He introduced himself in Spanish and fluently began a discussion that moved from what I read to be a rebuke to a heartfelt tease. Dave has never been one to hold a grudge. In this way we are quite different. 'What the hell was that all about?' I asked as Dave sat back down at our table. 'I thought you of all people would have wanted to rip that bloke's nostrils off.'

'I guess I felt sorry for him. Did you see his face?' I looked closely at the Spaniard. It was the first time I had seen him in good light. Two scars ran in crooked lines from the corners of his mouth to the base of each ear. The wounds looked to be souvenirs from a switchblade or penknife, like someone had set out to cut a smile into his face.

'He said he'd been told to walk the Camino by his priest,' continued Dave, 'but he didn't say why. There was something, I don't know, a bit tragic about him.'

I now saw a hollow look in the Spaniard's gaze. His bent grin took shape after he downed a shot of grappa. I let go of my hostility. We were all pilgrims for Santiago, departing from the same place on the same day, and I felt there was a special kinship in that. Dave and I never saw him again. I'm certain he had a lot further to walk than the two of us.

Regardless of the wet, the stage to Larrasoaña was a cakewalk. The road maintained a friendly gradient, with only minor rises and falls. Before long, we came to Zubiri, 'the town of two bridges', in the Basque country. We crossed one, an impressive Roman structure straddling the River Arga at the town's border. The bridge's central pillar is believed to contain relics of Santa Quitéria. Back before 'Santa' was affixed to her name, Quitéria was the daughter of a fifth-century Galician prince. The prince, a pagan, demanded she renounce her Christianity and marry a man of his choosing. She fled eastwards in defiance, walking across northern Spain and into France. She was captured in Gascony and decapitated by the prince's henchmen. The story then goes that Quitéria's body stood up, collected its head and made for the mountains.

In addition to taking a headless stroll through the hills,

Quitéria was said to have the ability to hold off rabid dogs with her voice alone. For this, she is the saint invoked against rabies. Legend has it that a rabid cow will be cured if walked three times around the bridge's pillar. I thought it a shame that these healing properties only applied to cows. The local dogs seemed violently diseased.

Dave and I lunched in Zubiri on chorizo that tasted as if it had been cut from the hide of one of those local wild dogs. The drizzle had become swirling rain. We chewed through the grit while sheltering under an overhanging apartment balcony on a street of considerable ugliness. Presently, a couple in their early twenties joined us to wait out the storm. Zoe and Joey were from America's deep south and within minutes it was clear they were a natural coupling. Joey was practically mute and Zoe could not be shut up.

'So, are you boys Christians? Do you believe in God Almighty and his only son, Jesus Christ?' Zoe asked, drawing breath for the first time in ten minutes.

'That's a tough question,' I said. Dave elected not to reply.

'Well, I would've thought it was a darn easy one. You are or you ain't. Which is it?'

Discussing my religion with zealots was not something I felt comfortable about. I had been baptised a Catholic and taken first communion inside a Catholic church. These were not just formalities intended to satisfy one side of my family; I really was a Catholic. During Sunday mass I would show the signs of the devout – rigid posture, genuflecting and deploying the sign of the cross. I could manage serviceable renditions of the Gloria and Agnus Dei. I'd even make sure to bring ten cents for the collection tray. But as a teenager my enthusiasm faltered. I eventually vanished from the scene altogether, like incense escaping a thurible. I partly blame our God-fearing parish priest, who, in addition to being predisposed to fiery homilies, was a fan of the Vatican II hymnbook, an abomination to the ears if ever there were one. But really I was just bored.

When my lax attendance at mass became the subject of gentle sisterly ridicule ('Tom's going to hell!'), my aunt – a nun, a great educationalist and the woman responsible for overseeing my first communion – let me off the hook. She described me as a young man with 'a broad sense of the Eucharist'. By this my aunt probably meant that I viewed the receiving of the body and blood of Christ as more than just a prescribed religious rite, but also realised that expressions of faith and obedience didn't need to be observed on a weekly basis. I used her point to justify ditching church completely. Nevertheless, I never regarded myself as an atheist.

The matter of my religiosity became confused when I enrolled at an Anglican school. In one divinity class we dealt with the prickly issue of the Catholic–Protestant dichotomy. The only Catholic in the class, I was ushered to the front of the room to act as spokesman and defender of my faith. All I knew to be different about the denominations was that Catholics believed in transubstantiation, purgatory and no sex before marriage. This elicited responses from the greying school chaplain ('So, in short, Tom believes in magic'), my friends ('Bad luck about your soul having to be cleansed in purgatory before getting into Heaven') and my enemies ('Trumble, married or not, you'll never get a root').

Apart from that instance, my being Catholic at an Anglican school was never really an issue. This had as much to do with my peers' indifference as it did with hiding my Catholic light under a bushel, as it were. Let's face it, being outwardly religious is rarely rewarded in the schoolyard. My education did, however, shape my quaint views on God and Heaven. My maker was a bearded gentleman of extreme old age who oversaw the administration of his house – Paradise. This was a place that kept all the truths of our existence, which were revealed to the worthy when they slipped into the afterlife. It was here that the three great mysteries were concealed: the meaning of life, what women want, and why Ron Barassi played Robert Flower on a half-forward flank instead of on the ball.

Nowadays there is no risk of my being mistaken for a paragon of Catholic virtue. But Catholicism has never fully left me. I regarded myself as a fence-sitter locked in a strug-gle between belief and non-belief. That neither side could claim ascendancy didn't worry me in the slightest. My faith, such as it is, had long been understood by no one but myself.

This was all meaningless to Zoe. A person's religiosity was a black and white issue: 'you are or you ain't'. There was no easy answer. Declaring I was religious might lead to discus-sions about intelligent design and the hereafter. Answering 'no' might lead to shrieks about my soul being condemned to hell or, much worse, an attempt to convert me. I looked to Dave for help. Not for the first time, he was inspirational.

'Zoe, I'll tell you what I am.' He reached into his bag and pulled out his ukulele. 'I am a musician and I think it's time for a tune.' His left hand worked the fretboard, plucking the tune of 'Sweet Georgia Brown', also known as the Harlem Globetrotters' theme song. 'Sweet Georgia Brown' would begin most of Dave's impromptu sets along the Camino. He would also invite requests. On subsequent occasions, most people would have the sense to gracefully decline and just enjoy Dave's soloing, but Zoe was emphatically not 'most people'.

'Oh, yeah, I got a request. You know any Christian songs?'

'Not really,' said Dave, 'but if you can hold a tune, then I can usually pick up the chords by ear.'

Zoe beamed, slapping Joey on the thigh excitedly. 'Ain't this guy the greatest?' Joey mumbled something inaudible. She began singing, her voice a blend of country-and-western, new-age gospel and billy-goat vibrato. It was a redemption story ('This song is about a man who nearly spent eternity in hell') that dealt with the difficulty of adolescence ('As a kid this boy liked cocaine and porn'), but which recognised the protagonist's business acumen ('He could pimp out any old hooker that no one else could sell'). After a lifetime of sin, his conscience got the better of him, so he embarked on a spiritual quest ('He upped and left and went looking for the Big Guy') and experienced an epiphany ('Before he found God, he thought that only titties and crack could give a man a high').

Dave was doing his level best to follow on ukulele. I could see we were both having the same thought – *get me the hell out of here*.

'Sorry to interrupt you guys,' I said. 'It's sounding terrific, but we really have to get back on the road.' I looked out at the driving rain. Dave's backpack was on his shoulders before I had even finished the sentence.

'Say, where you boys headed? We'd sure love to make your acquaintance again.'

I was ready this time. 'Well, we're not sure. We're just walking until we find what we're looking for.'

'Just like Jesus in the desert!'

'Spot on,' I said with a wink.

Three 'God blesses' later and we were on our way out of Zubiri forever. For some time after we'd left the shelter of the balcony we could hear Zoe singing fortissimo, beseeching Joey to join in.

'Poor bastard,' said Dave.

In our determination to leave the evangelists in our dust, Dave and I were the first of that day's pilgrims to arrive in Larrasoaña. The place seemed totally deserted. We ambled down the main road like cowboys in a spaghetti western stumbling into a ghost town. Impressive fifteenth-century homes bearing family coats of arms above doorways sat alongside garish modern designs. The sound of our poles striking the asphalt road echoed down empty alleys. Otherwise, it was silent. 'Siesta,' muttered Dave.

We found an albergue set back from the road, its door

invitingly ajar. Dave pushed the door fully open, exposing a long hallway in which a plump *señorita* sat at a desk, beckoning us to enter. She seemed greatly impressed with Dave, the first Australian she had met on the Camino who could fluently speak Spanish. She was less impressed with the pint of sweat I had decanted on her beautifully clean floor. We bought four cans of San Miguel and a night's accommodation before retiring to the albergue's lounge to discuss whether God really could redeem a pimp with a taste for pornography and cocaine.

A TOAST TO ST JAMES

It was raining incessantly as we walked out of Larrasoaña. The trees lining the path offered no protection. The rain fell heavily enough to burst through the canopy and obscure our sight. We had trouble making out the way-markers. Through the wall of water they looked like smudges of yellow rather than cockleshells.

I had first seen the cockleshell – the emblem of Santiago or, as I knew him back in my churchgoing days, St James – many years ago. It was embossed on my aunt's golden signet ring. I'd noticed it during my final one-on-one Bible-study tutorial before my first communion. Light had caught the ring's gilded edges and my eye. I'd asked my aunt about the shell on her ring, and the story she told seized my imagination in a way the Good Book never had.

What really set my pulse racing was the manner in which James' body came to be buried in Spain. The legend goes that before His crucifixion, Christ divvied up the known world among His apostles, instructing them to all spread the word. James was sent to evangelise the Iberian Peninsula. Over four decades he only managed to recruit a measly seven disciples. He returned to Judea in 44 AD a failure. It mattered not. James would do his best work from beyond the grave, a place with which he would very soon become acquainted.

James had sailed home at the very moment Herod Agrippa was 'laying violent hands upon some who belonged to the church'. He had barely wiped the Mediterranean salt from his eyes before he was charged with sedition. James was executed and became the first apostle to have won the crown of martyrdom.

This is where things got interesting. St James' decapitated body was loaded onto a boat that sailed west back across the Mediterranean Sea, through the Strait of Gibraltar and northwards up the Iberian coast. It was an impressive voyage considering it was a boat without oars or sails *or sailors*.

The ghost ship landed near the port city of Finisterre, where it was met by James' seven disciples, who'd somehow been alerted to the apostle's epic voyage. His followers sought permission from the region's pagan queen, Lupa, to construct a sepulchre in which to lay St James' mortal remains to rest. Lupa agreed, on the condition that they passed a series of tests, including slaying a dragon, reducing a pagan statue to dust and breaking in a pair of wild oxen. After the challenges were met, the pagan queen converted to Christianity and suggested a pleasant plot of green Galician land as an ideal burial spot. Pagan Spain had no interest in the tomb of a Christian, so James was forgotten until the year 813, eight centuries later, when the tomb was rediscovered.

A Christian hermit named Pelayo was wandering across a field when he spotted a star hovering low in the sky. The star led him to the mausoleum containing the relics of Santiago (St James in English, Jacob in Latin, Jacques in French, Giacomo in Italian). The city that was built around the tomb was named in honour of the saint and the light that had brought Pelayo to him: Santiago de Compostela, St James of the Field of Stars. The pilgrimage to Santiago would join the pilgrimage to Rome, to the tomb of St Peter – the prince of the apostles – and Jerusalem, to the Holy Sepulchre of Christ, as the most sacred to Christians.

These three pilgrimages were each assigned a symbol. Pilgrims for Rome, or 'Romers', wore the cross keys of St Peter. Those for Jerusalem bore the insignia of the palm branches with which Christ was greeted when he entered that city. These pilgrims are called 'Palmers'. For less obvious reasons, those who walk the Camino to Santiago wear the *concha* or cockleshell. These pilgrims are called 'Concheiros'.

No universally accepted explanation exists for the shell's association with the Camino. One theory is straightforward enough: the city of Santiago sits close to a coastline covered in cockleshells. After arriving in Santiago, pilgrims would traditionally journey three days west to Cape Finisterre, where they'd collect a shell and attach it to their garments as a token of their pilgrimage. Some dispute this, claiming that the Camino inherited the symbol from St James himself, and a miracle that took place a century before the pilgrim city was founded. A sailor from the kingdom of Galicia had fallen overboard to what should have been his death following an attack by a vessel of Moors, Muslims of Berber and Arab descent from North Africa. Days later, the sailor staggered ashore covered in cockleshells, a miracle given to St James.

There are yet more theories. Some pilgrims I'd meet along the way – kooky types mainly – would say the pattern of the shell reflected the Camino itself: its natural grooves a reminder of the many routes of the pilgrimage uniting at a single point. But the most compelling explanation predates the pilgrimage altogether.

Before its association with the Camino, the cockleshell was linked to another (non-Christian) deity. This connection is seen in the full Spanish term for cockleshell: 'concha venera', the shell of Venus. Think of Renaissance artist Sandro Botticelli's depiction of Venus emerging from the sea on a giant cockleshell. Many centuries before Christian pilgrims used this path, it carried pagans undertaking a quite different ritual. They were enacting a rite of fertility. Could there be a better talisman for such a quest than the *concha venera*, the shell of the God of Love? And it's not unknown for a pagan symbol to be co-opted by Christianity.

So, interest in my aunt's ring had been revived – sadly she had died some years before. The place where she acquired the ring is long forgotten. I was pretty sure she'd been out here during her extensive European adventures but I would never know for sure. It's hard to say whether she would regard my stroll along the Camino as a worthwhile enterprise. At that stage I was not even convinced myself. I hoped, at the very least, she would see it as contributing to a broadening sense of the Eucharist.

'*Buen Camino,*' announced a jolly Irish voice. It was Michael, greeting us with the standard Camino salutation. A lean gent in his sixties whom we'd met at Saint-Jean, he strode past us easily, the rain bouncing off his waterproofs.

'*Buen Camino,*' we muttered, miserable in the wet. *It's fine for you*, I thought, *this weather is positively Irish*.

'The weather reminds me of Iraq,' he said smilingly.

'Iraq?' I grumbled. 'But it's mostly desert there.'

He chuckled to himself in anticipation. 'From what I've been told it's partly Sunni but mostly Shiite. *Buen Camino!*'

Dave and I looked on in awe as Michael practically ran ahead. He moved like a man half his age, certainly a lot faster than us. Michael was one of a group of four pilgrims who'd left Saint-Jean at the same time as us. That morning we passed the other three in sequence.

We soon caught up to our particular favourite, a short, round French woman, resembling an aged Edith Piaf, who lugged a backpack twice her size. '*Bonjour,*' she sang out as we came up beside her, her voice reaching the limits of her upper register. She didn't speak English, but this scarcely got in the way of things. She seemed to be permanently optimistic. Nothing could dampen her spirits – not the atrocious weather, not the size of her pack and certainly not the small matter of our language barrier. She greeted us like family – standing on tippy-toe to warmly kiss us on both cheeks – before conversing in lightning-fast French. Dave and I nodded our heads interestedly, pretending to understand every syllable.

We had previously tried to find out her name via chest thumps and loud pronouncements ('Me, Tom. Him, Dave. You?'). '*Très bien!*' she would exclaim, as if we were children performing a pantomime. We'd named her 'Bonjour'. Each day so far we had overtaken Bonjour around noon. She started the day much earlier than us, enabling her to keep an identical itinerary to our own despite her slow pace.

Next was a tall Swiss man with protuberant eyes. His enormous frame appeared on the horizon shortly after we'd farewelled Bonjour. When he heard us approaching, he brought his marching to a sudden halt, swivelled around to face us, craned his neck forward and shouted, 'Hi guys!' We'd learnt that these words were his sum knowledge of the English language. Even on subsequent occasions when Dave and I encountered him separately, he would still greet us in the plural. We'd christened him, imaginatively enough, 'Hi Guys'.

Some pilgrims we nicknamed with more ingenuity, but not that much more. We dubbed the fourth member of the group, a chain-smoking Frenchman with silver-rimmed glasses, 'French Pipes', a reference to his severe sleep apnoea. I'd had the misfortune of selecting a bed that abutted his own in the albergue in Saint-Jean. The grisly spluttering and gasping that followed his apnoeic event, which caused him to literally stop breathing in the night, gave me no small amount of alarm. It sounded as if he were being smothered under a pillow. After the fifteenth event, I'd seriously contemplated using a pillow on him myself. French Pipes was mute, lending him a Jekyll and Hyde duality – dumb by day, thunderously voluble by night. He didn't respond in speech to my greetings. He would, however, acknowledge me by way of a friendly puff of smoke from his nostrils.

The River Arga is crisscrossed by the Camino a number of times before it forms a natural moat around the city of Pamplona. We passed over it via a medieval bridge, where a statue of St James atop a scallop shell stands sentinel. In front of us Pamplona's city wall loomed, the rain making it a bleak charcoal colour. The wall's collapse in the eighth century is said to have been the work of St James himself. The story goes back to the time of Charlemagne, ruthless expander of the Frankish empire. Aimery Picaud wrote about Charlemagne, forging a link between the Emperor and the Santiago pilgrimage in the historical annotations of his travelogue. He recast the Emperor's expansionist ambitions as a divine campaign to wrest the cities and towns along the Camino from the Muslims at the behest of St James himself.

In Picaud's version of events St James appeared to Charlemagne in a dream, instructing him to lead his army on a crusade to take back the ancient road. Having not succeeded beyond waging a three-month-long siege on Pamplona, Charlemagne dropped to his knees, saying, 'Oh, Santiago! If it is true that you appeared to me, let me conquer this city.' In a blinding flash the walls tumbled down.

Put simply, Picaud's history is twaddle, as spurious as the description of Charlemagne as eight-feet tall and strong enough to bend three horseshoes in his hand at once. Charlemagne took his army over the Pyrenees in 778, some thirty-six years before Pelayo had stumbled across the relics of St James. There was no road for Charlemagne to take back for Christianity because neither the Camino nor the city of Santiago de Compostela itself existed. What's more, Charlemagne was in Spain at the invitation of the Moorish Governor of Barcelona, Suleiman ibn-al-Arabi. Suleiman sought the Emperor's considerable military muscle to dispose of his enemy, Abd ar-Rahman, the founding emir of Córdoba. It was the ultimate power play, swearing allegiance to the Christian infidels to launch an offensive against the emir in the south. In return for his assistance, Suleiman promised Charlemagne the surrender of some Spanish cities. Pamplona, it would seem, required some coercion.

Saintly assistance or not, Charlemagne would pay dearly for his part in bringing down the wall of Pamplona. Suleiman had given the Emperor safe passage through the Basque region on assurances that Charlemagne's army would not damage the wall that protected the old city. Charlemagne's broken promise saw his rearguard massacred by vengeful Basques on its way back over the Pyrenees – the Battle of Roncesvalles – resulting in the death of our man Roland. It was Charlemagne's greatest defeat. The Basque people would not be subdued by any army, not even one led by one of history's most formidable conquerors. The story ended miserably for Suleiman, too; he was murdered by his former friend and ally Husayn of Zaragoza after Charlemagne's bloody campaign very nearly destroyed his city.

Crossing the medieval bridge, I decided to put St James to the test. 'Oh, Santiago,' I entreated. 'Make this rain relent and provide me with sustenance in the form of San Miguel.' Dave laughed nervously at two pilgrims who edged past us quickly.

'Ease up on that wailing, mate,' said Dave, smiling falsely at other confused bystanders. 'Someone might call for the men in white coats.' Then the rain stopped. We both looked up disbelievingly towards the clouds and then back at St James. The moment I began to reconsider my position on Picaud's history, the rain fell again, heavier than before. As we ran through the city gates and into the old town, I think I heard Dave shout, 'Don't *ever* fucking do that again!'

Pamplonans sheltered under awnings along the city's narrow streets; they were unmoved by the sight of two men running madly past with poles and backpacks. Idiotic young men sprint for their lives along these streets each year, warding off the sharpened horns of six 500-kilogram beasts with nothing but rolled-up newspapers. The locals may have thought we were bull-runners in training. Ours was certainly a brave re-enactment, full of expletives and skidding falls on the cobblestones.

We rounded a corner and found Pamplona's municipal albergue. We had our pilgrim passports stamped, claimed our beds, dumped our bags and then made for the showers.

An hour or so later we were out exploring in rain slightly lighter than monsoonal. We were not bothered. Water had completely soaked our packs, saturating our non-hiking gear. We simply couldn't get any wetter.

The rain relented in time for the end of siesta. Hundreds of people fell out onto Pamplona's sodden streets. The pulse of the city quickened. Laughing children kicked footballs, couples swooned, young mothers pushed prams and elderly gentlemen in coats and caps ambled imperiously, arms linked with their wives.

Dave had herded together stray pilgrims at the albergue and arranged for us all to rendezvous at the Plaza del Castillo for a tapas tour. Everyone assembled at the appointed time and nervously engaged in small talk. Dave shepherded them towards a bar, pairing up pilgrims of similar dispositions. He would ignite a conversation and then move on to do the same with the next couple. He made us seem as familiar to each other as old schoolfriends.

There was Lorenzo, a well-upholstered Italian with a gigantic smile, who wore a red polyester shirt and tight running shorts that barely contained his frame. He was talking to Jacob, a Seattle-based nurse working in palliative care for children. There was Nikki, a worried-looking Dane with sky-blue eyes who had recently returned to Europe from Asia, laughing skittishly with Liz, a budding Australian actress with an interest in the healing properties of reiki. Natalia, a diminutive Brazilian with dreadlocked hair and multiple body piercings, was talking to Constanza, a recently divorced teacher; she was walking to Santiago for the second time, and was notable as the only Spaniard in our party. I was talking to Kim and Phuoc of South Korea, seasoned hikers who had walked to Machu Picchu, through the Himalayas, up the West Highland Way and along part of the Appalachian Trail. One wondered where they found the time.

I scanned all of them, wondering what each hoped to gain on the road. My eyes settled on a face I'd seen before. It was Sally, standing slightly apart from the group, wearing yellow leggings that were impossibly bright against the grey light of the fading day. She caught me staring at her and began shaking her head pityingly. Evidently, my chakra problem had not improved. I quickly looked away.

Dave led us into a smoke-filled eatery borrowed from a Hemingway novel. We elbowed our way towards a bar covered with delectable *pintxos*, the Basque country's version of tapas, and began sampling. We feasted on venison with wild mushrooms, ostrich with cheese, as well as chorizo, ham, octopus, and other unidentifiable meats. We washed it all down with *cerveza* from the tap, toasting St James, Pamplona and each other as we went. We were pilgrims drawn from five continents and by the end of the night we were all hopelessly drunk.

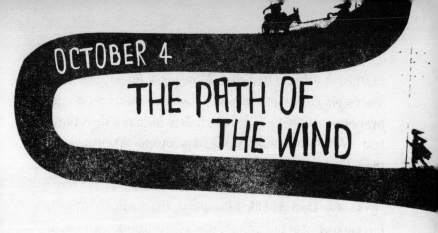

THE PATH OF THE WIND

The previous night everyone in the bar had fallen silent as a procession of grim-faced Basques had marched past the window. They walked mournfully, as if trailing behind a hearse. Some carried photos of menacing-looking men and others clenched placards. The rest held flickering candles. Constanza had explained that the photos were of political prisoners or detained terrorists, depending on your perspective, and the placards read, 'Bring them home'.

The protesters were marching against the Madrid government's policy of imprisoning convicted Basque country prisoners far from their native land – exiling them. These inmates had links to Euskadi Ta Askatasuna (Eta), which translates to 'Basque Homeland and Freedom'.

Since 1961 Eta has demanded that an independent state be created in the ancient Basque territories in northern Spain and southwest France. They've pursued this end through violent action. Over 800 people have died since Eta's first terrorist attack in 1968.

In March 2006 Eta announced a permanent cessation

to its operations. The Prime Minister of Spain, José Luis Rodríguez Zapatero, welcomed the announcement as 'the best opportunity for a peace process for more than thirty years'. Zapatero's optimism proved premature. Eta would end their 'final ceasefire' eight months later with an explosion. Since then, seven deaths have been blamed on Eta. Three weeks after Dave and I left Pamplona, Eta detonated a bomb in a parking lot at the University of Navarra, just metres from the Camino. Seventeen people were seriously injured.

The fight for independence is not unique to this part of Spain. Separatist slogans for other regions would appear along the entire length of the path. Separatists use the Camino to get their message to the outside world. No useable surface is spared as a canvas – not way-markers, not tree trunks, not even medieval bridges. With the exception of the Basque movement, Dave and I knew of none of these groups scream-ing out for independence. Sadly, nothing, it seems, attracts international notoriety like the odious militant arm of a political movement.

We left Pamplona, heading for Puente la Reina about 27 kilometres along the path. Here the Camino Francés would meet with the Camino Aragonés, the route from Italy via Arles in France and the Spanish province of Aragón. The Camino Aragonés links the Santiago and Rome pilgrimages. Two paths converge at Arles – an eastern route from the Mediterranean coast and one from the north, connecting the Camino to the Via Francigena, the pilgrim route from Canterbury to Rome. Those who walk the Camino Aragonés tend to start at Somport on the French–Spanish border, about 100 kilometres east of Saint-Jean.

The concept of a 'starting point' for the Camino is entirely modern. The starting point for the traditional pilgrim was his or her front door. A Danish woman I met in Roncesvalles had started walking from her Copenhagen home three months earlier and could not believe she had less than 800 kilometres to go. The 25 kilometres Dave and I had walked when we met her looked meagre alongside her 1600.

Tales of other pilgrims' feats were passed on like currency. There were stories of stamina, or obduracy, depending on your view, such as that of the Russian who had walked from his home in St Petersburg after a heated row with his wife.

'And where do you think *you're* going, Vladimir?' she probably asked, as he opened the door carrying a satchel and a bottle of vodka.

'Oh, sorry, Olga, didn't I tell you?' he would have responded. 'I thought I might walk to Santiago de Compostela in Spain. It's a Christian pilgrimage concerned with respect, something you'd know nothing about. I shouldn't be more than a year. Don't wait supper, *you bitter harpy*.'

There were stories of romance and rekindled passion, like that of a married couple who walked hand in hand from Toulouse to Santiago. As they stood before the Catedral del Apóstol at the end of their journey, they peeled their swollen hands apart, breaking their physical bond for the first time in months. Despite a stronger spiritual connection, their calloused flesh was so revolting they could no longer bear to be around each other. They both converted from Catholicism and successfully filed for divorce. Not really. I'm sure they lived happily ever after.

Stories of masochism – the pilgrim who walked from Paris barefoot or the man who rolled his way from León – or of obsession – the woman who trekked from Saint-Jean to Santiago back-to-back six times or the man who was setting off on his forty-fifth pilgrimage – I assumed to have been embellished but I couldn't be sure.

I was confident that neither Dave nor I would be admitted into the pantheon of extraordinary pilgrims. Short of stripping nude and walking the rest of the Camino on our hands, everything else had already been done. Dave and I would be nothing but anonymous names on a rollcall of millions. Our pilgrimage would be one of humility, and humbled is exactly how we emerged at the outer fringes of Pamplona following a night of excess. It was going to be a tough day.

At Pamplona's outskirts the morning sun sat above unsightly housing developments and wind-powered turbines. With pursed lips we pressed forward, up the short rise of Alto del Perdón. Relative to our first stage, to Roncesvalles, the climb should have seemed like cresting a measly hillock. Hung-over, it felt Himalayan. We took in the view at the hill's summit and surveyed a single-file procession of cast-iron statues of pilgrims, donkeys and a dog. The party leader bore the inscription 'Donde se cruza el Camino del viento con el de las estrellas', where the path of the wind crosses that of the stars. Below the inscription was the name of the company that had commissioned the statues – the same company as that which ran the wind farm. I wasn't in the mood for appreciating sculpture. To me, the piece looked as ugly as those modern windmills.

Noon approached. We were both famished, having skipped breakfast on account of our tender stomachs. We tripped down a series of sharp embankments, stumbled on loose shale, forded a small river and came to the little village of Uterga. A wooden stump with a San Miguel shingle hanging on a horizontal beam indicated a place of refreshment. The café was set back from the road behind an outdoor setting where Sally was talking to Warren. The twins quietly gnawed their way through enormous *bocadillos* while she grilled the group's leader.

'So, how do you three know each other?'

'We're all from Sydney's northern beaches,' said Warren. 'Jack and Steve are on holiday visas in England. The twins wanted to walk this track before they had to go pull beers in London. They figured that I'd like to come along.'

'You're here for a holiday?'

'It's more a training holiday. I wanted to do something that kept me active before I start military college.'

'You're a soldier?' Sally winced.

'You bet. Is there anything wrong with that?'

'Well, I suppose not. It's just that most people come here for spiritual or religious reasons or seeking inner peace.'

'I've got two words to describe that sentence – absolute *fucking* bullshit! From what I've read there have been just as many warriors along this road as pilgrims.' Warren had a point.

'Okay, jeez, but surely you're doing more out here than just trying to keep fit?'

'You're not wrong there,' responded Warren, winking at one of the boys. 'Here's the plan – we walk thirty clicks a day, sink a trolley full of piss to rehydrate, and cop a handful of roots along the way for fun.' The twins nodded their heads dreamily.

Sally scrunched up her face. *She asked*, I thought.

'C'mon now, Sal,' laughed Warren. 'Tell me you're not planning to bump uglies out here.'

'Excuse me?' said Sally, utterly revolted.

'I saw you eyeing off that Spanish bloke in the red singlet on day one back in Saint Gene.'

'Ah, Waz,' said one of the twins, 'I think that's pronounced —'

'I see you've found some new friends,' interrupted Dave.

'Here's a shitload of trouble,' said Warren.

'How are my chakras looking today, Sally?' I asked, raising my chin slightly to give her my best angle. She stood up, loaded her pack onto her back and threw me a cursory glance.

'No change,' she said over her shoulder while making for the road.

Dave laughed under his breath as he headed inside to order us lunch. The twins returned to their *bocadillos*. Sally pranced out of sight along the Camino. And Warren ran off behind a tree to meet a call of nature.

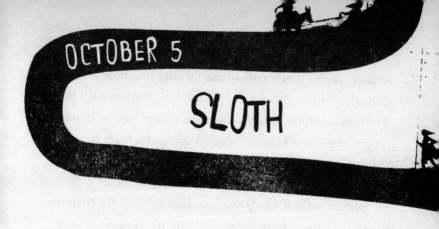

OCTOBER 5

SLOTH

News travels quickly along the Camino. From stories about albergues overcome with bedbugs to tales of pilgrims being arrested for lewd behaviour in León, information made its way along that trail at a cracking pace. Nothing travelled faster, though, than bad tidings.

Albergues, restaurants, bars and other pilgrim haunts were awash with rumours of an insidious sickness sweeping the Camino. Pilgrims were dropping like flies. Nikki, the kind Danish blonde with the nervous smile, had been flattened; a German student had forfeited his trip; and a Korean-American with a terrific appetite had not been seen in days.

Before long we all knew the symptoms by rote. It began with a dizzy spell, hot flushes and sweating. Then mild disorientation would set in followed by a piercing migraine. The sufferer would then violently convulse, expelling litres of diarrhoea and vomit like the possessed undergoing an exorcism.

The origin of the Camino sickness became the subject of countless theories. Everyone was an expert. The contaminated water was to blame ('Those fountains are full of muck'), or else rotten food ('You can't go wrong with the *tortilla*, but in these parts the chorizo is poison'). Some looked to poor hygiene ('Those albergues are filthy from oven to mattress'), others to promiscuity ('These kids, kissing and cuddling all the time; they'll be the death of us all!'), and, not infrequently, it was seen as a sign from above ('Jesus punishes those who stray from the path'). Apparently the only foolproof safeguard was to stop eating, drinking, sleeping and touching, while observing thrice-daily prayer. Either that or go home. It was worrying. There was, however, a more immediate concern.

I discerned Dave's limp as we were crossing the Puente la Reina (Bridge of the Queen), named for the eleventh-century monarch who financed its construction. I noticed him screw up his face and stifle an expletive after stumbling on a stone.

'Are you all right?' I asked. Dave was not one to make a fuss.

'Yes,' he hissed through gritted teeth. 'Why do you ask?'

'Because every time you put pressure on your left leg it's like Gordon Ramsay is standing beside me.'

'I'm fine,' he said sharply. 'It's just a little stiff.'

'Look out,' said Warren from behind, 'these two sound like they're about to have it out.' The cloudless day saw him kitted out in a camouflage-patterned singlet and his wraparound sunglasses.

'Morning, Warren,' sighed Dave.

'Ask me why they call this the "Bridge of the Queen".' He smirked, warming to his punchline. One of the twins obliged.

'Because it's the place where queens have their lovers' tiffs.' He laughed hard enough for his glasses to nearly come off. 'Go on, then, I wouldn't mind seeing a bit of a dust-up out here. How *do* a pair of fairies fight it out? Handbags at five paces?' He tapped us on our backs while overtaking us. As Warren strode on ahead, one of the twins turned around and apologetically shrugged. I looked at Dave, whose teeth were clenched. I decided to stay silent.

The landscape had changed colour. The green slopes of the Pyrenees had been replaced by sunburnt hills covered in vines. Somewhere near Estella we notched up our first significant milestone: 100 kilometres of walking. There was little fanfare. It marked only an eighth of our journey to Santiago. We still had a long way to go.

My guidebook described Estella as a 'new addition to the path'. As such, I expected our next destination to be full of housing developments and fast-food chains. Instead we found a charming little village contentedly nestled beside a river. With its attractive steeples and superb architecture, Estella could lay claim to being one of the prettiest towns of the pilgrimage. It looked anything but new. Of course, in the Camino context 'new' is a relative term. Estella was founded in the year 1090, a full three centuries after Pelayo's discovery under the star in Galicia.

Dave iced his knee in Estella's albergue while I made for the Palacio de los Reyes de Navarra (Palace of the Kings of

Navarra). It took no time at all to find Estella's Romanesque wonder. All roads seemed to lead there. I stood back admiring the façade's pillars, arches and porticos. Three of the seven mortal sins were depicted high on the broad head of the street corner column: lust was represented by a woman whose breasts were being attacked by snakes; sloth by a donkey playing a harp while a dog listens; and avarice by figures of naked men with coins hanging around their necks.

The depiction of avarice was particularly ornate. Perhaps the architect had been short-changed and the naked fools portrayed were his stingy employers. An unpaid bill would explain why the builder had limited himself to just three of the deadly sins. I tried to think of worthy representations for the remaining four. Anger could be a foot with a fresh set of blisters boiling up between its toes. Gluttony, a fattened-up Warren feasting on *bocadillos*, the twins looking on morbidly. Envy could be a sleep-deprived pilgrim jealously regarding a snorer's earplugs. And pride. I couldn't immediately imagine a depiction for the most serious of the cardinal sins.

As a child I had developed a fascination with the seven deadly sins. I attribute this to my formidable parish priest; it was a particular sermon of his that ensured my God-fearing initiation into the Church. With a pious smile, he talked us through each of the cardinal sins, instructing us to arm ourselves with the weaponry of Christian virtues (chastity, charity, temperance, kindness, diligence, patience, humility) lest we be beset by the scourge of Satan. Special attention was paid to pride, the sin that spawns all others, and sloth.

I noted that his description of sloth – and 'its wicked cousin despair' – as being the most depraved was met with sullen nods from the older congregants. He called it the unforgivable sin.

I took sloth to mean laziness, something all television-watching children know to be undesirable. But wanton and deadly? This all seemed excessive. The heinous transgression of sloth, I discovered much later, was seen in the Church as a consequence of committing *acedia*, a cardinal sin listed in the sixteenth-century Roman Catholic catechism. In subsequent catechisms, summaries of church principle and doctrine, 'sloth' would replace '*acedia*'. In Latin the word means to neglect something. In its religious context it means to exhibit a spiritual torpor or to refuse to perform the duties one must fulfil in order to be 'saved'. Despair, the wicked cousin, was seen as the conscious state of mind that led to *acedia*. This dark union led to the voluntary abandonment of all hope in salvation.

Despair, as I knew it, was a state of mind that was anything but voluntary. One despaired when one was subjected to terrible things. My parish priest was effectively saying the opposite – terrible things would happen to those who despaired. He even gave as an example the demise of the great traitor. 'Judas was not beyond salvation when he took his thirty pieces of silver,' intoned my priest. 'His fate was sealed when he hanged himself. This was his ultimate betrayal.' My mother shifted uncomfortably in her seat on hearing this. Even then I knew the priest was navigating dicey waters, but

I was not going to take my chances. Despair and its attend-
ant consequences (*acedia*, sloth and damnation) would be
avoided.

Maturity and rationality would release me from my mor-
bid obsession, but only by a degree. A child's fear is not easily
forgotten. On occasion, I still found myself fretting about the
cardinal sins, particularly sloth. Religious fence-sitter I might
be, but I do guilt and fear as well as any Catholic. Maybe a
small part of me – that inner child shaking in church, lost
in worry over the warnings thundering from the pulpit – was
drawn to the Camino for that reason. As a sinner I could at
least satisfy myself that I was finally on the right path.

Those who complete a pilgrimage are rewarded with
indulgences – partial reprieves of the time they'd spend
in purgatory to cleanse the soul of sin. For Catholics this
means that after death, temporal punishment in purgatory is
reduced, getting them into Heaven quicker. Put in another
way, to receive an indulgence is to be, say, let off for bearing false witness against your neighbour, but still having to
do time in purgatory for coveting his wife. Had Dave and
I walked to Santiago in a Jacobean year, when the Feast of St
James falls on a Sunday, we would have been granted 'plenary
indulgence', that is, the washing away of all our sins. It's
kind of like taking the purgatory bypass straight to Paradise.

These days this might seem an easy out. But in medieval times, when this road was teeming with *bandidos* and
scimitar-wielding Moors, pilgrimages were a life-and-death
proposition. The suffering endured on a pilgrimage was

thought to be serious enough to double as a punitive measure for criminals. The centuries-old practice of walking a
pilgrimage in lieu of a custodial sentence still happens in
Flanders, where one prisoner a year serves out his or her
sentence on the road to Santiago.

Indulgences still await pilgrims to Santiago even though
amenities are up and Christian-hating Moors are down.
Understandably, pilgrim activity increases exponentially in
Jacobean years. In 2004 numbers more than tripled. Over
150 000 people walked the Camino to get a direct ticket to
Heaven. As it happened, Dave and I were two years out for
the next Jacobean year, 2010, and so would only be granted
partial indulgence. At that stage, this seemed like a pretty
reasonable deal.

After siesta, Estellans started to appear like weary bears
surfacing from hibernation. They passed me on the streets,
doffing hats and offering warm greetings. *'Buenos tardes,
señor!'* Estella was built to accommodate those who walked
the Camino and the pilgrim trade still keeps the town's coffers
full. The Estellan treats the pilgrim very politely, as you would
anyone who is bankrolling your village. In this happy atmosphere I made for the next historical wonder, the Iglesia de
San Pedro de la Rúa, which I'd read about.

In the late-thirteenth century a Greek man went on
pilgrimage to Santiago. After negotiating the phenomenal
distance from Patras without incident, the pilgrim fell ill and
died in Estella, his identity unknown. He was buried in the
cloister of the church of San Pedro de le Rúa. The night of

his burial, the sexton observed a light shining from his tomb. They exhumed his body and went through his effects, and discovered a fragment of the True Cross and the shoulder-blade of St Andrew (martyred north of the Peloponnesus). The anonymous pilgrim had in fact been the Bishop of Patras. The bishop's remains are kept in a reliquary housed in the church. They kept the bishop's booty, too.

I rounded a bend, anticipating a crowd, and prepared to hand over a hefty admission fee to see something so impressive. Instead, I came to a couple of heavy locked doors with no evidence of any life inside. I sauntered dispiritedly back to the albergue. How could a church purportedly housing a piece of the actual cross on which Christ was crucified and the bones of an apostle be closed for business?

I was so preoccupied by the closed church that it became my topic of choice when hitting on a gorgeous pilgrim hovering at a bar we visited that night. I was three sheets to the wind when I approached her, so my memory is a little hazy, but I said something like: 'Hey, we've never met before, but can you believe that I wasn't allowed inside San Pedro's to see a bit of the True Cross? By the way, can I get you a drink?'

As it happened, she was not just attractive but learned, too. She informed me that there are enough True Cross fragments in Europe to construct a small ocean liner. Nevertheless, the remains of St Andrew – albeit a humble shoulder bone – would surely be a crowd-puller, I contended. She did not respond to me on this last point, instead sidling off to another conversation. Perhaps she regarded my interest in St Andrew's bones creepy. I returned to the albergue that night very much alone and made a rule – don't use saintly body parts in pick-up lines.

YOU WILL BE
WHAT I AM NOW

'In Estella,' wrote Aimery Picaud, '[the] bread is good, the wine excellent, [and the] meat and fish are abundant.' Nine centuries on, excellent wine can still be drunk in Estella. I couldn't comment as to the abundance of fish and meat, though; I'd been too drunk to notice. I peeled myself out of bed to a German chorus of admonishments spoken in English for my benefit ('Ya, Hans, zat snorink vas terrible!'). These were sure signs it had been a big night.

The sun was creeping above the hills that bordered the village. It was looking like it would be another spectacular day. After less than an hour of walking, Dave and I came to the *fuente del vino*, the pilgrim wine fountain. A large American had his mouth wrapped around the tap, and red liquid dribbled down his chin as his wife loaded up the camera with photos.

A number of us waited our turn like congregants in line for communion. Nobody spoke. This was the only wine fountain of its type. Drinking from it was one of those rituals that *had* to be observed. In my condition, it was masochistic to imbibe. I guess I was hopeful that a healthy swig from the fountain might alleviate my hangover. I filled up my water bottle and held it up for a visual and nasal inspection.

'What are you doing?' asked Dave.

'I'm allowing the wine to breathe while I observe its vibrant colour,' I responded, a vintner uncorking a shiraz from a promising vintage.

'How does it look?'

'It is a deep-brick cast with crimson hues. Its complexity of colour indicates a concentrated bouquet of fruit characters. But wait,' I took a deep inhalation, 'I detect smoky oak, chocolate and, yes, even liquorice. The aromas suggest a well-matured merlot, or perhaps a cabernet sauvignon, or —'

'Do you know what you are talking about?'

'No idea. I memorised that ten years ago from a bottle label to get my Responsible Service of Alcohol certificate.'

'Just drink the wine, you dickhead.'

And so I did. It was cold in an unrefreshing way, like the feel of a foodless spoon on the mouth, but, sadly, not quite so bland. After a sip, I could taste spicy and well-rounded rotten fruit flavours with dusty tannins; it reminded me of something . . . oh yes, that's it: fermented cowpat. I was left with a pilgrim drool and sunscreen aftertaste.

'How is it?' asked Dave.

'Delicious.'

After a few minutes of dry-retching, we staggered back onto the Camino only to be joined by Constanza, the young divorcee we'd met in Pamplona who was walking her second

Santiago pilgrimage. She rushed up, laying kisses on us both. Her greeting was welcome in light of the frosty reception I'd had from the Germans that morning. Constanza had also spent the night in a bunk near mine. But as it happened, she could only hear with the aid of a cochlear implant, a device capable of being switched off. While everyone else was contending with the snores, gurgles, coughs, burps and farts of the night, she was curled up in delicious silence. It went a long way to explaining her good humour. She was simply well rested.

As Dave and I basked in Constanza's ebullient greeting, Nikki the Dane came shuffling up the path. She held her pole limply, allowing it to skim along the road. She was nursing a paper-like object in her hand, occasionally bringing it before her eyes. She looked crestfallen, a state I put down to the Camino bug she'd picked up in Pamplona, until she noticed us. Her face lit up and she shoved the item into her jacket pocket.

'*Buen Camino*!' she said as she approached. 'Constanza and the lovely Australian boys. What a treat! You wouldn't mind if I joined you for a stroll?' Her greeting was an honest attempt at friendliness, but one that felt hurried and strained.

'Of course not,' said Dave. 'We'd be delighted.'

While the four of us climbed a slope flanked by native oak and pine trees, Dave and I fielded questions about how we knew one another.

David McNamara was the first person I met on orientation day at Melbourne University's Music Conservatorium, where we were both studying – him, piano; me, saxophone. I remember well that first day out the front of the Music School, standing apart from the larger groups of people somehow already known to each other. There were others like me, shuffling nervously at the side, hoping to spot a familiar face. We might have stood there stupidly for hours had Dave, lean and curly haired, not rounded us all up and pointed us towards the pub. He was at once sociable and good-natured, always ready with a one-liner that left groups of people clutching at their sides in hysterics. But to me his best trait was keeping an eye out for the ones who slipped off to the side. These were qualities most likely built into him at a young age.

Dave had grown up on the floodplains of the New South Wales Riverina. For friends and family alike, it must have seemed logical for the highly capable young Dave to follow in his old man's footsteps and continue his family's stock-and-station agency. Dave had other ideas. He had discovered a musical ear, a talent for performance and a natural ability on the piano. By age fourteen, Dave was able to play the complete songbooks of Elton John, Peter Allen and Billy Joel by heart, give a handy rendition of Beethoven's 'Moonlight Sonata' and was lead guitarist in a local outfit that once supported the band Spiderbait. He was also, as he is quick to point out, a reliable back pocket for the Finley Football Club, and was named as an emergency in Finley's Under-16s Team of the Quarter Century.

But you need not have spent long with Dave to realise he is more than just a country boy of friendly mien. He possessed an innate curiosity that couldn't be satiated in regional Australia. It was this that impelled him to move to Melbourne, to complete a music degree, to busk throughout Europe with his wife, to set up in Guatemala and learn Spanish, to then move to Granada in Spain and eventually to walk the Camino de Santiago de Compostela.

'So Dave brought you along for the ride?' asked Nikki.

'He most definitely did,' I said.

Dave had been determined to walk the Camino after first hearing it mentioned when he was travelling in Central America. He'd put out the invitation to join him on a 'stroll across Spain', as he so casually put it. I was a prime candidate.

I didn't tell Nikki and Constanza the other things that had pushed me onto the Camino, unwilling to unload my worries about the unemployment and uncertainty that waited for me back home. Even before I'd left, the excitement of resigning from my job had waned. In its place was anxiety. I was a strung-out man in his late twenties without gainful employment in an ever-tightening job market. There was no dreamy relationship or compelling responsibility to keep me in Australia. Dwindling savings notwithstanding, a walk across Spain seemed a capital idea: a way of delaying the decisions that had to be made.

'So are you both Catholic?' asked Constanza, tugging the small crucifix around her neck.

'Culturally Catholic,' said Dave. Constanza raised her eyebrows in question. 'I was raised a Catholic. But I've lapsed, you see. I'm an atheist.'

'Lapsed! What do your mother and father say about this?' she asked jovially.

'Mum doesn't seem to mind, and Dad doesn't say much at all. He died ten years ago.'

Nikki shot Dave a look.

Constanza blushed. 'I'm so sorry, I didn't —'

'Don't worry about it,' said Dave, brushing it away. He reached over his shoulder to retrieve his ukulele from his pack, and began strumming to hilariously improvised lyrics. This was Dave to a tee. In the blink of an eye we'd all gone from uncomfortably staring at our shoes to choking with laughter.

The hours melted away as the path cut first through open country and then hills lined with vineyards. Suddenly, I felt fire in my pistons, as if that fountain had contained a pilgrim elixir. We arrived in Los Arcos almost without noticing how we got there.

Fate has dealt Los Arcos the blow of being the largest town following Estella along the Camino Francés. I might have overlooked the derelict buildings and grimy streets had Estella's charm not been so fresh in my mind. The locals seemed to be aware of this injustice, too. We walked past three townsfolk, who looked unwashed; they regarded us forebodingly before one spat in our direction. It was clearly meant to intimidate, like a salvo across the bow of a ship.

Our time in Los Arcos was not all doom and gloom. The albergue warden was friendly, and that night Dave, Constanza and Nikki cooked up a paella fit for kings. But the town seemed determined to leave pilgrims feeling dispirited. As we walked out of town the following morning, we passed the local cemetery. The Latin inscription above the cemetery portal read, *'Yo que fui lo que tu eres, tu seras lo que yo soi'*, You are what I once was, and you will be what I am now. We hurried past, fearful a Los Arcan ghost might ascend from its plot and loose a volley of supernatural spit in our faces.

THE LAST CHANCE FOR FREEDOM

We were slipping behind our intended daily average of 30 kilometres. Any more than 20 seemed to tickle up Dave's leg problem – a burden he bore with, dare I say it, Christian resignation. Otherwise, we were in reasonable shape. In fact, it was all rather pleasant. The Camino certainly didn't feel like an onerous punishment. Those prisoners up in Flanders were getting off lightly. We left Nikki and Constanza early in the morning in the hope of outrunning a black storm gathering to the west. Rain was on its way.

We negotiated a steep descent and slid down some shale, before spotting a forlorn figure sitting on his pack at the path's shoulder.

'I knew you weren't cut out for this caper, Warren,' Dave joked.

'How are ya?' mumbled Warren, lighting a cigarette.

'The twins haven't gone AWOL on their drill sergeant, have they?' I asked.

'They've gone on ahead.' He frowned.

'Are you all right, mate?' asked Dave.

71

'I dunno, boys. This isn't what I had in mind.'

'What do you mean?' pressed Dave.

'Have you met Danielle, that massive sheila from Canada with more chins than a Chinese phonebook?' We both nodded. Danielle was an overweight clap-your-hands Christian we'd run into in Puente la Reina who we'd tried to avoid ever since. 'Yeah. Well, I got a lecture from her: unless I surrender to Jesus I'll spend an eternity in hell. That was scary enough, but, mate,' he paused and shook his head, 'that weird smile of hers nearly sent me over the top.'

'It's a pilgrimage. You were always going to get some religious heavies out here,' I said.

'It's not just that. Last night some flaky chick bailed me up in the albergue, talking about quantum physics or some shit.'

'What for?' asked Dave.

'No idea. It was something to do with us all walking the Camino at the same time. She said that if you look hard enough, you can see all the kings and queens and saints and all the others that have walked the pilgrimage.'

'What's the big deal?' I asked.

'Mate, I'll give you the red-hot tip: when I'm walking along this path I'm sure as shit not seeing St Francis of Assisi.'

'It's a bit kooky, but who cares?' said Dave.

Warren paused, pulling back on his cigarette. 'It's all about *energy* and *spirituality* out here; it's driving me fucking crazy. Everyone is so bloody alternative. They're all into alternative medicine, alternative religion, alternative food, alternative music. Christ, I even met a chick telling me about her job as an alternative dentist. What the hell kind of job is that? Does she punch her patients in the mouth to straighten their fangs instead of using braces?'

'Don't let it get you down, Waz.'

'It's too bloody late for that, Dave. I knew this wouldn't be a normal trip through Europe, but I expected more than this. Where are those hot *señors* I heard so much about and those big nights on the piss?'

'Uh, *señoritas*?'

'Whatever. They may as well be blokes. The only chicks in my age bracket are mad as cut snakes. The only normal sheilas are crusty old Frogs and Poms. As for the Germans, bloody hell, me grandfather would never forgive me if I even *looked* at a Kraut. To make matters worse, I haven't even had a beer since meeting you blokes back in Orisson.'

'Come on, mate, show some bloody Anzac spirit,' I said. 'This isn't how the diggers —'

'Piss off, Tom. I've got the rest of me life to worry about that shit. This is supposed to be a last hurrah before I go into the military. It's a last chance for some freedom.'

'Then let's make it a good one,' said Dave, hauling Warren up by the arm.

The three of us struck off down a gravel path, heading up a small rise before plummeting into a steep river valley. We were now in La Rioja, a tiny province wedged between Navarra to the east and the enormous region of Castilla y León to the west. We were headed for its capital, Logroño, a city famous for its happy citizens, fine wine and alluring tapas bars. In short, the perfect place to revive Warren's spirits.

The weather closed in on us around the time we came to Logroño's urban fringe. Gusts of wind kicked up dust ahead of an almighty cloudburst. To sharpen his reconnaissance skills Warren had devised an alternative route through Logroño's suburbs into the old town. We kept up a frenetic pace through the rain, which awoke some of my old injuries. It felt like sandpaper was being drawn across my groin and a spike was being nailed behind my patella. After thirty painful minutes making it double-time along the wet streets, we arrived at the three-storeyed albergue.

Warren pulled open a wrought-iron gate, revealing a drenched courtyard and a young woman sheltering from the rain under a ledge. She was bawling her eyes out.

'I need a smoke,' said Warren, pulling out his pack and taking cover below an awning at the other side of the courtyard.

'She doesn't look like she speaks English,' I said, joining Warren.

'Gutless bastards,' muttered Dave.

After a few minutes of comforting the woman, Dave reported back that she'd been refused admittance by the albergue warden. She had asked to stay a second night, a luxury prohibited in all but the privately run albergues. This rule is so strictly observed that pilgrims have been turned away for staying a second night in an albergue in the same city or village. In exceptional circumstances, when someone's injured or sick, allowances are made. But not always.

The woman, Esther, had explained to Dave in Spanish that staying in a private albergue would tarnish the purity of her journey; she hated the idea of people profiting from the pilgrimage. She had hoped the warden might waive the second-night prohibition on account of her feet being a mess of blisters. In spite of Esther showing him a doctor's certificate, the warden refused to let her in. So she waited in the courtyard for a miracle.

Warren, who had been listening to Dave's translation, tossed his cigarette away, walked over and cleared his throat.

'BUENEZ TARDEZ, SEÑOR!' he shouted, causing the young woman to reel backwards and raise her arms in fright. 'Dave, can you tell her I'm going to give her first aid?' Dave did as he was asked. Esther nodded.

Warren prised off her shoes and began to smooth ointment that he'd retrieved from his pack over her massacred feet. She yelped, prompting Warren to pull out a packet of pain-relief tablets. Her expression softened as Warren began to massage her heels. This was a side of him I hadn't seen before. It was like seeing the ghost of Sir Weary Dunlop.

While Warren worked between Esther's toes, Dave and I went to book in for the night, certain we could talk some reason into the warden. We were wrong.

The warden wore his moustache in an upturned fashion reminiscent of a silent-film villain. Our suggestion that his lack of compassion was un-Christian was met with a haughty smile. He was a very small man, drunk on status. He stamped our pilgrim passports and waved us towards our dormitory with a sanctimonious flutter. Without expressing gratitude, we hauled ourselves up three flights of stairs.

Dave and I returned to the courtyard to find Warren staring misty-eyed at his patient. Esther's tears had dried up. This might not have been the saintly intercession she was expecting, but then the Lord works in mysterious ways. The colour had returned to her face, which, without waterfalls of tears streaking it, was quite fetching. She returned Warren's look shyly. Romance was stirring. I thought of the many ways this scenario could go badly awry; it was clear the digger needed a chaperone.

The four of us found our way to Logroño's tapas-bar district just before the end of siesta. Esther stole sideways glances at her hero. Warren, meanwhile, had refused to book in to the albergue and proudly carried Esther's pack on top of his own. Within a matter of minutes, Logroño's streets were crammed with people emerging from siesta. It was time to hit the bars.

As the night wore on, Warren looked to be making reasonable progress with Esther, whose unpractised English was rearranged by Dave. The Manly boy's efforts faltered a little when he voiced his objection to Spain's withdrawal from Iraq, a policy Esther staunchly supported. It was left to Dave to avoid catastrophe. He guided the conversation back to our shared dislike of the albergue warden.

At bar three we were on to fresh tomatoes and olive tapenade on bread washed down by bottles of beer. Dave and I dedicated bars four to six to seafood (shrimp, crab, tuna, octopus), and bars seven to nine to the Spanish old school (chorizo, salami, spicy lamb). Each chunk of bread, tentacle of octopus and slice of chorizo was complemented with alcohol of some sort. At bar nine Warren was teaching Esther how to put someone in a headlock. By bar ten things got loose. Like a pack of racehorses freed from their saddle girths, we pinned back our ears and went wild. Tapas were replaced by shots of vodka, grappa, tequila, chartreuse, Jäger and some mysterious yellow substance that looked and tasted like a urine sample.

'*Shit!*' shouted Dave. 'Five minutes!'

It was like a gun going off inches from my ear. The other rule observed in all but the private albergues is the ten o'clock curfew. Wardens rarely had to enforce this rule. After a long day of walking, most pilgrims had turned in well before lights out. A week in and Dave and I had been forced to beg, barter and break our way into our accommodation on four occasions. With this albergue's windowless ground floor, chained iron gate and Gestapo-like guard at the door, we would be spending the night on the streets were we to break curfew tonight.

Warren and Esther seemed unconcerned. On my way out the door, I looked over to see Warren embracing his fair Spanish lady in an affectionate grapple hold.

Dave and I raced through the slippery streets of Logroño like a pair of bloodhounds pursuing a rabbit. We skipped over gutters, hurdled barricades and cornered sharp bends. Finally, we negotiated a tricky intersection and sprinted through the gate, crossing the courtyard and hurrying into the doorway. We passed the warden with seconds to spare.

'Quiet,' he hissed, after Dave and I had rejoiced with a round of high fives. We went up the stairs, giddy with excitement and slipped into the dormitory. It was dark and in the state we were in there was little hope of retrieving earplugs from our backpacks. After feeling my way through the room, I collapsed onto my bed – mercifully a bottom bunk.

My excitement was quickly replaced with queasiness. My stomach continued to lurch as if I were still on the mad dash through the streets. I could hear creamy condiments forging an unholy alliance with liquor and contriving an escape via the attic instead of the cellar. My head felt like the rotor of a helicopter.

In my university days, when these sorts of nights had been standard, Dave taught me a technique to combat the spinning-room sensation. The secret was to lie in bed on your back and put one foot on the floor. I had only moderate success with the technique that night, but in the end it was the unbelievable noise in the dormitory that was more distracting. There must have been twenty-eight souls all snoring.

I tried to get myself to sleep by thinking of the best collective noun for snorers. I settled on *a fucking nightmare of snorers*. I sat up, looked across to Dave's bunk and whispered, 'Can you believe this noise?' He didn't stir. I observed his left leg hanging off the bed, his foot resting on the floor.

JUST KEEP WALKING

Something was wrong. The snoring in the dormitory had become unnaturally loud. Then there was no longer a pause between the inhales and exhales, just one long continuous sound. The pitch climbed higher and higher until the snore became a scream. I was on my back, clawing the mattress, trying to get a grip. I could feel my teeth grinding as the walls either side of me seemed to bend and shake. I scanned the ceiling, searching for something to focus on to steady my spinning head. The screaming was now a deafening buzz. I shivered as dread wrapped around me. It was happening again.

As the building collapsed, I felt myself falling towards the ceiling instead of away from it. Beds, bodies and hiking apparel struck me, tearing off my clothes. The roar of buckling walls and debris falling somehow lessened the din of the buzzing, until everything went dark and silent.

I opened my eyes. I was lying on what remained of the albergue, a heap of rubble piled up, cone-shaped, like an island. I was as naked as the day I was born. At the far end

79

of the island, a bearded man wearing a carling felt cap and a brown cape with a wooden staff at his feet sat on a back-pack reading the Bible.

I stood up and searched around my feet for something to cover my private parts. All I could find was the shell of St James. Cockleshell in hand, I tiptoed across the rubble to discuss the catastrophic collapse with the old pilgrim. As I drew closer, I recalled something familiar about him. I was now only a few feet away and was certain we'd met before. Even though his face was partly obscured by the Bible, he looked just like —

'Santiago? Is it really you?'

'How are ya?' said the saint in a booming Australian accent as he put down his Bible.

'*Warren?*'

'Nah, mate. You look like you could do with some of this, my old son.' Santiago handed me his gourd. The lid came off with a hiss and I took a pull. It went down like nails. I thrust it back in his direction.

'Is this San Miguel?' I spluttered.

'Sure is. Good shit, eh?' He lit a cigarette, stood up and took a long drag. While this was going on, a Camino stray came sniffing around my toes and then started leaping up at my cockleshell codpiece.

'Get out of it!' shouted Santiago, kicking away the dog. 'Sorry, mate. Saint Gene's got a mind of her own.'

'Santiago, what's going on? Where are we?'

Santiago flicked his cigarette into the rubble and picked

up his Bible. 'You've been MIA,' he shouted. 'Now, act like you've got a pair and pull your bloody head in!' Spain's patron saint whacked me across the cheek with the Good Book, sending me back into the real world with a God-awful headache.

It felt like toothpicks were being scraped along the inside of my cranium and plunged into my frontal lobe. It even hurt to blink. I dragged my head off the pillow and looked across to the adjacent bunk. Dave was lying facedown on his mattress, fully clothed. His right arm hung lifelessly off the bed, while the left was twisted unnaturally behind his back. He was stirred by the sound of his mobile phone beeping. He reached into his pocket before opening his eyes.

'Who is it?' I croaked.

'Warren,' he gasped.

'What the hell does he want?'

'He says, "The Waz is back in town. What a night! See you soon."'

The albergue warden, still fuming from our curfew-stretching arrival last night, unleashed a tirade at us for not leaving before 8 a.m. He kicked us out without even giving me time to get dressed properly. We left in a storm of swear-words, stumbling into the sunlight with the enthusiasm of a pair of vampires. I frantically searched my pockets, looking for the solace that only a Marlboro Light could bring.

'I wonder if we're the first pilgrims to cop the finger from an albergue warden?' I asked.

Dave said nothing. I could tell from both his limp and his pinprick pupils that he was suffering terribly. The creases on his clothes spoke of an uncomfortable night. Compared to me, however, Dave looked positively stylish. I was barefoot, my shirt was half-unbuttoned and a just-retrieved fag dangled from my mouth. We were not the poster boys for the abstemious and devout seeking penance. We were more like vagrants looking for a street corner on which to panhandle.

Being unable to even look at food, I left Dave in a Logroño café. We arranged to meet in Nájera, a small city some 30 kilometres away. I staggered along a busy highway, passing rows of houses, drab streets and all the other symptoms of suburbia. One particularly decrepit house caught my eye. Encased in scaffolding, it sat rotting, a sulking demand for urban renewal. The sight of it pushed my mood into listlessness.

My familiarity with the hangover cycle (shock, odium, indolence, self-loathing) was itself a major concern. That I should be experiencing this during my life-changing stroll across Spain was an appalling development. It was the surest sign that nothing was really changing at all.

Dave and I had been on the Camino for eight days, and covered 170 kilometres. All it had so far amounted to was a lot of walking and a lot of drinking – a pilgrim booze fest. No life-altering moments. No crystalline realisations. Walking off a hangover in such a place was a step up from waking on a couch underneath a gangrenous souvlaki, but the novelty was wearing off fast. The endless Christian imagery I passed reminded me that my behaviour was more than just undesirable. Out here it was a sinful transgression.

Light-headed and wheezing, I struggled up a hill, bullets of sweat on my forehead. It was a sunny day, but the overnight rain had saturated the path, leaving it a quagmire of red clay. The boggy road was crawling with bugs, which nibbled greedily at my face and legs. My shoes were being sucked into the earth, at times tugged off completely. It was impossible to get into a rhythm. I was sinking.

'You look terrible,' said Sally from behind. She was skipping across the red sludge without getting so much as a splatter of mud on her immaculate lime-coloured leggings.

'Believe me,' I muttered, 'I don't need you to tell me my chakras are shattered today.'

'What happened to you?'

I groaned something about setting up Warren before guiding the conversation back to her. I soon regretted it. She started telling me about a *bombero* she'd met a few days ago.

'A what?' I asked.

'A *bombero*; it's Spanish for fireman. Anyway, it has been *so* passionate. We've actually met before.' In a previous life, as it turned out. Sally said that he didn't speak much English, but that they had been communicating in, well, other ways.

'We made love five times last night. We both cried with happiness for hours. Um, are you all right? You've gone really pale.'

It's hard to say what triggered it – Sally's libidinous affair, my nauseating headache, the stench of the mud or the insects crawling up my legs – whatever the cause, I just lost it. Out gushed all my woes. From unemployment and financial destitution to my sore knee and grisly hangover, I covered almost everything. I even told her about my nightmare.

'That's awesome!' exclaimed Sally. 'Don't you get it? The meaning of your dream is clear. It's a message that the things you have created are collapsing. All that is left in the dust and debris is *you*: naked, honest and exposed.'

'Warren was there, too, dressed as —'

'You're rebuilding yourself and your identity from the ground up. It's fantastic!'

I looked at her sceptically.

'Listen,' she said calmly, 'I have to hurry ahead to talk to a medium I arranged to meet in Burgos. Just answer me this one question: What is your intention here?'

I thought for a while, trying to conjure a good answer. I couldn't find one, so I trotted out the line I'd fed to family and friends before I left for Spain.

'Well, I'm on a kind of quest to sort out my life; a journey of self-discovery, you might say.'

'No!' she shouted. 'Forget all that crap. Just answer the question. What are you *doing* here?'

'I don't know, walking to Santiago, I suppose.'

'Exactly! That's all you need to worry about. There will be worse moments than this and when they happen, remember to just keep walking.' She adjusted the strap on her backpack and then left me, confused and worried.

'What do you mean "worse moments"?'

She didn't even look back.

I followed her up the hill. It was like watching the course

of a stone skimming across a millpond, refusing to be dragged into the darkness below.

This will not do, I thought. I needed to know whether this woman was a clairvoyant or a charlatan. I struggled gallantly through the mud, determined to meet her at the top of the hill. Calling on my last reserves of energy, I dug deep. But the faster I pursued, the further away she seemed to drift. Without turning around, she crested the summit and vanished. Dispirited, I half-staggered, half-crawled the remaining distance, eventually making the hill's brow. Blowing hard and coughing up an alarming volume of gunk, I threw down my pack and collapsed on the road. In front of me I could see vines knitted across the earth. Hills of singed grass and small peaks rising minaret-like in the far distance. But Sally was gone.

I was still 20 kilometres out of Nájera. To kill the time I thought of a story I'd read about the town and its place in Charlemagne's 'divine crusade'. So the legend goes, Nájera was the site of a battle between the knight Roland, Warren's old mate, and Ferragut, the Moorish giant said to have been descended from Goliath. Ferragut possessed the strength of forty men and could not be felled by any known sword, arrow or spear. But in Roland the giant would meet his David. This tale was used to illustrate the Christians' intellectual, physical and moral superiority over the Moors. In my beleaguered state I discovered another meaning.

Roland was sent to capture Ferragut's stronghold and liberate the Christian knights the giant had imprisoned. After a series of assaults on Ferragut's redoubt, the giant wearily offered a truce, challenging Roland instead to a battle of wits. The winner of this great duel would rule the kingdom of Navarra. Roland accepted.

Now Roland was no mug on matters theological. He was particularly well versed in Bible lore and the Holy Trinity, and knew by heart the Sermon on the Mount. But pity the fool who mistook Ferragut's physical size for an ogre's mental dimness. This giant could shame a mullah with his knowledge of the Qur'an, the Sunnah and the life of the prophet Mohammed (peace be upon Him).

The battle of wits tipped in Ferragut's favour following his stirring rendition of the Shahada, but shortly thereafter he became lost in thought, revealing, in a moment of suicidal candour, his one weakness to be at his navel. Roland seized the opportunity, unsheathed his dagger and plunged it into the giant's stomach. With Ferragut out of the way, the Christian army easily conquered Nájera. The Moors were massacred and the Christian knights delivered.

Only through my bloodshot eyes could I have really understood the morals of this story: violence will always win the day over debate and diplomacy; duplicity is an effective weapon in asymmetrical warfare; and, crucially, navel-gazing will invite one's doom. So I learned my lesson and ceased my moping.

It took me the rest of the day to make the town where

Ferragut fell. I stopped for a *tortilla* at the little village of Navarette. From there, the way-markers eventually led me over a sturdy bridge and into Nájera. I found an albergue on the fringe of town and pushed back the doors, revealing a small crowd of pilgrims devouring their supper. *'Buenos noches,'* I said. The shouting of an irate Frenchman who emerged naked from the shower cubicles at the side of the hall diverted their attention. *'Merde! No fuckeeeng hot watair!'*

A *cold shower*, I thought: *a fitting end to a shithouse day.*

SAINTS OF THE WAY

In the mid-fourth century an Egyptian called Mary undertook her own pilgrimage of sorts to Jerusalem. Although styled as a God-fearing Christian, Mary was in fact the entrepreneurial sort who had seen a golden opportunity.

From Cairo to Sinai, Mary granted sexual favours to lonely male pilgrims keen to chalk up a few sins before their absolution. She worked the streets of Jerusalem until eventually she became overwhelmed with spiritual uncertainty and set off to the Church of the Holy Sepulchre for guidance. When she arrived before the church, it is said that an unseen force kept her from entering. Mary, with a guilty conscience, attributed this to her impurity. Racked with remorse, she prayed for forgiveness below an icon of the Virgin Mary and could only then enter. She swore an oath of asceticism and went to serve out her penance across the River Jordan. She survived for fifty years as a Christian hermit, living off the wilderness in the desert.

If I believed in reincarnation, I'd say the soul of Mary of Egypt had found its way into a bearded Canadian called Boris.

Although it was hard to envisage him enduring the puritanical five decades that saw Mary canonised. He was not the self-denying type. Even so, I like to think that in Boris we met the purest embodiment of the patron saint of penitents in her unholy years.

We happened on Boris staring at a pair of young lady golfers tackling the first fairway of the Rioja Alta Golf Club. He was dressed in a loose-fitting grey singlet, black jeans and sandals. Although he wasn't formally attired, there was something imperious about him as he tugged at his beard. He looked like a contemplative Jesus.

'*Buen Camino*,' I said.

He turned around slowly and acknowledged us with a casual nod before returning his gaze to the attractive young woman completing her approach shot.

'Strange having a golf course in such an isolated spot,' I offered. 'Can't see too many pilgrims packing their clubs for a round.'

'It has its advantages,' he said absently, studying the golfer as she leaned over to replace her divot.

'Are you a golfer yourself?' asked Dave.

'For a while I wanted to be a pro.'

'Jeez, you must be pretty handy.'

'I'm not sure how good I am,' he said. 'I've never played a game in my life.' The Canadian followed the golfers' progress until they disappeared behind some trees. He then turned to us with a wry smile. 'I just liked the idea of giving ladies their golfing lessons. So, who are you guys?'

After we'd introduced ourselves, Boris said that we might be able to help him out. 'I'm looking for a lady from Texas.'

'What does she look like?' I asked.

'She's about five foot seven, brunette, hazel eyes and the kind of chassis that gets married men into trouble.'

'Doesn't sound like someone you'd forget,' I said.

'That's the goddamn truth. It's important that I find her. You see, I'm on a mission.' Boris cleared his throat.

In some ways, one must stay the hand of judgment when reflecting on Boris's journey. We were all walking to Santiago for our own reasons. Like many other pilgrims, Boris sought to experience something life-changing. He was out to bed as many women as he possibly could. And he was as dedicated to his cause as the most devout Christian was to theirs.

Boris had shagged his way over the Pyrenees, right across Navarra and into the province of La Rioja, performing miracles with women in the most imaginative of places. He was keen to let us know he was 'not crass about it'. There were no blow-by-blow retellings of his exploits, which would have been beneath his dignity. He had, however, hit on a way to ensure people knew just how lucky he was getting.

Boris, raised a Catholic, had borrowed liberally from the religious lexicon of his schooling to create his own sexually charged idiom. 'Angels' were the women he had scored on the Way; 'good Samaritans' were pilgrims who had vacated a room in an albergue to give Boris and an angel the privacy they needed; 'sepulchres' were towns on the Camino where his feelings towards an angel were consummated; 'tombs' were places where those feelings were rejected; 'pilgrim staff' I hardly need explain, and the 'Holy Trinity' was, well, you get the picture.

Boris explained that he'd seen the Texan from afar in Roncesvalles, but had already committed himself for the night to an angel he'd seen pulling beers behind a bar. Commitment was a serious matter for Boris. But he hadn't forgotten the Texan beauty.

'She might just prove to be my Blessed Virgin,' he said.

'Your what?' one of us asked.

'The Blessed Virgin was crowned queen of Heaven. Here, she'd be the crowning glory of my quest.'

Logistically Boris's mission was a nightmare. To stay in an albergue was to completely forfeit one's privacy. Finding inventive places to have sex was difficult enough, but finding a like-minded woman in such circumstances was nigh on impossible. For Boris this lent authenticity to his pilgrimage. The Camino was intended to be difficult, he explained. The ancient pilgrims had to hike through woods infested with *bandidos*, hold back bloodthirsty wolves with staffs and ford rivers teeming with unknown dangers. Boris had discovered a modern-day equivalent, with obstacles no less challenging and hazardous.

After interrogating us on the female pilgrims we'd happened on since leaving Saint-Jean, Boris pushed ahead in search of the Texan.

'That's one sick puppy,' I said to Dave. He nodded gravely.

The most memorable sight on the road east of Santo Domingo was a housing estate in the early stages of construction. Small fences marked out plots of land where pipes stuck out from the dirt like crosses above graves. Soon enough identical-looking houses would rise from the plat; a politician would hold a town-naming ceremony (my money was on Peregrino's Paradisio), and young families would take up residence in houses along Pilgrim's Place, Matador Mall, Toros Terrace, Santiago Street, All Saints Alley and other such kitschily named streets. The golf course where we'd met Boris adjoined the development and was probably meant as its centrepiece. I imagine plots would have been bought with the added enticement of free membership at the Rioja Alta Golf Club. I hoped for the sake of its members the club had reciprocal rights.

There was something incongruous about an American-style subdivision growing at the side of the Camino. It was the ultimate invasion of drab modern suburbia into wondrous antiquity, no less unsightly than walking up the road to Machu Picchu and seeing commission flats rising out of the Incan ruins or finding a caravan park amid the pyramids at Giza.

This section of road, west of Nájera, had been laid in the eleventh century by an unsuccessful monk called Domingo García. Domingo had been booted out of monasteries at Valvanera and San Millán after failing his studies. His dream of leading the monastic life shattered, Domingo returned to the forests bordering the River Oja around 1034 to live as a hermit. Shortly after coming home to the region of his birth, Domingo received a divine visitation from Santiago, directing him to join master road-builder Gregorio Ostiense in improving travel conditions for pilgrims.

This meant more than simply erecting a few road signs. Domingo happened to reside in a particularly hazardous section of the Camino. There were no roads or bridges, just dense scrubland, perfect cover for *bandidos* looking to ambush pilgrims. Domingo heeded Santiago's wishes and assisted Gregorio in his holy work, only for the builder to abruptly up and die. Domingo was left with unfinished bridges to complete and endless forests to fell. It was an enormous project. It turned out that Domingo might not have cut it as a monk, but by golly could that guy lay down a path.

He built a stone bridge over the dangerous River Oja, sliced through 40 kilometres of forest with a heavy sickle and converted a ruined fort into a pilgrim hospice. He died in 1109, aged ninety, but not before he'd constructed more bridges, expanded the road further westward and built a church in his village. He was canonised for his achievements. I am certain the patron saint of civil engineers, a man of tasteful constructions, would have been greatly displeased by the developments so near the city named in his honour – Santo Domingo de la Calzada, Saint Dominic of the Causeway.

After we arrived in Santo Domingo and had a bit of a poke around, Dave and I went to inspect a pilgrim museum, interested to see what we could learn about ourselves. There we watched an animated retelling of the miracle of the hanged innocent.

The cartoon was in Spanish, but it was easy enough to get the gist of it. A young man with a squire's haircut on pilgrimage with his parents to Santiago stops at a Santo Domingo inn. The innkeeper's daughter, a young woman with a heaving bosom and impossibly long eyelashes, falls hopelessly in love with him. What has all the hallmarks of a classic boy-meets-girl love story unravels on account of the pilgrim's rigid piety. Irate at having her advances thwarted, the rejected maiden hides a silver goblet in the pilgrim's backpack and accuses him of stealing. He is found guilty and condemned to hang.

Oblivious to their son's fate, the young man's parents continue on to Santiago, assuming their lad has gone on without them. On the return leg through Santo Domingo the parents are greeted with a macabre scene: their son still hanging from the gallows but miraculously alive.

The parents hurry off to inform the local constabulary, finding an obese sheriff devouring his dinner. The parents declare that their son still lives and demand he be cut down from the gallows. The sheriff scoffs that the pilgrim thief is no more alive than the cock and hen he is about to consume, whereon the fowls stand up on the plate and crow. The pilgrim is promptly cut down and receives a full pardon. The person watching the cartoon is left to speculate as to the fate of the innkeeper's daughter.

There are a number of flourishes around Santo Domingo that allude to the miracle of the hanged innocent, none more eccentric than the chickens kept in a coop in the west transept of the town's cathedral. Locals insist that they are direct descendents of the cock and hen that danced on the sheriff's table. There is also a piece of the gibbet from which the pilgrim was hanged displayed high above Santo Domingo's tomb.

A vexing issue for theologians is determining who should be ascribed the miracle of the hanged innocent – Santiago or Santo Domingo. Some versions hold that the pilgrim cheerily informed his parents that Santiago had supported his weight above the ground. Despite this, the miracle is popularly seen as the work of Santo Domingo. This seems fair enough. When it comes to miracles, Santiago could probably spare a few.

The work of St James from beyond the grave makes for impressive reading. He is credited with resurrecting a pilgrim's child who died in the Oca Mountains, felling Pamplona's impenetrable wall, freeing twenty Christians held prisoner in Zaragoza by the Moors, curing a paralysed man in the Santiago Cathedral, appearing on horseback to assist the Christian armies in the defeat of the Moors at several battles, and – my personal favourite – resurrecting a young man who'd castrated then killed himself at the behest of the Devil after he'd committed a sin of the flesh.

Santo Domingo's work looks positively lightweight in comparison. He transformed a felled tree into enough timber to construct his many edifices, healed a French knight possessed by the Devil and returned a blind German pilgrim's sight. Santo Domingo could do with a miracle with the glamour of the hanged pilgrim. Nevertheless, one thing is for certain: they don't make saints like they used to. Let us reflect on, say, Australia's own Mary MacKillop. Mary would achieve sainthood in 2010 for first healing a woman dying of leukaemia in 1961 and then curing another in the mid-nineties of inoperable lung and brain cancer. Good work to be sure, but pretty dismal when put alongside that of Santo Domingo and Santiago.

Leaving the pilgrim museum, I meditated on a miracle for the then-Blessed Mary MacKillop similar in stature to that of the hanged innocent. I thought of something miraculous, mumbled a prayer for the first time in years and eagerly awaited next season's football results.

I pictured the 2009 AFL grand final: a translucent nun in a red-and-blue habit intercepts a pass in the backline before slotting the winning goal outside fifty. *Hallelujah!* My prayers will have been answered! I imagined the Vatican expediting her canonisation, citing her responsibility for the miracle of the divine interception. I could see the statues they'd commission depicting her famous run with the Sherrin tucked under her arm. In Spain, where my prayer was received, the Blessed Mary MacKillop would thereafter be known as Santa María de la Diablo, Saint Mary of the Demons.

The following season the Demons finished stone motherless last.

SUBMIT TO THE RIVER

Not far out of Belorado, our day's destination, Dave and I came across countless pamphlets fluttering all over the path. This was the latest method for advertising private albergues. We collected as many as we could, intent on dumping them on the lawn of the offending place. Righteously, we marched on, eager to part with a few choice insults directed at the depraved warden. We found the albergue; a portly man stood at the door, grinning audaciously. We seethed at the sight of him.

'*Buen Camino,*' he announced. 'Please, please, come inside for a free drink.' Dave and I looked at each other. Did he say *free*?

We thoughtfully disposed of the pamphlets in a bin and went inside to inspect the albergue. Our host, Sancho, was all backslapping and hail-fellow-well-met. He poured us beer from the tap, refilling our glasses while regaling us with amusing anecdotes about German pilgrims. It must have been an hour before Sancho allowed us to see the bottom of our glasses.

'Gentlemen, you must stay here for the night,' he began. 'The day is nearly over. Please, please, I insist you stay.' It seemed impolite to not accept his offer.

Dave cleared his throat. 'Well, we had actually planned to stay closer —'

'Nonsense,' interrupted Sancho, 'it is miles to the next albergue.' He was very persuasive. The thought of walking any significant distance with a stomach full of San Miguel was most unappealing. 'Give me your pilgrim passports and I'll stamp them for you.' As if in a trance, we did as instructed. 'Good. Now that will be fifteen euros each.' We reached into our pockets and produced the correct change. At the very moment our transaction had concluded, Sancho's eyes went dull. 'Rodrigo will show you to your dormitory,' he muttered, waving towards a painfully thin figure brooding in a corner of the room.

Rodrigo skulked towards us with his hands clasped in front of him. His raven hair was greased back to his scalp and his tight shirt revealed the corrugated lines of his rib cage. He tried a smile that brought unnatural seams to his cheeks. The attempt was quickly abandoned. That face could no more smile than a scorpion could stay its sting.

Rodrigo led us out to a grey semidetached industrial block that had all the warmth of a morgue. He moved with stealth, like a supernatural creature luring prey to its dwelling. Rodrigo pushed open a thick door with a light movement; it was as though the building were obeying his command.

The block's harsh artificial lighting, low ceiling, and the

symmetrical rooms coming off the central corridor made me think of a mental asylum. I bit down on the sudden urge to drop my bag and bolt for the exit. At the end of the corridor, Rodrigo opened another door revealing a room big enough to squeeze in perhaps six beds. At least a dozen bunks had been crammed in. To access the bed on the far wall you had to climb over several others – a nightmare in the event you needed the bathroom after lights out.

'Take your pick, *por favor*,' said Rodrigo, 'and enjoy your stay.' He retreated from the room backwards, keeping an eye fixed on us. After he closed the door, we shook our heads as if emerging from hypnosis.

'What just happened?' asked Dave.

'No idea. Let's just get the hell out of this room.'

We draped our sleeping bags over the two beds closest to the exit and went exploring the albergue's principal building. The 'entertainment precinct', as it had been touted by the pamphlet, was a grimy room with a billiard table decorated with cigarette burns. Along the wall were three computers that I assumed had been bought at a garage sale in the late eighties. There was a settee covered with grisly-looking stains. The 'cinema' consisted of calico-clothed chairs arranged around a table supporting a broken projector. I felt a thirst welling up inside that only San Miguel could slake. So we went back to the bar. It was an altogether different place now.

The undesirables Sancho concealed before securing our cash had now emerged. Behind the bar sat a large woman wearing a maroon cardigan and a scowl. She was heavily made-up with too much mascara and scarlet-coloured lip-stick. Some beige substance plugged the cracks on her chin and cheeks. She looked like a burlesque dancer thirty years off the stage who hadn't realised the show was over.

'*Hola*,' she rasped in a two-pack-a-day voice.

'*Hola*.' I shuddered. '*Dos* San Miguel, *por favor*.'

She inhaled impatiently and, without moving her head, shouted, '*Elena!*' A girl with her hair pulled back tightly into a ponytail emerged from the kitchen. '*Si!*' she sneered like a petulant teenager, glowering behind her folded arms. The older woman waved our way, like a pest controller direct-ing an apprentice towards the cockroaches in the attic. The girl groaned and reluctantly set about tending to our order. Rodrigo, meanwhile, stood in his corner of the room, his head bowed like a gargoyle staring down from its perch, waiting to be summoned. Truly, we were pilgrims in an unholy land.

Our accommodation was on the very edge of Belorado and not, as we were led to believe, miles from the next albergue. I counted three in the space of the ten-minute walk into town. We strolled into Belorado's Plaza Mayor, admiring a rotunda of orange trees arranged at its centre and the set of bustling bars and restaurants at its circumference. Our drink-ing over the last few days had taken its toll on our pilgrim's purse. Tonight's meal would be self-catered.

We bought the ingredients for spaghetti bolognaise and returned to our albergue, expecting to find a rat-infested kitchen with Rodrigo shoving Camino strays into a bubbling cauldron. As it happened, the kitchen was the albergue's finest facility. The oven was clean, the stove worked reliably and the dining area was free of all albergue staff. There was, however, a pilgrim in a thick brown woollen jumper leaning over a pot of boiling broth.

'*Guten Abend,*' he said without looking up, his wire-rimmed glasses foggy with the steam.

'*Guten Abend,*' we responded.

'You are English, no?' he asked, brushing a lock of his blond hair out of his eyes.

'Australian, actually,' I said. This pleased the man. It seemed that even on pilgrimage, German enmity for Britons was rife. He whipped off his jumper, revealing a pair of leathery brown arms. He was dirty, but it was the grubbiness of the adventurer rather than the vagrant.

As Dave and I cut up onions and tomatoes, Johan told us his story. He had left his home in West Berlin in the mid-seventies to attend the University of Leuven in Belgium. There to study philosophy, he in fact just smoked copious amounts of weed, dropped out of university and went to travel the world. It happened that he did not get further than the subcontinent. Intoxicated by the beauty and danger of the Himalayas, Johan discovered a passion for mountaineering. He used as his base a monastery outside a small Nepalese village not far from Kathmandu. The monks there generously fed and housed him.

Johan was fascinated by the monks, who behaved as if their lives of abstinence had liberated them. So, impulsively, he dropped his old life and began anew. He quit the weed, shaved his head and spent the next twenty years meditating, reading and walking, gradually losing contact with the western world. He might well have spent the rest of his days in the mountains had he not been mugged in Kathmandu after being sent to gather provisions. 'It was a message that the time had come to head home.'

Much had happened in the intervening years. Both his parents had died, estranged from their son. Having no siblings, Johan had inherited the entire estate. There were wider changes, too. During Johan's self-imposed exile, Western Europe had seen an explosion of interest in eastern theology. Using a slab of his inheritance, he resettled in Innsbruck to be closer to the mountains and established a meditation school.

This trip was his holiday from running the business. Johan was walking the Camino in the old style, having stepped out his front door bound for Santiago. He walked over the Alps and into Italy, bound for Turin. He turned west for Milan, south for Genova and then headed along the Mediterranean coast for Monaco and France. He toured Nice and Marseille and then made for Avignon in the north before dipping back down to Montpellier, picking up the Camino Aragonés at Toulouse.

Johan had no idea of the distance he had walked. Our rough calculations put his two-month-long journey at 2000 kilometres with another 550 remaining to Santiago. We estimated Johan averaged a little over 30 kilometres a day, a manageable distance across easy terrain and in agreeable weather. But Johan had kept that average over the Alps and the Pyrenees, while lugging a backpack filled with a tent, warm clothes, cooking utensils and a sleeping bag.

We sat down to eat, and noted that Johan's smile oscillated between friendly and deranged. He was deeply enigmatic. The cryptic phrases and pithy one-liners that punctuated the telling of his life story only complicated the matter. Were these truths learnt from the disciples of the Dalai Lama or the ramblings of a madman?

Like all vital characters in the best fiction, he was ambiguous. I felt like I was meeting the gravedigger from some Shakespearean play or other. I couldn't remember why exactly, but the gravedigger scene in *Hamlet* was supposed to be important. From memory it had to do with the circle of life. So I asked him why he was walking to Santiago.

'Are you not satisfied with my earlier answer? That I wished to get away from work?'

'Yes, but why did you choose to walk the Camino de Santiago and not just through the Alps or the Pyrenees?'

'It was just a good little walk.'

I tried a different tack. 'Okay, what have you learnt on the Way?'

'Nothing that I have not known before,' he chuckled.

'And what is that?'

He paused, his eyes narrowed. 'The Camino is like a great river. All one can do is submit to its current. To fight the Camino is to fight against that which resides in us all.' Johan fell into a fit of cackling as he cleaned up his dishes, and stowed them in his enormous backpack.

'I must find a campsite before it becomes too dark,' he said, hauling his enormous pack onto his shoulders. 'Farewell, my young Australian friends. Do not stand still in the river for too long, or you will drown! And beware the flat plain to come. This path is at its most treacherous when things seem easy!' He hooted his way out of the albergue. We followed him out the door and watched as he vanished into the dark, the gravedigger exiting the stage.

LOS DOS SANTIAGOS

After consultation with Dr Google, I diagnosed Dave as suffering from chronic tendonitis. He met my suggestion of a rest day with staunch opposition. Country blokes are made of stern stuff. City folk, however, will blink at the first sign of trouble. My knee was hurting badly, too, and a day off the path was probably what it needed.

Disagreeable though our accommodation was, the fact it was a private albergue had its advantages: we could stay for a second night and avoid having to limp to the next town. We rebooked at the reception desk, manned by the retired burlesque dancer, and went to the bar for breakfast. The cheerless bartender received our orders as enthusiastically as a house cleaner might greet a rodent. She took off to the kitchen with a grunt and returned half an hour later, practically hurling our breakfast plates onto the table.

'*Gracias, señorita*,' said Dave.

'Hmph,' she responded.

'Troll,' I muttered.

Continental breakfasts are always disappointing, but this

was utterly depressing. For four euros apiece, Dave and I were treated to two pieces of stale bread smeared with strawberry jam and a bitter *café Americana* each. 'I think my knee has mysteriously healed,' I said while suspiciously eyeing the green sheen on the strawberry jam.

'Is it too late to get a refund and keep walking to the next town?'

'I would have thought so,' said Dave, shovelling another teaspoon of sugar into his coffee to soften the blow. We forced down breakfast and then repaired to the sofa. The morning light streaming through the window showed up the mould evolving in the seams of each arm. Before long, I thought, these couches would grow legs and go searching for a better albergue. After an hour or two of listening to Dave work on his ukulele technique, I went for a poke around Belorado.

It was midday by the time I reached town. The next wave of pilgrims wouldn't hit for hours. For now, Belorado belonged to the locals, who it seemed kept to themselves at the local bars. I walked across the abandoned Plaza Mayor and found somewhere for a coffee. The bar was reasonably well patronised. There was the usual smattering of old boys in brown cardigans grouped in fours, playing cards, their crowded ashtrays thickening the air with carcinogens. Another was hunched over his drink at the bar talking to the barman, who was leaning in towards him conspiratorially. They looked like a pair of *bandidos* plotting a heist.

I ordered an *Americana* and made my way to the far end of the bar, where a drunk immediately accosted me. I had clocked him when I walked in, gibbering above the din. The barman shooed him away when his tone warbled towards something more threatening and offered me an apologetic shrug. The drunk, meanwhile, continued talking to himself while moving around the tables, studying each card player's hand. The old boys all ignored him. They knew his story and it no longer held any interest for them. I wondered if this was what Johan meant about staying still and drowning on the Camino. I drained my coffee, left a tip for the barman and returned to the Plaza.

Whatever construction was taking place in Belorado's streets seemed to be paused for siesta. I negotiated my way around the spades and cement mixers left abandoned in the middle of the road. Presently I found the Iglesia de Santa María, a sixteenth-century church built below limestone cliffs.

The church was empty. I walked up the aisle towards the stone retable, an ornamental shelf, with enclosed panels holding revered objects, behind the altar. Two contrasting figures rested on adjacent columns. They were the images of Santiago Peregrino and Santiago Matamoros, St James the Pilgrim and St James the Moor-slayer.

The two depictions of Santiago were polarised – one made him look beatific and benevolent, carrying his pilgrim's staff; the other formidable and terrible, on his horse, wielding a sword. Santiago earned the name 'Matamoros' at the Battle of Clavijo in 844, and, from what I can make of it, it seemed to suit him better than 'Peregrino'.

Like his brother John, James was a hothead. The two burst onto the scene in a small Samarian village, calling on God to rain down lightning on a group of sceptics who had questioned the legitimacy of Christ's claim to be the Son of God. Jesus rebuked them for their tempestuous outbursts – 'The Son of man is not come to destroy men's lives, but to save them' – and dubbed them '*Boanerges*', Greek for Sons of Thunder.

James' other distinguishing feature was his ambition. This, too, was a familial trait. Subsequent to the near dust-up with the doubting Samaritans, John and James secretly lobbied Christ for a seat either side of Him in Heaven. This unsavoury incident caused much displeasure among the other ten apostles.

Nevertheless, the gospels relate that James was unflinchingly loyal. He was the fourth person Jesus recruited as a disciple and, with John and Peter, made up the chosen group. These three witnessed some of Christianity's most important events, including the Transfiguration – when Jesus became radiant and conversed with Moses, Elijah and God – and Christ's agony in the Garden of Gethsemane – the difficult moment between the Last Supper and His arrest.

In short, James was one of Christ's most important disciples, and Pelayo's discovery of his relics could not have come at a better time. By the ninth century, most of the Iberian Peninsula was under Moorish rule. The relics of Mohammed that the Moors carried into battle were supposed to be very powerful. Pelayo's find ensured the Christians had something of equal worth. These were the holiest sorts of relics available, the kind perfectly suited to spearhead the Reconquista – the reconquest of Spain for Christianity. The relics were said to possess supernatural properties. St James' timely appearances on horseback at the battles of Clavijo in 844 and Las Navas de Tolosa in 1212 attest to the spirit of the Son of Thunder being imbued in those old bones. Useful supernatural powers notwithstanding, the relics' greatest gift to Christian Spain was more practical.

Having a holy site in the northwestern tip of the Iberian Peninsula meant that pilgrims had to trek across the heart of a Muslim-dominated land. Monarchs lifted tolls for pilgrims and offered Christians tempting enticements in exchange for settling along the path. This was particularly so along the Camino Francés, where hordes of pilgrims from the Continent made their way to Santiago.

Religious military orders were drawn to the Peninsula, charged with providing protection for the Santiago pilgrims. The Camino was directly responsible for the organisation of the Order of La Terraza, the Order of Calatrava, the Order of San Julián del Pereiro and the Order of Santiago. At various stages these orders took their places alongside the potent forces of the Hospitallers of St John and the Knights Templar. These two orders, founded in Jerusalem in the eleventh and twelfth centuries respectively, were initially concerned with nursing sick Christians back to health and protecting pilgrims. But the onset of the crusades brought with it a surplus of European sponsors eager to lend financial assistance towards recapturing the holy places. Knights Templar and Knights Hospitaller became the two charities of choice, and they were rearranged into fully-fledged military organisations. All cashed-up and seething with Christian righteousness, they would expand their operations beyond the crusades in the Holy Land. With this boosted military presence and through sheer weight of numbers, the Christians would drive the Moors south.

As a sign of gratitude for his intervention at Clavijo and for turning the tide in favour of Christian dominance in Iberia, an oath was sworn to pay homage to Santiago in the form of an annual stipend. The *Voto de Santiago*, the Vow of St James, was marked with a monarch or a high-ranking official delivering an *ofendra,* an economic tribute, at the Catedral del Apóstol in Santiago on 25 July – The Feast of St James. This tradition still endures. Today the *ofendra* usually comes in the form of civic improvements to the path or upgrades to pilgrim amenities and facilities. All this would have been very satisfactory for an intemperate man with a thirst for power. But nothing would have pleased James more than being made patron saint of Spain, the land he failed to subdue in life.

My eyes fixed on Santiago Matamoros, restless in his panel. The saint I could see before me was the essence of Christian defiance, the terrible knight sent from Heaven who had brought the Moors to heel. This was the image of St James as medieval Christianity had imagined him: captured in his great moment on the fields of Clavijo. But in that pose I saw something malicious. His pious doppelganger standing in pilgrim garb nearby was of little relief. In the company of the Moor-slayer, St James the Pilgrim appeared meek and docile. I made for the door posthaste, lest I be trampled under the wrathful hooves of that white horse.

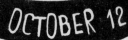

HOLY UNIONS

The following morning was the most tranquil on the Camino to date. There was no wind to spirit away the fog at the base of the Oca Mountains. The mist lifted late morning, unveiling a path up a slope covered by pine and oak trees. Dave and I moved fluidly towards San Juan de Ortega (St John of the Nettle), a village tucked into the side of Alto Carnero, the highest point of the Ocas. The town was named after Juan Velázquez, who had dedicated his life to the care of pilgrims after St Nicholas of Bari saved him from drowning while on pilgrimage to Jerusalem.

Juan learnt his trade under Santo Domingo, continuing the master builder's work after the latter's death. Juan extended the Camino further west towards Burgos, and built five bridges between Logroño and Atapuerca. He also maintained a pilgrim's hospice on the western slope of Alto Carnero. In death, Juan was canonised, and dubbed the patron saint of hospice-keepers. In addition to that dull charge, San Juan was named the intercessor for barren women, a position that requires some explaining.

It was said that a swarm of white bees filled the air whenever San Juan's tomb was opened. The white bees were seen to be the unborn souls of children, kept safe by the saint pending their incarnation in the wombs of the faithful. San Juan was himself born to aged parents and after his canonisation became known for helping people overcome sterility. These saintly powers piqued the interest of Isabel la Católica, the fifteenth-century monarch who was thought to be infertile. Some time between setting up the Spanish Inquisition, expelling Jews and Muslims from the Iberian Peninsula, instigating the discovery of the New World and uniting Spain under Catholicism, Isabel visited San Juan's tomb to pray for a son and heir. Her prayers answered, Isabel named two of her children Juan and Juanita in honour of the saint. The fate of Isabel's children would suggest that in her prayers she forgot to include St Teresa of Avila, the patron saint invoked against bodily ills.

With the exception of María of Aragón, Queen Consort of Portugal from her marriage to King Manuel I, Isabel's offspring endured tragic lives. Isabella died while delivering a son; Catherine of Aragón was cast off after failing to deliver Henry VIII a male heir; and Juan, Prince of Asturias, died of tuberculosis aged nineteen, a short time before his wife delivered a stillborn child. But of all Isabel's children, Juanita's plight resonates most strongly with the Spanish.

After her mother's death, Juanita became one of the most powerful regents in Europe. She acceded to the thrones of Castile and Aragón and mothered a son who became Holy

Roman Emperor Charles V. But she is more memorable for her obsession with the occult and her jealous rage.

Many have delighted in grotesque depictions of Juanita's refusal to bury the corpse of her husband, the philandering Philip the Handsome. For months after his death, Juanita refused to have Philip's body interred, rejoicing each morning to find him tucked up in his casket instead of in his mistress's bed. No one knows exactly when she finally had his body committed to the earth. It was presumably some time after they were calling him Philip the Embalmed but hopefully before he was Philip the Foetid, Rotted Mess. They were, however, calling his widow 'Juanita la Loca', Juanita the Mad. The tomb at which her mother had prayed was in the next village and I was keen to take a look.

Our early morning energy had been sapped by cresting Alto Carnero. The towering pines denied us a view back down towards Belorado so we pushed on down the hill for San Juan. We walked into the town, and past a small Romanesque church, out the front of which were screaming kids running about wildly after their first communion. This was where San Juan's remains lay.

'Just a second, mate,' said Dave, pulling me back as I went to make my way into the church. 'I think I might keep walking to Agés. There's a bit of pilgrim traffic on the road today.' The competition for beds in smaller towns had increased since Santo Domingo. The first-in-first-served rule meant there was little time for sightseeing. 'You go and check out the church; I'll go and get us set up in Agés.'

'Are you sure?'

'Positive,' said Dave, turning on his heel. 'I'll see you later on.'

I passed the proud parents loitering out the front with their smartly dressed children and entered the church. There was no one inside. I searched up and down the church's nave, eventually finding a staircase down to San Juan's tomb. Tentatively, I made my way down, my hiking boots echoing eerily through the unseen cave below.

The stairs led to a crypt containing a dimly lit alabaster sarcophagus raised on black marble with silver lettering spelling out the name 'San Juan de Ortega'. A tall bearded man wearing sandals and a black singlet was running his hand over the panels of the tomb.

'I thought the only tombs you visited were the ones where girls knocked you back,' I said.

Boris raised his head slowly. 'Hey, man.'

'Are you interested in Camino history?' I asked.

'Not at all.' He continued to pass a hand across San Juan's tomb. 'I just came down here to be on my own and found this beautifully carved coffin. I have sometimes thought of becoming a sculptor myself, you know.'

The conversation and the echoes that we awoke in that cold crypt made me uneasy. I began to back towards the stairs. 'I'll leave you to it, then, Boris.'

'Hey, wait up. I'm coming, too.'

We moved silently back up the stairs, through the church and out onto the Camino. With some difficulty, I fell in with

Boris's pace. It was much slower than when we last met before Santo Domingo, when he'd raced ahead in search of his Blessed Virgin. This was the gait of a pensive pilgrim.

'Hey,' I said after a while, 'did you manage to find that Texan?'

Boris missed a step. 'We just had lunch back at San Juan. Things didn't go exactly to plan.'

'What happened?'

'Nothing, man, that's the whole problem.' A slight mist crept into Boris's eyes. 'I had me an old-fashioned Texan rejection.'

'American girls are real heartbreakers,' I said. Boris shot me a quizzical look.

'Speaking from experience?'

I hesitated out of reluctance to rake over some unpleasant memories. Normally, I'd have kept my peace and just offered him a consolatory tap on the back, but I saw the Canadian's teary eyes. He looked like a man whose misery needed company.

I told him how we'd met in Scotland on a student-exchange program. The exact nature of our courtship need not be elaborated on beyond the fact that it contained all the usual bits – knowing looks across the bar, outrageous flirting, close talking and so on. It's certainly fair to say that the internationality of the affair heightened the intensity. We were, after all, both foreigners on foreign soil.

'I've heard the Australian accent goes over well stateside,' offered Boris.

I nodded. But there was more to it than just accents. She was from New York and carried herself with a New Yorker's confidence that, along with her looks, was enough to still a crowded room. I'd simply never met anyone like her. I felt privileged just to be in her company, not to mention calling her my girl. I was in awe of her.

After we finished our semester, I followed her back to the States on my way home to Australia. We spent a perfect month together, touring New England, partying hard, hanging out with her friends and all the while confessing our undying love for one another. But it had to end. At the airport gate shortly after, parting in floods of tears (more mine than hers), I looked back and, like General MacArthur, declared pathetically, 'I will return!' Six weeks later she rang to call it off.

I was crushed, and for the longest time thought this was the source of my problems. I spent a year saving up for a flight, certain that mouthing a couple of romantic platitudes face to face would win her back. I arrived the week of her college commencement, literally walking in on the graduation party. Whereas once her friends had swarmed about me to hear my exotic accent and make my acquaintance, they now looked at me as they would have an impostor. My girl walked forward looking magnificent, unchanged except for the fact that she was smoking. She spared me the indignity of staying a minute longer in that hostile room, leading me out into the humid June night.

Before she even spoke I could tell I was toast. It was written on her face. While she gently broke the news, a clean-cut college boy came outside. They exchanged a look intended to convey that all was well and that she didn't need his help. He returned to the party. Right then I developed a sudden urge to start smoking. I snatched the pack from her lap.

I briefly indulged in self-righteousness, even though I knew she'd done nothing wrong. She had already broken the news over the phone a year ago and it was breathtaking arrogance to think she would rekindle things at the mere sight of me. I couldn't even satisfy myself that she was making a terrible mistake. I'd met her new man on the last trip: he was a good guy with an honest smile and a bright future in commerce.

Once I'd calmed down, we embraced in that cold fashion lovers do when they've become friends instead. She stood up, leaving me her cigarettes, and returned to her party without looking back. I spent an unhappy fortnight emptying out several Boston bars of Budweiser before going home. I arrived back in Melbourne heavy-hearted, four grand lighter and with a serious nicotine addiction.

'Have you heard from her since?'

'I get the occasional update from a mutual friend.'

'How's she doing?'

'Great. She's coming up to her first wedding anniversary and has just entered the second trimester.'

'Ouch,' said Boris. We rounded a bend, walking past a couple of German girls picnicking on the side of the road. We returned their Camino salutations and went on until Boris grabbed my arm and faced me.

'Hey, man,' he said, looking at me intently. 'I think you really need to get over this girl.'

'Get over her? Mate, I'm *well* over her. I last saw her four years ago.'

'Four years ago! That's a full Olympic cycle. You really have to move on.'

'I have moved on; I was only telling you because it seemed the Texan had got you down.'

'What gave you that impression?'

'I don't know, I thought —'

'Listen, I'm going back to have a chat to those girls. I'm getting a sudden urge for some sauerkraut. I'll see you in Agés. In the meantime, I think you should try and find yourself a pilgrim girl and get over this New Yorker.'

'I am over her!' I shouted out after him, watching as he strolled towards the Fräuleins, most likely plotting a Holy Trinity. I turned around, chuckling at mistaking a teary eye for heartbreak, my left hand frantically searching my pockets for a cigarette.

BARKS OF BOILING HATE

It is little wonder to me that Brazilian author Paulo Coelho chose a dog as the manifestation of the Devil in his Camino book, *The Pilgrimage*. Loosely tethered to the front gate of almost every property we passed was a vicious, hateful dog, each possessing razor-sharp teeth and a bloodcurdling bark.

Wild dogs threatening the passage of pilgrims along the Camino have been an issue for almost a millennium. Old Picaud notes that the function of the pilgrim's staff was to both act as a 'third foot' and defend 'against the wolf and the dog'.

And here's the rub: I hate dogs.

I know this places me firmly in the minority, but it is a position from which I will not resile. Without exception, every dog I have encountered, be it domestic, wild or stray, has sensed my antipathy and returned the sentiment. This means I attract a lot of livid snarling, nuzzling of the crotch and snapping at the heels. I have even had a dog communicate its distaste by urinating on my leg.

I don't understand, either, the relationships dogs have

with most other human beings. Presidents grovelling over Scottish terriers, chocolate labs or springer spaniels on the White House lawn is, for me, confounding rather than endearing. All that gravitas traded away for a chance to stuff around with the flea-infested family pet. Surely brokering peace between Palestine and Israel is of greater importance than feeding the dog and cleaning up its shit.

Ultimately, it's the willingness to forsake one's sensibilities around a dog that, frankly, I do not get. This first occurred to me some years ago when a high-school crush accepted my invitation to go to the movies together. This being my first ever date, I presented myself at her family home determined to make a good impression. Like the sounding of a nemesis's horn signalling an imminent attack, a dreaded chorus of growls came from within the house.

The moment the mother opened the door an Alsatian built like a draughthorse began to circle me, occasionally darting in to sink its fangs into my calves. While this was going on, a Shih tzu bounded up, jumping headfirst into my crotch. 'Dear, oh dear,' exclaimed the mother. 'Rusty and Lilly are behaving very strangely.'

'What on earth gave you that impression?' I wanted to ask. 'Is it that Rusty just tore a hole in my Achilles or that Lilly is hanging from my testicles?'

The attack was not nearly as offensive as the suit-wearing father who declined to shake my hand for 'personal reasons' but allowed the little bitch to lick his face and mouth. I looked about the room, searching the faces of the mother, the sisters and my date for something like the horror I was feeling. None of them seemed fazed that the man of the house was prepared to trade saliva with a Shih tzu that had probably had its nose up Rusty's arse. The girl and I did not proceed beyond that date.

Even the most ardent dog-lover would find it difficult to feel affection for the Camino canines. Out here, the dog is not man's best friend, he is the spawn of Satan – glowering, snarling and barking at any pilgrim who comes near. I felt vindicated. It was as if a cloak had been lifted so the world could see their true nature at last. The embodiment of manic rage struggling at the end of a chain that we had regularly encountered since leaving Saint-Jean, however, was nothing compared to the dogs of Agés.

We were enveloped by another thick mist the morning we made for Burgos. It was a complete white out, concealing the creatures responsible for the most hideous barking ever to have assaulted my ears. These were barks of boiling hate. Malicious paws would slice through the opaque whiteness centimetres from our faces, or snouts with bared teeth would emerge from the mist only to snap back in a jangle of chains. At times multiple barking jaws would appear close together, like three-headed Cerberus guarding the gates of hell.

I would like to say that I swiped back at their outstretched claws with Herculean courage. Nope. I was reduced to a pussycat cowering behind my unshakeable companion. Dave seemed completely unperturbed. He walked on with the joviality of a weekend golfer.

The barking lessened as the fog lifted. Visibility, it seemed, was the antidote to their rage. It was a beautiful blue-sky day. The road went up through pine trees and dense scrub. Our speedy ascent fleeing the dogs had meant that we unintentionally left Atapuerca behind us in the white soup.

Some years before, construction workers cutting a rail link to nearby mines discovered human remains in caves near the small village of Atapuerca. The local police were despatched to investigate whether the bones belonged to victims of foul play. Sure enough, there was evidence of cannibalism, but the crime had been committed nearly one million years ago. The trail having gone extremely cold, a group of palaeontologists took over the site and discovered a quantity of human fossils that comprise over 90 per cent of all known European pre-Neanderthal remains.

With lukewarm enthusiasm, Dave and I had agreed the night before to take the 3-kilometre detour at Atapuerca to visit the caves. From where we were now, however, we would have to walk back another few kilometres to find the detour.

The dusty remnants of my ancestors don't move me. When I've visited palaeontological exhibits, I haven't known what to do. I normally just click my tongue in contrived disbelief and mutter something like, 'Jeez, this bloke was around a hell of a long time ago'. Also, walking backwards on a pilgrimage feels almost heretical. Back on the path, Dave and I looked around stupidly, each waiting for the other to make a decision.

I blinked first. 'You don't reckon that we could just —'

'Absolutely,' said Dave.

We resumed our steady ascent, compiling a list of justifications for bypassing one of Europe's most important archaeological digs. There were weighty theological justifications ('This is a Christian pilgrimage and those people weren't Christian'); there were pragmatic justifications ('We need to keep moving if we want to make Burgos by night'); there were philosophical justifications ('Big deal if they were around one million years ago, what difference does that make to the here and now?'); there were spiritual justifications ('Maybe the fog was the universe telling us *not* to visit the site'); and finally there were justifications of indifference and priority ('Stuff 'em: let's get to the next town for a beer'). It was less the watertight logic of university-educated men, more the grunting of a pair of Neanderthals.

The path climbed and we walked on until we saw a crucifix attached to the top of a cairn. This Alto Cruceiro mountain cross marked the beginning of the next section of the Camino. For the next 250 kilometres the road would not rise or fall more than 150 metres. That said, it was not the place to view the great flatness of the Meseta Central (which translates to 'inner plateau'). Obscuring our view was the city of Burgos. You could almost smell the smoke from the chimney stacks and taste the dust kicked up by the B-doubles.

The popular view among pilgrims who had walked the pilgrimage was that we were approaching a period of intense boredom. My attitude to this was, well, terrific. With all the excitement we had experienced, a week or so of dullness was probably in order. And flat terrain seemed the best place to recuperate from sore knees in preparation for scaling the hills that rise barrier-like before Santiago. Johan, the mountain-loving monk, was the only person to have said anything seriously negative about the Meseta – 'beware the flat land to come'. This was hardly surprising. He was most likely projecting his distaste for even terrain. The approach into the first city of the Meseta was, however, cause for mild depression.

Before long we were trudging past factories, overpasses and highways to the clang and rattle of industry. Sensing a lull in the mood, Dave did what he does best in these situations: pulled out his ukulele and started up with a song. Like wandering minstrels, we sang our way into Burgos on the shoulder of what must be one of Spain's loudest and busiest highways. We composed several tunes in that countrified-gospel style favoured by Zoe the evangelist with lyrics dedicated to three of our favourite pilgrims. We titled them 'Boris and the Hunt for the Holy Grail', 'French Pipes and the Word that Went Unheard' and 'Jesus Loves You, Warren'. We called ourselves 'Santiago and the Moor-slayers'. It was the easiest 10-kilometre stretch of the Camino to date. At the end of it stood the Burgos Cathedral.

There are structures along the Camino that are no less iconic than the yellow way-markers and the cockleshell. The cathedral at Burgos is one of them. Since the thirteenth century, its gothic spires have guided pilgrims in for a religious pit stop before the long haul across the Meseta.

To bypass this architectural wonder would be like

declining an invitation to stroll along the Champs Élysées, or rejecting a trip to the top of the Empire State Building. What kind of cultural impotence must one suffer to show no interest in such a sight? What sort of heathens would pass up the opportunity to admire it? Santiago and the Moor-slayers, that's who.

After dropping our gear at the multi-storey Albergue Divina Pastora, we left to tick the Burgos Cathedral off our must-see checklist. It would make up for our indifference towards them bones back in Atapuerca, we reasoned.

We were so excited at the thought of seeing the cathedral that we thought we'd take the edge off our nerves with a *cerveza*. As it happened, we picked a bar with a stand-up piano and a barista thrilled at the prospect of a bilingual pianist entertaining his patrons for free. Our one beer turned into many. This is not so hard to believe as that, by demand, Santiago and the Moor-slayers went on to perform three one-hour sets.

It would be an evening of rare events. It was the first and only time that Santiago and the Moor-slayers would ever enjoy a paid gig (we received two rounds of San Miguel Grandes – the equivalent of a pint – on the house); the first time I would be cajoled into an encore performance of 'Tiny Dancer'; and, I'd wager, the first time the good citizens of Burgos would have ever heard of Peter Allen, let alone clapped along to 'Tenterfield Saddler'. Dave's playing had drawn pilgrims into that bar as if it'd contained the True Cross itself.

As the night wore on, all the old faces emerged. First,

in the bar, then on the makeshift stage. Liz, the Australian reiki-master, performed a sultry version of 'Fever'; Nikki, the nervous Dane, a faithful rendition of 'Penny Lane'; Bonjour shunned the crowd's request for 'La Vie en Rose', instead proving herself a stunning soprano with the 'Habanera' from *Carmen*; Boris sang two tunes from the Burt Bacharach songbook before sidling up to a *señorita* at the bar; and an Argentinean foursome did 'Don't Cry for Me Argentina', barbershop-quartet style.

The atmosphere was only once disturbed, by an earnest female voice with a southern drawl shouting repeatedly, 'Play something Jesus would sing! Play something the Good Lord would sing!' The bar fell silent; all eyes turned to us. 'Sorry, ladies and gentlemen,' retorted Dave, as quick as a flash. 'Jesus couldn't make it tonight. But I'm Dave and this is Tom and we are Santiago and the Moor-slayers.' The bar erupted into laughter, and I felt I could hear the collective sigh of relief before everyone joined in on an extended rendition of 'Piano Man'.

Passing up the opportunity to see the Burgos Cathedral is difficult to defend. But if Burgos's role is to spiritually fortify the pilgrim before the great trek across the Meseta, then it achieved that purpose. In that Burgos bar brought to life by Dave's music, a group of pilgrims filled up on a different kind of spirit, readying themselves for whatever lay ahead. From the sound of it, the only real challenge that lurked out there was trying to invent ways of not getting too bored. Not exactly life-and-death stuff. Even so, for those of us seeking life-altering conversions of Road to Damascus proportions, we needed a night of this kind. There was still a long way to go.

Time had run away from us. The albergue doors would be closing in a matter of minutes. We shook hands with the barista, skolled our beers and, with the others in tow, made off at a frantic pace for the albergue. Between the high Romanesque and gothic façades, below the statues of rearing horses and the solemn faces of the Castilian kings and queens, I saw the twin towers of the cathedral lit up, radiant. Without the slightest pang of regret we ran on, beating the lockout with seconds to spare.

And the next day, we would walk across the Meseta.

PART TWO

THE GREAT FLATNESS

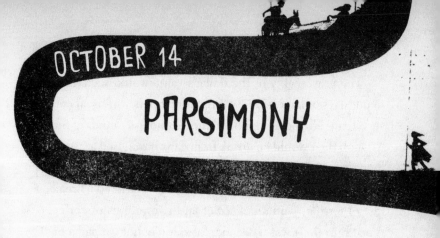

PARSIMONY

The television in the café was screening the morning news. Despite having mastered the Iberian lisp when asking for a *cerveza*, I remained embarrassingly unilingual and so was unable to follow what the silver-haired anchorman was saying. Footage of screaming Wall Street traders, however, needed little translation: the financial crisis had gathered momentum since I'd left Melbourne. This was less concerning to me than the value of the Australian dollar, which a quick check online showed to be declining rapidly.

I recalled rejoicing when the dollar had nudged the sixty-five-euro-cent mark shortly after I'd bought my aeroplane ticket. Instead of heeding the advice of all-knowing grandmothers and buying up euros there and then, I held off, hopeful the dollar's value might attain even loftier heights. The gamble hadn't paid off. Right now the dollar seemed destined to be on par with the Kenyan shilling. Dave and I joked that by the time we reached Santiago we would be trading in body parts: 'Did you say two euros for a San Miguel? Why, that's six and half million Australian dollars! What can I get for a kidney?'

The grim reality of the dollar's value would see an end to our days of largesse. It was time for a policy of fiscal conservatism. No more pilgrim menus or endless rounds of San Miguel. Beer would be drunk from cans purchased at supermarkets and dinner cooked in albergue kitchens. To celebrate the new era of pecuniary responsibility we ordered a breakfast of *tortilla*, *pain au chocolat* and two rounds of coffee. A last hurrah. It was a disgraceful splurge, but we had a big day ahead of us.

Over the last week, Dave and I had been averaging 20 kilometres a day. With a whopping 500 kilometres to go, we needed to crank it up if we were to make Santiago by All Saints' Day. The less physically demanding terrain of the Meseta seemed a good place to begin. We set ourselves a 30-kilometre stage, which would take us to the tiny village of Hontanas.

We made our way out of Burgos in brilliant sunshine, leaving behind our old selves with the morning traffic. In the place of the big-spending beer guzzlers who struggled across relatively short distances were two frugal pilgrims with an ambitious plan. We would cover 500 kilometres in seventeen days.

Dave and I were pumped. By now we had written off Johan as a demented madman with a prejudice against flatness. We had conquered the Pyrenees and the undulating land of Navarra and La Rioja with consequences no worse than sore legs and joints. How hard could an amble across 250 kilometres of flat land be for hot-blooded Antipodeans from the flattest continent in the world? We were like wild animals preparing to be set loose in our native habitat. We tightened the straps on our packs, hawked up some phlegm, discharging it man-of-the-world style at the side of the path, and set off at a thunderous clip. At this rate we'd be knocking the scab off a San Miguel by three.

West of Hornillos del Camino, a good 15 kilometres out of Burgos, the terrain took on a disorienting sameness. The strain I was feeling through my leg muscles gave me the sense that I was setting a good pace, but the landscape felt like it was moving with me. There was not a tree or a bush in sight nor even a rise or bend in the road. Just boundless rows of harvested wheat stalks sprouting on both sides of the path out to the horizon.

The scarcity of landmarks made judging distance nearly impossible. There was the occasional cairn by the road, and sometimes a tractor trailing dust would shunt us off the path, or we'd spot another dizzyingly straight road running perpendicular to the Camino, marking out huge parcels of land. But these were quickly subsumed into the great monotony of the Meseta.

Dave seemed to gain strength out here, perhaps recalling the landscape of his childhood. He sped ahead, leaving me in his dust. I gave up my attempt to keep pace with him, electing to tough out the remaining distance to Hontanas on my own. I had plenty of mental fodder.

The morning news reports of the economic crisis back in the real world were weighing heavily on my mind. Multinationals sliding into bankruptcy and national economies on the brink of collapse would inevitably drag Australia into recession. These were concepts last discussed when I was a pimple-faced adolescent trying to master an on-drive. I could no longer take refuge beneath the blanket of youth and leave the worrying to my parents. I knew that recession and its hardships (unemployment, a tight job market, financial destitution) would be waiting for me on my return home. It would be a disastrous time to be unemployed, worse still to be unemployable.

My curriculum vitae read like a list of ho-hum party tricks (cinema choc-top seller of the year; grade-six-standard alto saxophonist; captain of my school's year-nine cricket team). A brief flirtation with journalism had spawned an underwhelming folio of published work, mainly colour pieces printed in suburban rags and the odd major daily. My standout articles included a piece on a rare sighting of the Orange-painted Snipe in rural Victoria and a hard-hitting exposé of the fat dog epidemic in Melbourne's northern suburbs. To escape another year as a glorified copyboy I took a job in the state's conservative party office for reasons attributable to 'making a difference'. It seemed a disingenuous gesture, my having never voted for the side of politics in whose employ I now found myself. But I learnt to hate the other side, came to embrace my new team and then distrust them, and eventually to dislike both major parties. I left without having made the slightest difference.

Mine was a résumé that spoke of a peripatetic approach to employment. It showed me stopping off briefly in hospitality and education administration, uprooting for journalism, throwing that in for policy development, and then drifting into data entry. I had wandered through these jobs like an itinerant, unsure of the route to my professional destination. Ultimately, my working life had been a wayward collection of failed experiments that amounted to desperately little.

In truth, I was no more employable than when I'd left university. Before coming to Spain, I'd held down a two-month job punching gas-meter reads into a computer, hardly the kind of work that would skyrocket me into the highest tax bracket. With everything happening in the world, it would be about as good a job as I could expect when I returned home.

So, what had I been doing for the last six years that was so engaging as to prevent me from securing long-term employment? And what was I doing in the middle of a wheat farm while my contemporaries were battening down the hatches and bracing themselves for economic hardship? I imagined my friends and siblings doing responsible things, adult things, like securing their assets, paying off their credit cards, cancelling holidays, reassessing their budgets. The best I could come up with was a no-more-beers-at-the-bar strategy. Suddenly, the pilgrimage seemed extraordinarily self-indulgent.

Dave was a speck on the horizon and growing smaller by the minute. I increased my cadence, seeking those assurances other unemployed people give each other. But in every sense I was on my own. Dave was an outstanding musician who could supplement his income with relief teaching and private tuition. There was a certainty in that, just as there was certainty in his marriage and Dave and Rachel's various assets. He was beyond my line of sight. I was hemmed in on either side by wheatfields with nothing else afore or astern.

I began to question whether I was on the right path. As the sun dipped low on the horizon, I slipped into paranoia. Had I misinterpreted a way-marker back at one of those intersections? Was I supposed to be bearing north instead of holding this westerly course? Eventually, a large cairn came into view. Knowing that only pilgrim hands would ever construct such a thing, I answered a resounding 'no' to those questions.

'Who are you talking to?' It was Dave, seated on his pack behind the cairn.

'No one. What's the matter with you?' Dave's cap was pulled all the way down over his forehead.

'I have a minor problem.' I detected a strain in his voice.

Christ, I thought, *we're* both *coming unstuck*. Anxiety was the part of the package I brought to the team. Dave's part was reliability. I readied myself to remind him of this until he pulled his hat off.

Vivid red spots framed by scratch marks dotted his head. 'Fucking bedbugs!' I cried unhelpfully. Dave's nemesis of the animal kingdom had announced itself in a place where the weaponry to halt its advance (antiseptic, repellent, insecticide) was scarce.

'It gets worse,' muttered Dave, pointing out bites on his arms even angrier and redder than those on his head.

We should have been expecting this. We'd quickly learnt that the images we had of rotund *señoritas* at albergues making up our beds with freshly pressed linen were fantasies. There were never any sheets or pillowcases. At best, a pilgrim might be issued with a disposable bedcover and pillowcase made of a cheap synthetic fabric. These provided protection from bedbugs in the same way a raincoat protects against nuclear fallout.

Dave had waited for me, hoping to borrow a long-sleeved shirt so he could conceal his wounds from wardens in the next town. Bedbug outbreaks over the summer had forced the closure of a handful of albergues, and Dave didn't want to risk being refused entry. He needn't have worried. We found an understanding albergue warden in Hontanas. She spirited Dave away to the laundry, fumigated his clothes and gave him a can of heavy-duty insecticide. He emptied out the can spraying his bag and mattress. From that point, this became written into Dave's daily routine – coffee for breakfast, Mortein for tea.

While Dave dabbed calamine lotion on his bites, I went off to prepare dinner. Given the events of the day, I chose to delay the onset of our fiscal restraint and shouted us three rounds of San Miguel and a pilgrim's menu in the albergue's restaurant.

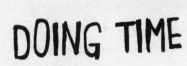

DOING TIME

I needed to get off the Meseta as quickly as possible. The thought came to me while cracking open my third San Miguel the night before. The anxiety I'd felt the day before proved I was not handling the flat parts of this pilgrimage very well, but the reasons why remained amorphous.

Maintaining the distance we covered from Burgos to Hontanas would put us back in the hills in eight days. That was too long. Over dinner I'd pitched a revised itinerary to Dave that would begin with a 35-kilometre haul to the town of Frómista. If we could keep up that sort of distance we would take at least a day off our Meseta time. To sway Dave to my thinking I talked about it like it was a jail term, as if *doing* the Meseta were no different to *doing* time. Dave did not need much convincing. The new plan meant stealing into the pre-dawn dark and therefore avoiding the attention his bug-riddled state might attract.

We were away the next day before the long-haul hikers had even packed their scroggin. We set off at a ferocious speed but at the first peep of dawn I felt the creep of anxiety again. The precious few physical distractions in the land-scape should have come as a relief from the visual tedium. Instead they became symbols, portents of trouble ahead – projections of my paranoia. Had that cairn collapsed across the path to warn me against proceeding? Were those sun-flowers' drooping heads nodding forlornly at pilgrims heading towards ruin? Was that poplar leaning dramatically over the path the aftermath of a terrible storm or bracing for one to come?

Maybe Johan was not a mad monk after all. Nasty things might not have been lurking out here, but the Meseta seemed capable of inducing them within. Not having a physical chal-lenge to distract them, pilgrims must trek the wilderness of their mind – a far trickier landscape to negotiate. Who knows what fears and anxieties were concealed beneath the crags, until then hidden by the brightness of modern life?

Some Camino books will have you believe that this kind of internalising leads to all sorts of metaphysical experiences. When Shirley MacLaine took on the Meseta she ended up going on a vision-quest to Atlantis and the lost continent of Lemuria. My snoring-induced nightmare back in Logroño suggested that I was prone to visions of saints. I was not really looking for more evidence to support this.

Fascinating as it would be to converse with Santiago on the Battle of Clavijo or talk road construction with Santo Domingo or swap rabid-dog stories with Santa Quitéria or discuss turning tricks in the Holy Land with St Mary of Egypt, none of that would be helpful. What saintly wisdom could assist me in getting my life back on track or making sense of the last six years? Even the idea that it'd be saints who appeared before me seemed optimistic. I would be more likely to encounter the spectre of a drunk Templar swigging from a gourd in a paper bag, and trying to bum a cigarette.

I tried chatting with Dave to keep myself from going nuts, but he was not in a talkative mood. The bites on his arms hadn't improved overnight and there was fresh evidence of insect activity at the tip of his nose. It looked like a bug platoon had withstood the insecticide, stormed the citadel and hoisted their flag on its ramparts. The bites were so vicious you almost wanted to scratch them for him. He developed a new mannerism: bringing to within inches of his head an outstretched hand, like a claw poised to rip his face off. Then he'd grit his teeth, breathe deeply, and return his hand to his side.

I lowered my eyes to the path and started counting steps in the hope of warding off black thoughts. I lost count somewhere after two thousand, so started again. It was an extremely long day.

Valladolid, not far south from where we were, had spawned one of Europe's most odious figures. The Dominican Fray Tomás de Torquemada's grisly life achievements earned him the nickname 'The Dark Prince of the Spanish Inquisition'. Pope Sixtus IV anointed him the first Inquisitor-General of Spain in 1483, a position he embraced with relish.

The Iberian Peninsula quickly became a place where survival hinged on presenting oneself as rigidly pious. Witches, protestants, homosexuals and Moors were among those firmly in the Inquisitor's sights. But for Torquemada, Jews were his chief concern.

With Vatican support, he pressured Isabel and Fernando, the Catholic monarchs, to issue the Edict of Expulsion in 1492. It was the vile pinnacle of his career. Jews of all age were given four months to leave the Iberian Peninsula on pain of death. The doctrine of *sangre limpia* (pure blood) was made a state-sponsored ideology that would result in 100 000 trials and the violent deaths of 2000 people.

Paranoia and insecurity most likely drove Torquemada's obsession with *sangre limpia* – he was himself born to well-placed Jewish *conversos* (converts to Christianity). The doctrine came to underpin a quest to root out *marranos* (Jews who had only pretended to convert) and other heretics.

The punishments meted out by Torquemada and his cronies sitting on the ecclesiastical tribunals were brutal. Following the public or private *auto-da-fé* (Portuguese for 'act of faith') – a sort of nightmarish marriage of Catholic mass and judicial sentencing – the condemned would be paraded through town wearing the *sambenito*, a cross-covered yellow shirt shortened at the waist to expose the genitals. Immediately after being marched through the town square, the condemned would be led to the local church and flogged.

Irrespective of age and gender, heretics who maintained their innocence would be subjected to incomprehensible torture as a means of extracting a confession. The condemned would then be tied to a stake and presented with three options: recant and kiss the cross, and death would be delivered by garotting; recant only and a fire would be set alight underneath the stake, fuelled by dry timber to hasten the execution; refuse to recant, and the wood used for the fire would be green, prolonging the agony. The methods of torture and execution varied until the Inquisition's disbandment in 1834, over three and a half centuries after it was established.

Towards the end of his life, Torquemada became increasingly fearful of being poisoned – haunted, one hopes, by the ghosts of those he sent to die. He refused to eat anything unless a 'unicorn's horn' was nearby to use as an antidote. Unjustly, he died peacefully in his sleep in 1498.

The Vatican formally revoked the Edict of Expulsion in 1968, not long before its five hundredth anniversary. Spanish governments have since scrambled to provide compensation to Sephardic Jews – descendants of those expelled in 1492 or Jews who define themselves by the customs and rituals that originated in the Iberian Peninsula. Among their entitlements is the right to apply for citizenship after a year of legal residency in Spain. A belated play at atonement for the less palatable parts of Spain's Golden Age.

Frómista seems arrestingly large in the context of the sparse countryside that surrounds it. Despite being plonked in the middle of a paddock, Frómista has grand public buildings, suggesting that the town has profited greatly from those bloody interminable wheatfields. They were of only fleeting interest. I needed a beer.

I had noticed that all the bars along the Camino – from Larrasoaña to Logroño – were patronised by identical-looking elderly gentlemen. There was always a foursome of card players at the window, each with a Camel Filter sagging out of his mouth. Two slightly younger men smudged in dirt from the field would meanwhile be nattering away about something of great importance (a bad harvest, the bitterness of the coffee, Atlético Madrid's run of poor form). And in the darkest corner of the bar, a tired old drunk would be pouring money into a machine that always looked as if it were preparing to haemorrhage coins but never did. It was not a lively scene.

There was something immediately different about the bar in Frómista. There was the usual accumulation of cigarette butts, serviettes and crumbs on the floor and a thick cloud of smoke trying to escape through the door. But here it was quieter than in other bars. There was no murmuring or hawking up of tar phlegm. No one turned to look at Dave and me when we walked in, either. The reason swiftly became clear.

She was profoundly beautiful, of course, drinking quietly at the bar, puffing thoughtfully on her cigarette. Her backpack leant against the smooth skin of her leg, making me, for the first time in my life, jealous of a piece of luggage. Wisps of dark-brown hair had broken ranks with the rest of her pinned locks and hung tantalisingly about her neck. Her smile could have moved the most hardened cynic to believing in boy-band lyrics. But it was her smoking, the very thing that modern folk would deem antisocial and unattractive, that defined her potent looks.

She smoked her cigarette the way it should be done, drawing in its contents slowly and deliberately. It was like watching an old cigarette commercial – she was all silver-screen glamour. It perfectly contrasted with my recent habit of pulling back desperately on a fag, determined to suck in every last milligram of nicotine. This woman's smoking transformed a seedy health risk into an exotic extension of her spectacular body.

While I was stuck on unpilgrim-like thoughts, Dave went to the bar to order a round of San Miguel. I took my seat alongside the crusty old Frómistans. They were all staring at her with moistened eyes as if Aphrodite had just dropped into their dank watering hole for light refreshment. Frómista and its citizens, I feared, would never be the same again. But then, I wasn't sure I would be, either.

DIVINE CLARITY

That I fell immediately for the girl in the Frómista bar was unsurprising. Romance was rife along the ancient road. Constanza and Lorenzo had been spotted holding hands in Santo Domingo; Warren and his Spanish patient Esther had not been seen since Logroño; and Boris had fallen in love seven times over 350 kilometres. Now I had become the latest victim of St Valentine.

Her hazel eyes and brown hair were consistent with Boris's description of the Texan. He was wrong about her chassis though. It could get more than just married men in trouble. The sight of her had silenced the anxious voices in my mind like the orator who stills the room with a knife on glass. On the downside, her looks caused my romantic prowess to regress to schoolboy standards. I didn't even ask her name during our first chat. I wasn't fazed.

My interaction with the girl outside the Frómista albergue (I said, 'Hi'; she gave me a 'Howdy' pronounced with a southern American twang) gave me the spiritual nourishment I had craved since stepping onto the Meseta. That night, I slept soundly and woke refreshed and invigorated. Dave's bites had settled down as miraculously as my anxieties. Everything seemed okay again. The dramas of the last couple of days were placed in their proper context – minor inconveniences overcome with the help of antiseptic and the sound of a Texan drawl. We treated ourselves to a shortened stage to Carrión de los Condes, an easy 20 kilometres up the road. We left Frómista with light hearts and the sun on our necks.

Boris, Liz and Nikki caught us up outside Revenga de Campos about an hour along the path. The conversation strayed towards our post-Camino lives.

'I'm planning on becoming a concert pianist,' said Boris, as if it were a *fait accompli*. 'A master of Liszt.'

'I'm going to break into Hollywood,' said Liz. 'I bought a ticket to California from Madrid last night.'

The fact that Boris had never taken a piano lesson in his life and that Liz had progressed no further than her local amateur theatre were immaterial. Sure, there might be challenges and setbacks: all the greats endure such trials. There would be peaks and troughs, but they were part of the artist's vicissitudes, and so to be expected. They *would* make it.

This is what happens when so many people on a circuit break are pointed in the same direction. We were cut loose from the real world and its trying exigencies. Anything was possible. Out here, the pilgrim who doesn't suffer delusions of grandeur is the deluded one.

Nikki kept quiet until prompted by Boris to reveal her

plans. She thought seriously for a moment before smiling vacantly. 'I'm going to be *happy*,' she announced, giggling. We all let her declaration hover in the air unremarked upon. Nikki seemed not to care. She stared straight ahead, but her focus seemed fixed on something inward.

Dave and I kept our goals modest. We'd both pare back our commitments, such as they were, and devote ourselves to music. We already had the genesis of a band in Santiago and the Moor-slayers. All we needed to do was expand the repertoire and get a gig.

We were no longer walking to Santiago. We were walking to Carnegie Hall; to the Kodak Theatre to accept an Oscar; to a sold-out gig at Red Rocks. The two long rows of cockle-shell-embossed bollards that lined the road from Frómista to Carrión formed our guard of honour. Nothing on the Camino thus far had rivalled this buzz. We carried ourselves like champions, knights of the pole and the cockleshell. We were not the first to enter Carrión in such a manner.

El Cid came here 900 years ago to avenge his daughters' mistreatment by the dishonourable counts of Carrión who married them. Frankly, the Cid had no business being self-righteous. He was an unscrupulous man, switching sides and religions for personal gain. Spain has embraced his self-styled image of the virtuous champion, raising statues of him holding glorious poses all over the place. We passed one in Burgos. No one, though, could dispute his skill with the sword.

The Christians called him 'Campeador', an old Spanish contraction of the Latin *campi doctus*, meaning 'master of the military arts'. But the name bequeathed by the Moors is the one that stuck – El Cid, The Lord. Offending the Castilian warrior was unwise in the extreme. The counts would fall to the ground in sections for their folly. The village where they were brought to justice still bears their name: Carrión de los Condes, Carrión of the Counts.

We booked into an albergue run by Benedictine nuns. Securing a bed required a three-euro donation, strict observance of the curfew and a dish to be added to the communal dinner. These three contributions were in keeping with the Benedictine tradition and were rewarded with the mother superior's blessing. The obligation to bring a dish to dinner didn't leave any time to explore the town, so Dave and I again talked ourselves out of our vow of poverty and joined the others at the bar. We found a place with tables and chairs spilling out into an attractive plaza. While the others held a table, Dave and I went off to order a round of Miguel.

We managed to squeeze in five rounds before it was time to head back to the albergue for the communal meal. At the market we remembered how light our wallets were and only shelled out for a can of tuna, a five-inch-long chorizo, a dozen beers and a bottle of mineral water. The sisters seemed less than impressed when they saw our contribution. I thought about reminding them of the starving children in Africa, but not even I have that much cheek.

The kitchen was a hive of activity. Nikki, Liz, Jacob and Boris laughed away as they threw miscellaneous ingredients into a boiling pot of pasta. French Pipes was encased in plumes of smoke alongside two of his countrymen before being shouted at by a sister for smoking inside. Michael the Irishman was cooking up a stew while singing 'Dirty Old Town'. The Argentinean quartet was gathered at the bench slicing up chorizo, *jamón* and other smallgoods. Bonjour was whistling in the corner, laying out an assortment of cheeses on a platter. And tossing the most enticing tomato and iceberg lettuce salad imaginable was the Texan.

I noted that Boris was paying the Texan scant attention. In fact, an atmosphere of mutual indifference flooded the space between them. This was outstanding news. With the bearded Canadian out of the picture, perhaps the hulking Australian had a chance.

About forty of us squeezed around a table big enough to accommodate half that number. The mood was nonetheless upbeat. Dessert had been subsumed into the main course, making for an exotic – if not delicious – assortment of foodstuffs. At one stage I had a spoonful of tuna, a lettuce leaf and a cinnamon doughnut all bobbing away in my lentil broth. Dave and I weren't alone in having made only a modest contribution to the meal but no one had skimped on the alcohol. Only the sisters were sober.

When the dishes had been cleared and the dining area tidied, the nuns ushered us towards the vestibule for our reward. They waited patiently for us to fall silent before an unusually tall nun leant over and pressed play on a cassette player. As the room filled with the sound of Gregorian chants, Boris whispered, 'That young one off to the left is really hot.'

This was the first time I'd seen Boris drunk. As the night had progressed, his voice took on a tissue-paper tone and his smile a sickly sweetness. When he spotted a target, he would slither his way over, pitch forward into a suggestive lean and commence a stare that teetered on the brink of a leer. I knew he was serious about the nun because he was involuntarily rubbing his hands together. This, I had noticed, was a gesture that accompanied only his thirstiest desires.

'Take it easy, mate. She's a nun!' I said. Boris looked hungrily at the young sister and mentioned something about her teaching him the rhythm method. I told him I thought he'd said he was a Catholic.

'I was *raised* a Catholic, but I've become something else since walking this trail.' He was trying to catch the eye of the little nun by raising his eyebrows seductively.

'A heretic?'

'Not quite. I've been reading about some of the pagan rituals that took place on the Camino before this was a Christian pilgrimage.'

'What rituals are those?'

'Ancient pagan rituals of fertility.' Boris was grinning broadly now. 'Apparently, there are a whole lot of fertility symbols along this path – like images of Aphrodite and Venus – that all predate Christian artefacts. I'm happy to stand here and participate in this little Christian ceremony, but if that girl expects me to receive a blessing from her superior, then I think it's only fair that I give her a blessing of my own.'

'You are a very odd man, Boris.'

A diminutive nun in the same brown-and-white habit as the other sisters appeared solemnly from a side room. It was the mother superior. The lines on her face spoke of her devotion – wrinkles for piety, creases for chastity, folds for temperance, furrows for diligence. But I could find no evidence of patience in that dreadful frown.

'*Silencio, por favor!*' she screeched. The tall nun quickly pressed stop on the cassette player. The mother superior cleared her throat and clasped her hands together. At the moment she opened her mouth to break the silence, French Pipes let loose a flamboyantly loud fart.

A pair of Italians broke into fits of hysteria and had to leave the room, while those in the vicinity of French Pipes (his name having evolved into a double entendre) slowly backed away. The mute Frenchman looked about, arms raised in the air, as if to say, 'It wasn't me!' The youngest sister bit down on her lip to stifle a laugh and the other three looked fearfully towards the mother superior. They knew what was coming. A horrible squeal cut through the pilgrim laughter that had taken over the room. With backs stiffened and hairs raised, we all turned anxiously to the tiny mother superior. She was on the warpath now.

Under the circumstances the giggling nun did a noble job of translating the mother superior's message. It was a homily of fire and brimstone; the rude interruption having enhanced its toxicity. The message was loud and clear: 'You must not desecrate this house. To do so is to spit in the face of the apostle himself. You are here to celebrate the glory of God. Kneel before Him! Submit to His will.' This went on for an excruciating length of time before the mother superior came around to each of us, whispering a prayer and drawing the cross on our foreheads. She prayed for a particularly long time in front of Boris and French Pipes.

Before the doors were locked, the smokers were allowed to slip outside for a last-minute shot of nicotine. I leant back on a wall across the street, puffing away on my Marlboro Light. The Texan was off to the side, smoking in her enchanting way. For the briefest moment our eyes locked. I smiled gamely and threw her a wink. It was too dark to say for certain, but I like to think that she blushed bashfully before averting her gaze. It had been a spectacular day. I finished my cigarette and flicked it into the street, watching as it danced in a festival of golden embers. The world was my ashtray.

OCTOBER 17
THE PERFECT RENDERING OF PRIDE

I could have sworn I felt the moment the Camino virus entered my body, the foul thing jerking me awake at some evil hour after lights out. On first thought, getting sick straight after a day of unbridled joy seemed unjust. But the timing of it was so precise that I put it down to design, as if I had been picked up to maximise the impact of being hurled back down.

The coffee and *tortilla* Dave pushed in front of me at breakfast brought on abject queasiness. All I could see was last night's soggy cinnamon doughnut drowning in lentil soup. It was taking me down with it.

Dave frowned. Even the most sinister of hangovers wouldn't affect my appetite in such a way. 'Are you right, mate? You look terrible.'

'I'm fine,' I said, suppressing a shake. 'I just need to get back out on the road.'

'Why don't we just take the day off? I reckon we can afford another rest day.' This was not true. After yesterday's short stage, a day off would nudge the required daily average north of 30 kilometres if we were to meet the All Saints' deadline. That demanded a level of discipline our sporadic first two weeks on pilgrimage suggested we would be unlikely to achieve.

'It'll pass. Don't worry so much.' I stepped outside to get some fresh air. A new dawn was breaking. The morning sun backlit a statue depicting a pilgrim walking into the teeth of a gale, his coat flicked back by a gust of wind. Somewhere inside me, too, a storm was brewing.

The first serious sign of trouble was just outside of Carrión. Fortunately, nearby there was a roadhouse with amenities to cope with my dire need. It was an eruption major enough to indicate I was in no condition to walk the 26 kilometres to Terradillos de los Templarios. Dave suggested that we return to Carrión. Deep down I must have known that this was a foretaste of the catastrophe that lay ahead, but I insisted that we barrel on.

There is nothing remarkable about the stage from Carrión to Terradillos, save for one thing – it contains the longest stretch of the Camino Francés without a town. For 18 long and lonely kilometres the path bears due west without a bar, restaurant or albergue in sight. Three kilometres in and Dave made one last attempt to convince me to turn around, practically begging that we head back to Carrión. Even after I was forced to jog behind a bush, I refused to concede defeat. I was certain that the worst had been left in the roadhouse. I think I was still high on the previous day's triumphs – there was nothing this pilgrimage could throw at me that I couldn't overcome. Dave knew better. While I was on the toilet he had bought a couple of large bottles of water and a roll of paper.

When we reached the heart of no-man's-land, with over 9 kilometres of townless road in front and behind, a wave of nausea oozed over me. I recognised the nasty little forerunners – the hot flush, dizziness, acidic saliva in the mouth – but they came all in a rush. I only had a second to drop my pack before a great roar of vomit was ejected from my mouth. I could feel an unseen hand wringing out my stomach like a wet towel. The pain was dreadful. I thought of the martyrdom of St Elmo, disembowelled with a windlass on the rack. It seemed preferable. The four Argentineans walked along the path next to me. Gone were yesterday's bright smiles. They looked as grim-faced as the Horsemen of the Apocalypse.

Dave stood beside me, a look of worry fixed on his face. I turned my head towards the horizon of yellow grain and cobalt sky, searching for an object to focus on. In the far distance I could make out what might have been a church steeple, but it brought little comfort. From here it resembled one of Blake's dark satanic mills that we used to sing about at school.

I could now admit to being unwell. The moment I thought everything had been expelled, another heave would stain the path with a fresh patch of lentil-flecked fluid. With Dave's help, I walked about 500 metres in just over an hour. The time between each vomit shortened until with one last spasm it was over. I rolled over on the ground, emptied out. The vomiting had done more than just draw the venom from my stomach; it had gouged out the hubris of the previous day.

A biting anxiety came over me. A thought flashed: I could die out here. Dehydration could do it. I indulged in the fantasy, but it was unsatisfying. I was not enough of a hiker or a Catholic for friends and relatives to proclaim that at least I'd died doing what I loved. In fact, there would be a complete lack of meaning to my passing. If written truthfully, messages at the base of a cairn marking the spot I died would only puzzle passers-by: 'Here lies Trumble, a man who thumbed his nose at the corporate sector and then died'; or 'Trumble died here: he wanted to get back into music'; or 'Trumble died at this spot . . . that is all. *Buen Camino!*' This scared me more than death itself: the knowledge that I'd achieved nothing of significance.

I trawled through memories for something to suggest mine would be a story of a life of promise tragically curtailed. In my mind's eye I came on a twelve-year-old looking up at a formidable football coach. 'You have potential, boy,' he said, 'but in this caper, potential is a dirty word.' I remembered that boy resolving to make something of that potential, working hard at things besides football at school, entering university with the same attitude. Then something went wrong.

Not often can we picture the day our internal pendulum swings the other way. But I remembered it clearly at times such as these. I can smell it and hear it, too. The sweet mustiness of marijuana in the air, the foreign voices cackling across the bar, the easy euphoria and then the plunge. I remembered the throbbing in my ears and the shaking walls and the fear.

In that lonely wheatfield my mind raised something else

to replace the image of that cocky young kid. It was the sight of someone older, someone drawing back slowly on a cigarette to ward off that new-found dread.

Dave splashed water in my face. I stood up and wobbled across the path before collapsing in a small clearing on the other side of the road. I peeled open my eyelids to see Dave making his way towards a car, next to which a Spaniard was turning sausages on a barbecue. At first I thought I was hallucinating. But hearing Dave's explanation of our situation to the Spaniard made it clear this was no oasis.

The Spaniard was happy to give us a ride to his own albergue in Terradillos after the day's hungry potential customers had walked past. He diagnosed my sickness as the result of poor water quality and mentioned it was just as well that he was doing discounts on *agua mineral*. I doubted he was right. Dave and I had drunk from the same water fountains and he seemed fine. Besides, this bug had been tormenting pilgrims well before we reached the Meseta.

Dave bought some water and food. I sat on one of the Spaniard's spare chairs, my head ringing. I longed for solitude. I had met earlier expressions of condolence from passing pilgrims with a stoic wave and a one-liner about the lentil soup looking better on the way out. But I could no longer do it. My armour had been cast off and there was nowhere to hide. I was exposed. I wanted to be on my own, to ride out the storm and then move on as if it had never happened. The Camino had other plans.

A heavy hand came down on my shoulder. I looked up

to see a pair of brown bulbous eyes inches from my face. 'Hi guys!' The Swiss giant drew up a chair beside mine and began tut-tutting his sympathy. Seconds later a gentler hand rested on my arm. '*Bonjour,*' came a whisper, lacking its customary *joie de vivre*. Liz and Natalia began administering reiki, placing their hands on the wounded parts of my body to promote healing, or so they said. Meanwhile, I saw someone out of the corner of my eye who looked to be performing callisthenics. It was explained that she was conducting an interpretive dance to help me overcome my crisis.

After the two-pronged reiki treatment had exacerbated my dizzy spells, Nikki performed an eastern remedy passed on to her by a guru she'd met in Goa. She closed her eyes, clapped her hands together and started running her palms down my arms to my fingers, clasping an invisible evil spirit before casting it off into the air. French Pipes wandered over and blew a couple of concerned puffs of smoke in my face, perhaps deducing from my pallor that I was suffering nicotine withdrawal. Boris was hovering about, alternately expressing worry and checking out Nikki.

One of those silver-haired pilgrims who had described the Meseta as the dullest section of Camino walked over to the makeshift bar and ordered a bottle of water. He stood next to me and with pursed lips offered a consoling tap of my elbow before quickly heading off. I tried to imagine how he would have viewed the scene: a deathly pale pilgrim sat with a middle-aged man in wire frames who puffed smoke in his face, while three women ran their hands over his body and another danced nearby without musical accompaniment, and a giant with eyes falling out of his head bellowed 'Hi guys!' each time a new pilgrim joined the gathering. It might have looked like some ancient Camino exorcism. In the end, I didn't care what it looked like, I just wanted some peace.

Dave and I zipped past other pilgrims in the Spaniard's sedan. It was the first time in sixteen days I had been in an automobile. I broke out of my reverie and realised with a shock what this meant. The pact I had forged with Dave was broken. His only stipulation, that we *walk* the entire length of the Camino Francés, had been breached. The Camino had wooed me to an isolated spot, smitten me on the side of the road, humbled me before a parade of friends and put a car in my path – a temptation I could not resist. The story of our Santiago pilgrimage would now contain an ugly addendum, a 17-kilometre car trip across the Meseta.

Dave looked out the window from the back seat at the pilgrims making for Terradillos. The sight of his crestfallen expression gave way to another realisation. The Camino had not brought me down; I hadn't needed its help. Worse still, I had brought Dave down with me. Dave would brush off my apologies, saying it was 'just one of those things', but he was being typically generous. My friend had pleaded with me from the start that we return to Carrión, a place equipped to deal with my illness. My pride, however, had pushed me out the café door and into the wilderness.

My mind cast back to those three deadly sins depicted on the street corner column at the Palacio de los Reyes de Navarra in Estella. I now had an image for the transgression that begets all others. It was me walking from the Carrión roadhouse, deaf to my companion's appeal to reason. It was the perfect rendering of pride.

I stared out the window. There was another black church looming out of a wheat paddock. I felt the cool grip of *acedia* take hold, despair beyond the reach of salvation, the unforgivable sin.

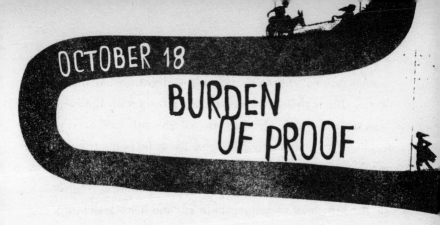

OCTOBER 18
BURDEN OF PROOF

Embarrassingly, my illness was only of short duration. Apart from an ongoing aversion to lentil soup, the physical effects had mostly worn off. My enthusiasm, however, had taken a battering. The Camino was knocking down the wobbly hopes and false pretences that had lately propped up my life. This walk suddenly seemed deeply arduous and there were still 400 kilometres to Santiago.

Dave and I left the albergue later than normal. My guilt over breaking our pledge was compounded by Dave's kindness. He'd spent the whole night fetching me water and checking that I hadn't choked on my own sick. In the morning he was jovial as ever. Once we'd resumed walking, I could nevertheless sense a measure of disappointment – slightly forced laughter and a faltering smile – that we'd hitched a ride. He was not his usual self. I pulled out my iPod, hoping to find distraction in music. I should have realised that the Meseta wouldn't allow for that sort of escapism.

I'm generally pleased to meet a fellow Australian abroad, and am given over to the bonhomie countrymen share. Dave would agree with me on this approach. His instinctive friend-liness means that he can agreeably put up with the most miserable of bores. Meeting Edward was different.

I didn't immediately dislike him. I found him intimidat-ing. I recognise that my subsequent loathing for Edward was probably down to my shortcomings. Intimidation is, after all, the precursor to envy, resentment and hatred, all symp-toms of insecurity. And maybe I did envy Edward; there were enough reasons to. He was one of that tribe of obnoxiously over-educated swots in their mid-twenties who take time out from their prematurely impressive careers to trek through Afghanistan before coming home to write their memoirs. He was, to put it simply, brilliant.

Envy alone, though, cannot explain the black hatred I felt for Edward after our first meeting. This, I attribute to the delight the prig took in reducing me to a featherweight mediocrity.

'I'm a lawyer,' said Edward after rebuking Dave for attempting to shorten his name to Ed. 'That is, I *was* a lawyer.'

'Where were you working?' I asked.

'One of the big firms in Melbourne,' he said with a dis-dainful cough, wiping a speck of dirt from his sleeve. 'I chose that firm because of its *pro bono* opportunities. I should have been a criminal barrister, really. There were certainly enough influential people pushing me in that direction and I didn't like the corporate stuff all that much. Unfor-tunately, I was constantly being seconded to oversee big mergers and acquisitions.'

'So what is it that you want to do now?' I asked. Edward ignored my question, pressing on with his backstory – the promising young lawyer who eschewed a high-income profession to follow his dream.

'It meant that I could never get out and help the people who *really* needed me. I left the firm the day after they gave me a promotion. Now I'm an aspiring writer.' It was important for Edward to make these points. This information would eventually grace the jacket cover of his first great tome.

I looked at him closely. His pale-green kurta, the garment of choice for Lahore shopkeepers, spoke of his subcontinental travel. His espadrilles, the flat-soled shoe of the medieval Basque peasant – totally inadequate for walking a pilgrimage – showed his solidarity with the downtrodden. He had just the right amount of stubble and his curly brown locks were the right sort of unkempt. Taken altogether it was the look of a man who intended to convey a certain carelessness about his appearance. The kind of carelessness that suggested he was a tormented genius who recited beat poetry to the music of Leonard Cohen at art society gatherings. The kind of carelessness it takes hours to perfect.

'I'm walking the Camino as inspiration for my first book,' Edward continued.

'For religious reasons?' I asked.

'Not at all,' he scoffed. 'When it comes to religion, I share the disdain of Karl Marx, who said —' Edward cleared his throat —' "Religion is the sigh of the oppressed creature, the heart of a heartless world, and the soul of soulless conditions.

It is the opium of the people."' I imagined that the memo-rised quote had probably come in handy before, reminding people of the sheer size of his knowledge.

'I intend on exploring the illusory qualities and false pretexts of the pilgrimage as spiritual quest to support my broader contention that God is a servant of demagoguery.'

Dave and I looked at each other blankly before one of us asked, 'So your book is a philosophy?'

'My philosophy will find its way into the book, but the book is first and foremost a story about the artist's growth to maturity, an exploration of the self.'

'Sounds great,' said Dave as earnestly as he could manage.

'Is it a travelogue?' I asked.

'Oh, no,' he said. 'I would never do anything so drab and unoriginal.'

'I see,' I said.

'But the story will take as its setting those places I have seen in my travels. For instance, the book begins in Barcelona —'

'Ah, *Barcelona*,' said Dave with a heavy lisp. 'What a per-fect place to begin a story.'

'To be honest with you,' said Edward, 'I was hoping to find, as George Orwell did in 1937, a place with, *and I quote*, "The working class in the saddle".' Edward looked at us expectantly.

'So you didn't like it then?' I asked eventually.

'I loved it,' he said haughtily. 'Anyway, I won't go on. You two probably aren't all that interested in books.'

'As a matter of fact,' said Dave in a rare tone of indignation, 'my friend here is considering writing one himself.' To the tip of my nose I flushed deepest crimson. Edward swivelled sharply in my direction. 'Is that so?' he asked, his lips moving into a leonine grin.

My plan to write was an old idea that had crystallised on the Camino. I hadn't confided this information to anyone beyond Dave. I suppose I was concerned that it might invite comparisons with Boris's intention to become a concert pianist.

Many words could be used to describe my first attempt at a novel yet none serve quite so well as 'crap'. It was meant to be a story warning of the perils of pursuing self-fulfilment. Instead, it read like a second-rate romantic comedy that waded through a labyrinth of cliché before finding an escape in a fairy-floss conclusion. Somewhere between Carrión and Terradillos I'd abandoned my writing ambitions once and for all. Edward was nailing the lid on that coffin.

'What are you reading at the moment?' asked Edward.

'Right now? Not much.'

'I thought you wanted to be a writer,' he laughed. 'The best writers are voracious readers.' I said nothing. 'Okay, what is it that you last read?'

'*The Great Gatsby*. I really —'

'Still on the high-school stuff, are we? What about before that?'

'*Death in the Afternoon*,' I lied, hoping that Hemingway was of sufficient stature to parry further interrogation.

'Oh, dear,' said Edward with a frown.

'What's wrong with Hemingway?'

'Nothing, I suppose. It's just that . . .' Edward hesitated to feign spontaneity. 'I've developed this theory about the authors people our age read. It's like this – tell me you read Scott Fitzgerald and I'll call you a child. Tell me you read Hunter S. Thompson or Jack Kerouac and I'll call you predictable. Tell me you read Dan Brown and I'll ask you to leave. Tell me you read Dostoyevsky and I'll call you a liar. Tell me you read Hemingway and I'll call you a bore, but tell me you read Faulkner and I'll buy you a drink.'

'So what's your theory?'

'That most people read the wrong things.'

'I'm sorry I'm not up to speed with Faulkner's work,' I said with a philistine grunt.

'No need to apologise,' said Edward with a smirk. 'You're not on your own with that one. I don't mean to sound rude, but how do you expect to become a writer if you don't know the works of a Nobel Prize winner? You *are* aspiring to write a book, aren't you?'

'Well, I was, but —'

'*Ei incumbit probatio qui dicit, non qui negat,*' intoned Edward, proving his legal bona fides.

'Excuse me?'

'"The burden of proof rests on who asserts, not on who denies,"' he explained, chuckling like one who has just manufactured the cleverest of ironies. 'Tell me, what is your book about?'

'I've abandoned the idea, Edward.'

'No need for modesty amongst friends. What was it about?'

'He's going to write a travelogue,' said Dave, 'and it's going to be a damn sight better than the shit you'll churn out, *Ed*.'

'Oh. I see.' Edward marked out a pause before executing his *coup de grace*. 'I'm sure it will be a really *fun* read.'

Unfortunately, Dave's attempt to come to my rescue was not enough to slow Edward down. He spent the next two hours describing the complex literary devices he planned to mobilise in his first novel, until we arrived in the town of Sahagún.

'Ah, Sahagún!' Edward practically shouted. 'Can either of you two tell me why this place is significant, beyond being the resting place for saints Facundo and Primitivo?' Like an irritating schoolteacher he asked the question without waiting for an answer. 'Sahagún marks – almost to the kilometre – the halfway point between Saint-Jean-Pied-de-Port and Santiago de Compostela.'

I'd imagined that arriving at this point would rank as a significant moment on the Camino. But the milestone only intensified the sense that I'd failed before even reaching the halfway point. I'd let Dave down and now some prick had picked apart the one post-Camino idea I'd had. I quickened my pace, eager to leave the town behind us.

On the western side of Sahagún sits the River Cea, whose other bank is covered by ash trees and poplars. I had read about this place. Locals believe these trees to be the remnants of one of Santiago's most celebrated miracles. The apostle's intervention is recorded in an episode of the Song of Roland. For this reason, I half expected to find Warren humming the Reveille somewhere in the woods.

Charlemagne ordered his soldiers to camp on the banks of this river the night before the decisive Battle of Sahagún, As was custom, the Christian soldiers planted their lances in front of their camp before preparing their arms for battle against Agolant and his Moorish army. They awoke at dawn to find some of their lances had grown branches, leaves and bark. They cut them down carefully, and from their roots a forest grew.

Forty thousand Christian knights were slain in the battle and the Moors emerged victorious. It was discovered that the lances that had taken root the night before belonged to those who had fallen in battle. Locals believe the black poplars – a genus of tree that has no business being in this region of Spain – among the forest of ash are the offshoots of the flowering lances. This is an enduring sign of God's divine power.

'I think I'd prefer God sent me Santiago on horseback than a flowering lance before a fight,' said Dave. 'What do you think, Edward?'

'I don't pay much attention to fairytales,' he scoffed. 'I'm more interested in *real* history.'

We walked on to where the Camino diverges into two paths out of Sahagún before they reunite in the small town of Mansilla de las Mulas, 30 kilometres further along. The more popular northern road takes pilgrims via Calzadilla de los Hermanillos, a village whose Mozarabic-style architecture Edward would not shut up about. Fascinating though Calzadilla sounded, Dave and I decided on taking the road less travelled. Without Edward, this made all the difference.

MEDITATIONS

The Meseta stretches some distance beyond León, but this, the largest city along the Camino Francés, is the symbolic end of the great plain. But from where we were, León still seemed out of reach. My inglorious performance along the flat road was something I'd be happy to put behind me. Dave would feel the same way, I suspected. So we set ourselves an ambitious stage of 45 kilometres, which would take us into new surrounds and the city.

Boris joined us for breakfast. He was also eager to return to a bustling city. Spain's rural heartland had not yielded the torrent of *señoritas* he was hoping for. The three of us set off before daybreak after chowing down on croissants and coffee. I wasn't yet at full walking capacity and found it difficult to maintain Boris's speed. It was as if the promise of city bars packed with women had pushed the Canadian into a higher gear. He gradually drew away from us.

'Must have a girl lined up in León,' I said, in a poor effort at humour. Dave remained silent. I looked towards my friend and noticed an unfamiliar expression on his face.

'Are you all right, mate?'

'I'm fine,' he said, in a way intended to end the conversation.

'What's wrong?' I persisted.

'Nothing at all.' There was tetchiness in his voice. I quickly looked for the source of Dave's irritation. His bed-bug bites had nearly disappeared and he no longer appeared to be struggling with his tendonitis. There was only one other thing it could be.

'I'm really sorry about the other day,' I said softly.

'Forget about it,' he mumbled.

'Seriously, though, it must —'

'Just forget about it,' he snapped. 'Listen, are you going to be right if I step it up a bit I wouldn't mind a stint on my own.'

'Go for your life,' I said, concealing my surprise. 'I'm nearly back to normal.'

He walked off without responding. I slowed down, allowing the space to grow between us. Soon enough I was on my own.

The morning mist lifted to a cloudless noon. I could make out the dark outline of the Cantábrican Mountains on the northern horizon. Those peaks would follow us west, reaching formidable heights before receding into the Galician hills beyond León. The sight of them told me I would soon be reacquainted with uneven terrain.

The thought of scaling the mountains teased a line of

sweat from my brow. I didn't feel ready for sharp ascents. I felt, instead, the need for nicotine. I let my pack slip off my shoulders and sat down opposite a large cairn to catch my breath.

A rusty cross sat in the middle of the cairn and around its base were photos and messages of peace, a canvas for spiritualists and a monument for Christians. This was not the cairn's original function. The pre-Roman Celts used piles of stones to mark high-mountain passes. Roman travellers had brought this tradition to the ancient road. Piles of rocks were easily recognisable landmarks for foreign pagan worshippers trekking across unknown land to the sea. They named these rock piles *murias* to honour Mercury, the god of travellers. I was staring at a tradition that had endured for millennia.

I pulled a cigarette packet from my backpack. Before lighting up, I glanced around to make sure I was on my own. This was the first cigarette I had smoked since taking ill and I could do without being reminded of that fact. The coast was clear. I took a long pull.

'Should you really be smoking?' asked a voice from behind the cairn. I nearly swallowed my cigarette and looked around. At first, all I could take in was a pair of hot-pink leggings arranged in the lotus position. After my retinas had stopped burning from the bright colour, I made out Sally sitting with her eyes closed. She looked as if she were preparing to levitate to Santiago. I let out a long groan in response.

'You've been unwell,' she said, her eyes remaining closed, her posture perfectly aligned.

'How do you know that?'

'I was there, helping you with my dance, don't you remember?' An image of the kind road-trauma victims repress flashed in my mind. I recalled a figure pirouetting in front of me while reiki hands clutched at my stomach. I felt a sudden wave of nausea.

'How could I forget?' I said, suddenly losing my appetite for the cigarette. 'I don't mean to offend you, but I felt equally shithouse before and after your routine. What were you doing?'

'Capturing an important moment. It was a manifestation of your internal upheaval.'

'I don't see how that was supposed to help.'

'That's because you expect immediate change without consideration,' she said patiently.

I pulled myself up to my feet and rubbed my temples. 'Why would someone need to capture a moment of humiliation? I'd sooner move on and forget it ever happened.'

'And that, I think, is the problem,' she said, opening her eyes momentarily to fix me with a stare before closing them again. 'I'm proud of you. I knew you'd make progress.'

'Jesus! Is there any danger of having a normal conversation out here?' I picked up my backpack to leave.

'Hang on,' she shouted. 'I'm not through with you yet.' Sally jumped to her feet and strapped on her small pack.

My strength was returning. I was moving more easily than I had since taking ill. Sally seemed to float along the path beside me. The afternoon sun gilded the wheat stalks, which shook in the breeze. The Meseta seemed peaceful for the first time since I'd been on it. I looked to Sally, smiling as she walked.

'Say,' I said in a soft tone, 'how are things going with you and that fireman?'

'Wonderful. So don't get any ideas.'

'What? No. I wasn't trying to —'

'Oh, dear,' she muttered. 'You still have some challenges to overcome.'

'What challenges? Can we please stop talking in cryptic codes and discuss the problem?'

'Okay, what's your problem?'

'Right now?'

'Yes.'

'Well, to be honest, I'm a bit worried about Dave.'

'Forget about him for the moment. He's travelling his own path, confronting his own challenges.'

'Hang on, you said back in France that his energy was centred and his chakras were all aligned.' I couldn't believe I was actually talking this shit.

'You need to focus on your own journey. He must confront those things alone, just as you must . . .' She sighed, before grabbing my arm. 'There are more things to come, more disappointments ahead. You have done well to come this far. Focus on what's important. Until then —'

'I know, I know. Keep walking.'

As we came upon another cairn, Sally stopped in her tracks and dropped her pack. She lowered herself into what looked like a praying mantis position.

'What are you doing?'

'Meditating,' she said. 'You're welcome to join me, but there will be no talking.'

'What about those disappointments?'

'*Shhh!*'

'I'll see you later,' I said, continuing on down the path.

'Only if the universe says so,' she whispered, eyes closed once more.

I walked through Mansilla de las Mulas and off towards León preoccupied with my latest encounter with Sally. I still wasn't sure whether she should be deified or committed. There was no use dwelling on it. I needed to get back to the real world.

The increased amount of traffic on the roads indicated I was nearing the city. The promise of seeing something busy and lively imbued me with a new enthusiasm. I walked on, faster than I had in days. Soon enough two figures appeared in the distance up ahead of me. As I approached, I could see one playing a ukulele and the other tugging at his beard while laughing wildly. We rendezvoused in front of a three-lane highway.

'How's the day been, gentlemen?' I asked.

'Uneventful, mate,' Dave said with a grin, turning around with an outstretched hand. 'How about yours?'

'Unusual,' I said shaking his hand, accepting without question his reversal in mood. Maybe Dave just needed a bit of time on his own after all.

We dashed across the highway, weaving in front of semi-trailers and behind speeding sedans. We emerged near some hills that once crested revealed the panorama of the Irago Mountains breaking through the evening smog. Before us spread the sprawling mass of León, the cathedral's spires illuminated in the setting sun.

We were clear of the Meseta.

PART THREE

ABSOLUTION

OCTOBER 20
PROBATIONARY SALVATION

León has all the ingredients of a 'must-see' European city. There is its cathedral (one of Europe's finest), its mixture of architectural periods (Romanesque, gothic, medieval), the Barrio Húmedo (an old quarter the rival of any in Spain), its ancient past (the city's name is a contraction of the Seventh Roman Legion, which was stationed here from the year 68), and the Iberian ubiquities (crowded bars, tapas, pulsating night-life). And yet, as I discovered, León remains relatively unknown.

Perhaps its lack of a touristy icon is to blame for its anonymity. Ask people about what Barcelona is known for, and they'll say Gaudi. Granada? The Alhambra. Pamplona? The bulls. And Madrid? Ah, *everything*, they'll say. But ask someone about León and you'll get dead silence. Guidebooks, too, seem determined to preserve the city's obscurity. While Barcelona and Madrid are lavished with superlatives ('spectacular', 'lively', 'wondrous'), the words used to describe León ('conservative', 'tasteful', 'restrained') could equally apply to a nursing home.

León was once at the epicentre of Spain and its spiritual and strategic interests. It was the military redoubt from where Christians launched their offensive against the Moorish Emirates to the south, and the administrative hub for the affairs of the Reconquista. By the end of the fifteenth century, the Christian armies had seized the regions of Extremadura and most of Andalusia. Eight hundred years of Moorish dominance had come to an end and the Spanish Golden Age had begun. León had lost its relevance. Were it not for the Camino, León would be little more than 'that place in the wheat'. I was not bothered by any of this. To me, León seemed as spectacular as it must have been in the days of the great kings who ruled it.

My opinion of León might have been less favourable had I not just emerged from 250 kilometres of great flat nothingness. Before I'd left Melbourne, I imagined my pilgrim self to be bronzed and outdoorsy, at home in the wilderness, liberated from the urban grind. It had proved a preposterous fiction. The unease I'd felt on the Meseta revealed that I belonged to crowded places, breathing car-exhaust fumes in the shadows of tall buildings.

In other circumstances I might have described our accommodation as a charmless monolith in Communist-bloc grey. To eyes eager to view anything other than wheat, however, our albergue was an architectural wonder. It also doubled as a regular hotel. This had its advantages. In this place curfew was a notional rule and there was the opportunity to stay consecutive nights.

Dave and I arranged a day of rest. With Boris in tow, we booked in for two nights and went searching for a bar. We tore up that old town like bulls charging the matador's cape.

I awoke the following morning miraculously without a hangover. Our eight-berth dormitory was fitted with four large windows that reached up to the ceiling. Sunlight flooded the room, and was accompanied by the sounds of horns, worn brake pads and quarrelsome commuters. I felt rejuvenated. By the look of things, Boris and Dave weren't quite so lucky. Dave was passed out facedown, and Boris had fallen off his bunk, mistaking his boots for a pillow in his sleep. I decided to slip out quietly to explore the city on my own. There was much to think about.

Our time in the wheat had led to unexpected developments. Somewhere out there things had become fractious between Dave and me. I was still uncertain as to how much the broken pledge had rankled him. Our handshake outside the city had eased my concern but only to a point; it seemed to mark the beginning of an uneasy truce. And even a cursory glance at the history books will tell you how uneasy truces end.

I'd downgraded my initial (and somewhat melodramatic) judgment of my prideful behaviour from a mortal to a venial sin – from one that would lead to damnation to one that would lead to probationary salvation. Frankly, I had bigger concerns. The Meseta hadn't so much presented me with new dilemmas as unveiled existing ones. These things were known to me and yet remained ambiguous, as if they were drawn too close to my eyes for me to properly see them. The only way I could get a handle on what was happening was to keep moving to Santiago. For now, an amble around León would have to do. With guidebook in hand, I began at the town church.

From afar, León's cathedral was a chaotic assembly of flying buttresses and decorated portals and pinnacles. At close quarters you could appreciate its incredible detail. A group of worried-looking men had been precisely carved across the lower curve of the arches above the cathedral's entrance. These men, I read, depicted after the Last Judgment, were those who had been condemned to eternal damnation. They stood to the left of St Michael; on his right stood the elect, euphoric as they prepared for Paradise.

Growing up, when church attendance was not necessarily followed by a wedding reception, a wake or Christmas lunch, mass made me feel like I was sitting in the belly of a stone beast. The air would hang heavily and there were endless oppressive reminders of Christ's pain on the Cross. The effect was not a cheery one. The León cathedral was different. Its stained-glass windows – all 125 of them – made it seem like the air I was breathing had acquired a colour. Medieval architects had imagined a cathedral made of walls of glass; they called it Pulchra Leónina, the House of Light. Though beautiful, the end result wasn't very practical: the nave has collapsed in on itself twice since the thirteenth century.

My next stop was the Basilica de San Isidoro. As I passed through its vaulted doors, I doubted very much if I'd ever again find myself in the company of such important people.

The tombs inside the basilica's royal pantheon are crammed with the remains of eleven kings, twelve queens and twenty-three princes and counts.

Before entering the tombs, I went to inspect the museum's booty. I wandered past jewelled chalices, church vestments, and yet another fragment of the True Cross before arriving at a mummified finger encased in a glass box.

Under most circumstances, the idea of looking at a shrivelled phalange would excite me as much as reading Britney Spears's biography. But it wasn't just any finger; that digit had been busy.

It had written breviaries and missals for mass, books on history, theology, language and astronomy. It had penned powerful political treatises and compelling expositions on the human condition. And it was responsible for the *Etymologiae* (Origins), a twenty-volume encyclopaedia covering rhetoric, grammar, dialect, food, tools, agriculture, war, jurisprudence, beasts, birds, the world, elements, Jews, pagans, philosophers, Heaven, earth, prophets, geography and much more.

The finger belonged to Isidoro of Seville. Isidoro was a rising star within the church before he wrote his magnum opus. He would go on to become Archbishop of Seville in 600, a position he held until his death in 636. Over this period he converted the Arian Visigothic royalty to Christianity and built schools as a means of curbing the influence of Gothic barbarism. It worked. Isidoro is regarded as a pivotal figure in bringing civilisation to the Iberian Peninsula.

He was canonised and made a Doctor of the Church – a title he holds with only thirty-two others. But it is the timeless epithet given to him by French historian Charles de Montalembert that resonates most strongly: '*le dernier savant du monde ancien*', the last scholar of the ancient world.

I bent over, bringing myself closer to Isidoro's finger. Up close it looked like cracked ebony. Beyond my field of sight I detected someone staring at me. I looked around to see a little girl. She gazed at me with widened eyes, perplexed. I made a scary face and she ran off screaming. I made an apologetic shrug to the mother, who shook her head and frowned. Through a torrent of tears the little girl was bawling out, '*El hombre está loco!*' I confirmed later with Dave what she had said – 'that man is crazy!' It was time to head to the bar.

In 1928 Alfonso XIII set about converting Spain's most historic buildings into a chain of luxury hotels. The idea was to generate tourism in Spain's poorer regions and preserve the country's culturally important buildings. The Paradores de Turisimo de España is now a state-owned hotel group of converted monasteries, fortresses, castles and palaces. The Convento de San Marcos was chosen as the site of León's *paradore* in 1961. It was also said to contain a plush bar where a tired pilgrim might quench his thirst.

San Marcos was originally built as a pilgrim hospice in 1152. The building was ceded to the Order of Santiago – a monastic order by name, an army of ruthless knights by nature – soon after, from which the knights were supposed to protect the stream of pilgrims passing by. Ensuring pilgrims weren't horribly slaughtered by Moors was in fact a corollary to the knights' real purpose. The Order's motto, '*Rubet ensis sanguine Arabum*', my sword is red with Arab blood, gives an indication of what they were clearly more interested in doing. They took the red cross of Santiago as their emblem – the bottom of the cross resembles a sword, a fitting emblem for soldiers of Christ as well as those bent on blood-tinged rampages – and then set about eradicating Islam from Extremadura.

By the late-fifteenth century, the Order was at the forefront of politics and war across the newly united Spanish kingdom. Once the Moors had been muscled off the Peninsula, however, the knights of Santiago were proving more hindrance than help in concentrating power under a single crown. Fernando and his queen Isabel la Católica had no intention of disbanding the knights of Santiago for fear of turning public opinion against them. So Fernando installed himself as the knights' grand master and defanged the Order, transforming it into a purely honorary association of nobles. To quell disquiet among the knights, King Fernando rebuilt San Marcos into palatial headquarters, essentially bribing them not to make a fuss.

The Order continues to exist under the Spanish Crown. Membership can only be attained by noble ancestry, Christian descent, proof of being a practising Catholic and legitimate birth. So, even in the modern age the Order demands pure

Christian blood and allows no bastards. The Order is currently composed of sixty-five knights and novices. They are, among other things, charged with the defence of the belief in the Immaculate Conception of Mary. Antiquated, yes, but a darn sight better than an army of Moor-slayers.

I approached the *paradore* from the Plaza de San Marcos, pausing at a sculpture of a pilgrim leaning against a stone cross. His head was ricked backwards, as if he were gazing in awe at the grandeur of San Marcos. I could also read fatigue on his face and in his slouching posture. I almost felt a surge of guilt for having indulged in a rest day.

From close up the pilgrim's expression morphed into one of longing. *Behind that stately façade*, the statue seemed to say, *no beds are kept for us weary pilgrims*. I took a seat alongside the statue and we looked on mournfully, like a couple of old men on a nostalgia trip.

Pilgrims have no business being inside stately buildings made for the wealthy. Our home is the unforgiving path, the vertiginous slope, or the plain, our refuge the hospice and the albergue. To enter San Marcos for a beer seemed like a betrayal of my stony kinsman, who was forever cemented in its shadow.

My reverie was eventually disturbed by a familiar image in the periphery. It was the Texan, beautiful as ever. She walked slowly along the far end of Plaza de San Marcos, pausing to take a photo of the relief of Santiago Matamoros carved above the *paradore* entrance. She turned to search the plaza as if perceiving the eyes that were trained on her.

The Texan glanced at the stone cross but didn't dwell on the two pilgrims at its base. She swivelled back around and resumed her walk.

Sometime later I broke out of my stone cast, like a gargoyle coming to life at night. I patted the sculpture on his head, gave him the Camino salutation and turned for the Barrio Húmedo. There was nothing to be gained from this musing. I would be better off with a San Miguel enjoyed in the company of real pilgrims in preparation for the final push to Santiago.

THE WILFUL CANADIAN

We were now in a region where it rains ten months of the year. It poured the morning we left León, as if to remind us that our T-shirt-wearing days were a thing of the past. These were terrible conditions in which to walk a massive 38-kilometre stage. We had no option.

The rest day had pushed the daily average back above 30 kilometres. The flattest section of the Camino was behind us, but the next couple of days would be at worst undulating terrain. This would be our best chance to claw back some time before we hit the mountainous region. Having shirked one stipulation of the pledge – no cars on the Camino – I was more determined than ever to meet the All Saints' deadline. It might have proved the only thing to be proud of at the end of this pilgrimage.

We scampered across León's saturated streets, wearing slickers for the first time since stepping onto the Meseta. It was our greyest morning to date. Boris tagged along. He was welcome to, but his incessant singing – he kept repeating 'I'm gonna have a Galician girl' to the tune of 'I'll Never

Fall in Love Again' – was becoming tiring. His company also meant I didn't have the opportunity to clear the air once and for all with Dave. Never mind, I thought, a moment would present itself.

After an hour or so of walking we came to La Virgen del Camino. In 1505 the Madonna appeared to a shepherd and told him to instruct the Bishop of León to build a church in the town. The bishop was not disposed to taking orders from a humble shepherd, so, as proof, the shepherd placed a stone into his sling and hurled it skywards, where it grew in midair into a boulder. The bishop, suitably impressed, fell in line and ordered a church to be built.

The story of how the church came to be built was far more impressive than the church itself. The original building had been replaced in the sixties with what looked like one of those Uniting Church structures that brood on street corners in outer suburbia. I wondered why the Holy Mother had gone to the trouble. Rain collected in dirty puddles as we sought shelter. The scene was depressing enough to at least dissuade Boris from singing.

Nikki was there, looking up at the church. One of her hands hung limply by her side, her fingers anxiously flicking the card-like object I'd seen her cradling way back at the Estella pilgrim wine fountain. It looked like a photograph, but it seemed rude to ask. The three of us sidled up alongside her and exchanged muted greetings. Her breathing came in whimpers, like the sound gusts of wind make when passing through phone wires. Her gaze never shifted from the church.

'This is all a bit grim,' said Dave.

'Bloody grim,' I agreed. Nikki's eyes remained glued to the façade of the church. She was transfixed, it seemed, by the sculptor's depiction of Mary, raised slightly above six worried men either side of her, presumably the twelve apostles.

'Come on, Nikki,' said Dave softly. She turned towards Dave, her smile unnaturally wide.

'Let's go,' she chirped, placing her hands in her jacket, tucking the photo out of sight.

The rain eased slightly, but our moods remained bleak. Boris finally broke the silence.

'So, Nikki,' he began in a voice that was so soft and fluffy it felt like cotton wool was being inserted into your ears. 'We've been walking this track for three weeks and none of us know your reasons for being out here.'

Boris was entering risky territory. Since we'd met Nikki back in Pamplona, she'd been reluctant to share these things with others.

'I just like taking big walks,' she said, trying to keep things light. Dave and I laughed to ease the awkwardness.

'What about that photo?' persisted Boris. Dave frowned.

'That's, uh, that's someone I know.' Her voice faltered, and she changed the subject frantically. 'So many people know about this pilgrimage. When I was studying with my guru in India, I met these guys in Bombay who decided to walk the Camino. I found their enthusiasm, how do you say —?'

'Infectious,' said Boris.

'Infectious!' she said triumphantly, sensing that she'd successfully redirected the discussion. 'You boys are so smart. So I thought I'd walk the Camino, too. The funny thing is, those silly guys didn't even end up coming here.' She giggled and then sighed.

'So that photo is one of those guys?' asked the Canadian.

'Boris —' said Dave with a shake of his head.

'You know what?' said Nikki. 'I think I might stop to meditate.'

'Here?' said Boris. He swivelled his neck around to accentuate his point. We were at the edge of León's urban sprawl and it was still drizzling. Rolling out the meditation mat in a Glasgow housing estate would be more pleasant than along this section of the Camino.

'Looks like as good a spot as any to me,' said Dave. Nikki smiled gratefully at Dave and then hurried up a street that looked to be leading into an industrial area. We walked on.

'It's a wonder you've managed to get anyone, *ever*, to sleep with you,' said Dave once Nikki was completely out of sight.

'Just trying to work out what makes that girl tick.'

'Maybe you should give it a rest, mate.'

'What's wrong with asking her about why she's walking the Camino?'

'Because clearly she's walking for private reasons,' said Dave in his definitive tone.

'Never mind,' said Boris with a mischievous grin, 'leave us on our own and I'll coax it out of her.' Dave stopped suddenly. His blood was up now.

'Boris, don't make the mistake of thinking the rest of us are *anything* like you.'

'All right,' I said, in a rare attempt at mediation. 'We've all had a long morning —'

'What's that supposed to mean?' cut in Boris.

'It means, not all of us are here to root our way across Spain.'

'I should hope not, man, I mean you being married and everything.'

'Now what's *that* supposed to mean?'

'Nothing. It's just that you're a little defensive about this girl.'

'Boris —' Dave stopped himself and took a breath. 'You're . . . not a complicated man, are you?' This was about as cutting as Dave ever allowed himself to get. He stepped up his cadence and walked ahead of us.

'What was that all about?' Boris asked, turning to me.

'Something's eating away at him,' I said. 'And you're not helping.'

'Okay, there's some weird shit going on here. I think I might give you two some space.' Without another word, he slipped into a nearby café. I had no desire to follow him inside and smooth things over.

I caught up to Dave at Villar de Mazarife, 23 kilometres out of León. It was past midday and we were due for a lunch break, but Dave was keen to push on through the town.

'Everything all right?' I asked.

'I'm not ready to stop walking just yet.'

'Listen,' I said after a pause, 'I've been wanting to clear things up about the pledge.' He stopped suddenly to face me, his fists clenched in frustration.

'Would you get over the fucking pledge? I don't care about it! In fact, it never worried me in the slightest.'

'Really?'

'For Christ's sake! Yes, really.'

'Well, then what was that lecture about with Boris?'

'You can't be serious? Didn't you see how he was behaving?'

'Yeah, but we both know what he's like.'

Dave let out an exasperated sigh. 'Look, Nikki clearly has things going on in her life. That photo she carries around with her is someone close to her who's died.' The same thought had crossed my mind, but I couldn't remember a time when she could have told Dave about it. We'd always encountered her together.

'When did she tell you that?'

'She didn't; I just know. Let's stop discussing Nikki and this bloody pledge –' Dave's sarcastic lilt returned – 'I'd rather hear about the next town and seeing as you're the nerd in this team, I'm guessing you can give me the rundown.'

'And you'd be right,' I said, not totally convinced Dave was back to his old self.

We were now headed for Hospital de Órbigo, I explained – the realm of Christianity's most prestigious military orders. The town's eponymous hospice was, at various times, run by the Hospitallers of St John and the Knights Templar. This was not the town's chief attraction; its bridge, the Puente de Órbigo, took that honour.

The bridge achieved landmark status along the Camino after it had been the stage for one of Spain's greatest jousting tournaments. It was renamed 'Paso Honroso' (the passage of honour) for the event. With its themes of romance, courage, bravery, political intrigue and built-in pathos, the story of the Paso Honroso could have easily come from the pen of Sir Walter Scott. In fact, the tourney's hero, the Leónese knight Don Suero de Quiñones, is widely considered the inspiration for Cervantes' Don Quixote.

Don Suero certainly possessed a quixotic sensibility. He challenged the best lancers in Europe to meet him on the Órbigo Bridge. The reason? To impress a lady who had scorned him. The Don pledged to wear an iron collar to symbolise his binding affection for the woman who'd rejected his advances. The collar would not be removed until he had broken 300 lances across the armour of his challengers.

The tourney began two weeks before the Feast of St James in the Jacobean year of 1434, at a time when the road was teeming with pilgrims. Word of Don Suero's joust drew knights from across the Continent keen to exercise the birthright of the nobility. For what better way to prove one's worth than on the lists with steed and lance?

They came in droves. The banks of the Órbigo were covered by battle tents, fluttering pennants and the wooden lists constructed along the length of the bridge. After three weeks of competition, and having snapped the requisite number of lances, Don Suero unlatched the iron band from around his neck, breaking the bonds of his unrequited affection. The crowd cheered as he led a procession back to León, from where he would journey to Compostela as a pilgrim.

Don Suero's victory did not come without a price. His habit of taunting opponents by wearing a woman's blouse into tilts put him offside with sections of the nobility. In defeating most of the knights who dared to cross the Paso Honroso, he also made a large number of enemies. Gutierre de Quijada was among those whose honour had been robbed at the Paso Honroso. Twenty-four years would pass before Gutierre had his revenge – ambushing and killing the Don in cold blood.

Dave and I arrived at the thirteenth-century bridge not long before sunset. In my own quixotic moment I imagined myself at the top of the lists, mounted on a charger bearing my insignia. I could hear the blacksmith's hammer correcting the dints in fractured armour above the clamour of ladies-in-waiting, musicians, knights and jesters. In the foreground stood my opponent, arrayed against my chivalrous purpose. He wore the florid heraldry of Boris the Sordid, and smugly eyed me off from the far end of the lists, while scantily clad members of his all-female retinue attended to his saddle girths.

The first of our three tilts would begin in plumes of dust kicked up by our steeds. Bravely they would bear our weight along the palisades that lined our noble passage. Lances would then meet armour in an explosion of splintered wood and wild applause from galleries built along the bridge's arches. Don Tom had emerged victorious, halfway to proving his fealty to the Fair Maiden of Texas.

THE BRAVE FRONTIERSMAN

The fact that I didn't know the Texan's name might seem odd given how much I fancied her. Most people would have long since taken steps to ascertain the name of the future mother of their children. Not me. Not knowing the Texan's name only intensified the hold she had over me.

This little mystery would have an expiration date, of course. There would be occasions where I would need to know her name, such as during the solemnisation of our wedding vows. Meanwhile, I whiled away rain-drenched stretches along the road by imagining her name.

From the way she carried herself, her posture, her bearing, I could tell she'd been born into stature and old-world class. Traditional parents, I surmised, would most likely have passed on a name that had been in the family for generations – Frances, Deborah, Victoria, Roberta or Jacqueline? The Texan wasn't a woman to stand on ceremony, though; she'd of course prefer the kind of diminutive that only cute American girls can pull off.

If there was any justice in the world, she'd have a surname

that evoked the same sort of breeziness she herself did. It'd almost certainly be alliterative with the first name. Having filtered all possibilities through these criteria, I concluded that the Texan went by the name of Franny Faucheaux, Debbie Dubois, Vicky Vanderbilt, Bobbi Belucci or Jackie Johnson. I found saying these names out loud soothing, playing around with the pronunciation, using different accents or redistributing the emphasis of certain syllables.

The weather cleared the morning Dave and I left Hospital de Órbigo. We had easily walked the 15 kilometres to Astorga and inspected the city's cathedral, Roman ruins and Gaudi-designed palace well before midday. Astorga marks the intersection of the Camino Francés and the Via de la Plata, a converted Roman trade route carrying pilgrims from Seville via Zafra, Mérida, Cáceres, Salamanca and Zamora.

There were noticeably more pilgrims around now, including an influx that had joined the Camino Francés from the south and those lazy sods who had skipped the Meseta and picked up the trail at León. From hereon the demand for beds would increase significantly, so we drew up a stage-by-stage itinerary that meant we'd avoid stopping at the larger regional centres. This new plan saw us leave Astorga for the unremarkable township of Santa Catalina de Somoza, 10 kilometres to the west. We thought we would have no problem getting a bed there. As it happened, the Texan shared our logic.

Dave spotted her first. Her brown hair was pulled back tightly in a ponytail, which moved side to side like she was in some hair commercial.

'Let's catch up to her,' said Dave.

'Yeah, I'm not sure. I just don't want to interrupt —'

'You know what they say,' said Dave. 'Faint heart never won fair lady.'

The Texan had stopped at the side of the road, admiring the mountains in the north while sipping from her water bottle. Dave hung back behind me, prodding me forward with his walking pole. We were now close enough for her to hear our footsteps. Sweat dribbled from my brow. The time had come. I cleared my throat.

'Oh, look out! Here's a bagful of trouble! How are you, mate?' I fairly shouted at her. My attempt at casual familiarity caused her to choke on a mouthful of water. She swivelled around, alarmed, and wiped the spilt water from her face. Dave emerged from behind me, palms raised in the universal symbol for 'we're non-threatening'.

'Oh! Howdy, Dave. Howdy, Tom. How y'all today?' she asked with a smile. Every last drop of blood drained from my face. She knew my name.

'G'day, mate!' I bellowed. The Texan's smile morphed into an expression of puzzlement.

'. . . Howdy,' she repeated, perplexed. I felt panic take hold while a grotesque silence wrapped around the three of us. Dave strolled forward.

'So, where y'all heading, *Texan*?' he said in a southern accent that was so ridiculous that it sent her into a laughing fit.

'"*Texan*". So that's what you boys call me?' she asked,

putting on a Calamity Jane twang. 'Well, I like that. I'm headed for a little town called Santa Catalina. It can't be more than a couple of miles up the road. Say, where're you headed?'

'Santa Catalina,' I gushed. Dave snickered.

'Well, okay then, let's get going.' She returned the lid to her bottle of water and set off with the carefree exuberance of a girl ambling her way to a line dance.

The Texan was captivating. Up close she was even more beautiful than I'd originally thought her. There was, of course, more to her than just a pretty face. She was fluent in Spanish, passionate about jazz and country music and interested in fine arts and theology: a scholar and musician who drove cattle across the prairie. I pieced this together from what I could overhear of the conversation she was having with Dave, who was kindly attempting to involve me in the discussion. She seemed far more interested in Dave's bucolic upbringing than my bland mutterings. Her very presence left me woefully inarticulate; it was all I could do to string a sentence together. Only the uneven cobblestones of Castrillo de los Polvazares an hour out of Astorga jolted me into action.

'So,' I began enthusiastically, practically cutting off Dave mid-sentence, 'have you seen what's happening in the financial world? A crisis, wouldn't you say?' A jarring silence followed. I suppose this was my attempt at sounding sophisticated, but the effect was more like the child who interrupts his parents' conversation to show them a finger painting he's done with his dinner.

'I'm not gonna lie to ya,' said the Texan eventually, 'I

haven't been following current world events the last few weeks.' She turned to Dave, encouraging him to finish what they'd been talking about. Things were not going well. I figured we only had an hour before we came into Santa Catalina. Who knew what obstacles there might be between here and the albergue? Some stud with swarthy good looks fresh off the Via de la Plata might be hovering around the corner. Or, worse still, Boris might suddenly materialise from behind a hill. It was time to pull out the big guns. Dave, it seemed, was getting on well talking about home and the Riverina, so I picked up the theme of country living in the voice of the Australian larrikin.

'Me family's got a house down the coast,' I boomed, heedless of whomever was talking, 'it's bloody beautiful down there, mate.' Dave cast an inquisitive eye in my direction. I pressed on gamely, broadening my accent even more. 'I bloody love that clear air. It's the only way to live. Out there all you need is a stubby and a good barbie.' Dave's face contorted into a cringe. He pursed his lips together and disengaged from the conversation. He was never going to ambush my strategy, but nor would he encourage it.

'Oh, yeah?' said the Texan interestedly.

'Me family's property is on a lake system four hours east of Melbourne. It's down in the southeast tip of the mainland.' This was all utterly useless information to the Texan, of course. It was just a canvas for exhibiting a Far North Queenslander's brogue, a pitiful mix of Steve Irwin and Alby Mangels. Any Australian child could have detected the forced nasality soaring above my leafy suburban burr. The Texan, however, was none the wiser. I was hoping she would conclude that it was a voice chiselled by a raw climate, moulded around camp-fires and crafted out on the paddocks – an outback patois.

'That sounds real nice,' she said dreamily. Dave puffed out his cheeks. As a legitimate man of the land, he probably took this kind of deception as a slight, but he was too kind to expose the charade. 'Bloody oath it is,' I said. The Texan seemed responsive. She was now regarding me with vague curiosity. Dave coughed violently; something nasty had caught in his throat.

I decided to rebuild myself in the image of the knocka-bout Australian male. I took as my inspiration those heroes of the ballad that had clogged up the English curricula of my school years. In my mind the transition from unemployed urbanite to brave frontiersman of the bush was utterly seam-less. Suddenly, I was a modern-day Clancy of the Overflow, talking in rhyming slang about picking up spiders with my bare hands and shooting rabbits (bloody pests) while living 'most of the year' on a country homestead.

'Have you ever seen a shark before?' the Texan asked after I had detailed my run-ins with dangerous Australian fauna.

'Oh, shit, yeah,' I said broadly. 'Everyone has seen one of those. But it's the Joe Blakes you want to watch out for.'

'Joe, who?'

'Joe Blakes, you know, snakes. When I was a kid out on the farm, I saw this gigantic king brown near the dam.' I was really talking shit now. 'It was the biggest I ever saw.'

'What's a king brown?' the Texan asked.

'A very deadly snake. Knock you off in five minutes, it will. Anyway, it was bearing down on me and I would have been rooted had me old man not been there.'

'What did he do?'

'He stomped his feet on the ground. Snakes are afraid of the vibrations. Anyway, the king brown was off quicker than a bride's nightie.'

'Oh,' she giggled.

'That must be Santa Catalina,' interrupted Dave, eyeing a cluster of houses and hoping that they might signal an end to this desecration of our culture.

'So, which albergue are you staying in?' asked the Texan.

'The first one we come across, mate,' I said, lifting the peak of my cap and spitting at the side of the road.

'You mind if I join you?'

'No dramas at all,' I said, aiming for nonchalance as my heart felt as if it were about to burst. The first albergue we saw doubled as the local bar and restaurant. It was not the most salubrious venue for romance, but then a ready supply of alcohol never hurt a courtship.

'Well, I'm gonna hit the showers,' said the Texan after we had our passports stamped. 'I'll see you two boys later.'

'Yeah, righto.' I watched her as she glided up the stairs.

I turned to Dave. 'That went all right.'

'Bloody oath, *mate*.'

Dave conversed with some pilgrims in the restaurant while I continued to talk crap to the Texan at a table outside. The sight of her discreetly made-up in the evening light sent me into a flutter. To conceal my nerves, I fell deeper into my performance. I was no longer Banjo's ideal of the Australian bushman; I was something infinitely more grotesque. Curiously, the image I chose to portray – the laidback type not given to ponderous self-reflection, determined to live in the moment – is the exact opposite of how I am in reality. That was unsettling enough, but what in subsequent days would really cause me to wince was remembering the words I used – ones that I'd never have dreamt of saying in regular conversation.

In one particularly memorable sentence I referred to the barman as 'cobber', a San Miguel as 'sherbet', the Texan as 'darl' and a drunkard carrying on outside as a 'drongo'. There was something tragic about it all. I couldn't maintain the fraud for much longer. So when the Texan casually dropped into the conversation that she was eagerly anticipating rendezvousing with her fiancé in Santiago – a medical graduate from Harvard finishing a one-year posting with *Médecins Sans Frontières* in West Africa – I felt as much relief as I did misery.

If my pouty frown did not betray my hurt feelings, then the reassertion of my moderate inner-suburban accent surely did. The Texan almost immediately understood what had just happened. She was only momentarily perplexed when the carefree Aussie larrikin reverted to a strung-out guy with a complex about his employment status. She clicked her tongue in an all-knowing way, offered an apologetic smile and then kissed me on the cheek. She then repaired to the dormitory leaving me to fix up the bill. Only at the end, when all had been lost, did I truly approximate something unmistakably Australian – a piece of roadkill discarded at the side of a road.

Dave came outside, took me back to the bar and ordered a couple of shots of yellow grappa. Things began to unravel shortly thereafter. About fifteen young Atlético Madrid fans arrived to watch a Champions League game on the television. For unknown reasons, Dave and I adopted Liverpool FC for the night; we had a soft spot for the away team, I suppose. When Robbie Keane scored in the fourteenth minute, we drained our beers, ordered another round of shots, hurled abuse at the locals and gave a plausible rendition of 'You'll Never Walk Alone'.

The night threatened to turn ugly when the home team scored late in the second half. At first, the locals delighted in a bit of harmless roistering. This escalated into something more sinister when I accidentally shoulder-charged some bloke waving his scarf in my face. Dave intervened just when it seemed inevitable that I would start a pub brawl. In his inimitable fashion, Dave suggested that in retribution they should shave my head with the set of clippers the bartender kept behind the bar. The strategy was translated to me in a manner that implied this was the only way I could prevent a glassing. So, with Dave supervising, I was ushered outside for the trim.

I was quite forcibly made to sit down on a chair; watching

on in anticipation was the red-and-white-clad mob of Atlético Madrid's regional fan base. A ferocious-looking man with guts that seemed ready to burst through the vertical stripes of his team's colours was presented with the clippers. His aggressively shaved pate was proof enough that he was something of an expert on the matter at hand.

Ten minutes later I emerged from the crowd and was handed a mirror by the bartender. I might not have been able to pull off the knockabout Australian farmer, but, my word, did I look every bit the football hooligan. I didn't mind the transformation either. I looked hard and tough, right at home on the terraces at Anfield. Dave's silence suggested I should probably reserve judgment until I'd sobered up.

THE LUCKY GODSON

I sat bolt upright, momentarily uncertain of my whereabouts. Everything seemed to be in order. The sun had begun its march over the horizon and light was streaming into the dormitory. But something was troubling me; latent memories slowly made their way to the surface.

Events of the previous night formed vague shapes in my mind. There was the Texan, the shots, the beers, the football, and something else. Frustrated, I kneaded my weary eyes, trying to coax out the missing memory. The palm of my left hand moved along my forehead and, sickeningly, it passed over my hairline. Where normally it would have met with moderate resistance from my fringe, my palm instead cruised effortlessly across my shaved head. And then it all came flooding back.

I ran to the bathroom to survey the damage, catching my reflection in the mirror and recoiling in horror. For the first time since I was born, the topography of my head could be clearly seen. All that remained on my scalp were miniature rows of stubble in the unmistakable shape of male pattern baldness.

The fate of my hair was plain to see, its destruction inevitable. My forehead was a relentless sea eroding the shoreline. And testosterone, it seems, carves away at a hairline much faster than Mother Nature sculpts the land. Going bald was not unexpected, of course; it's something of a family tradition. I was just not expecting to be beset by the affliction so soon. I had assumed that hair loss would happen well into middle age: something to go with retirement and grandchildren. I imagined a receding hairline at that stage of life might lend my looks greater distinction. There was nothing distinguished about this hairdo. I returned to the dormitory, put some clothes on and packed up. Dave was waking up with a grim hangover, moaning with every movement. I walked downstairs and into the courtyard for a cigarette.

We weren't far from our destination and here I was, recovering from another binge after having spent the day impersonating someone else to impress a girl. When nothing came of that, I'd had my head shaved to satisfy some strangers while playing at being a football hooligan. I was still a child, and not in a boyish, young-at-heart sort of way.

This pilgrimage was beginning to feel like a missed opportunity. Maybe I'd done more out here than just break the pledge. Maybe I'd also blown a chance to finally migrate beyond a forgettable stage in my life. The Camino seemed only to aid my relentless adolescence that was stretching on into my late twenties.

As I lit up, I caught my reflection in a window behind the glow of the morning sun. The hemisphere of light floated above my shaved head like an aureole. A new light was also being cast on my trip, revealing it to be nothing more than a continuation of prolonged juvenility.

I went to wait for Dave by the side of the road. He staggered out of the albergue not looking in a good way. Today we would be taking the Pass of Foncebadón, a terrible stage in which to be nursing a hangover. Looking down from a formidable 1505 metres was the Cruz de Ferro, the highest point of the Camino Francés, marked by a large cairn and iron cross. We would then plunge 900 metres over 10 kilometres down into the village of Molinaseca.

This was an important landmark for the spiritualists. It had become a place where people deposited mementos (trinkets, tokens, messages), literally and symbolically leaving things behind. The only thing I could imagine leaving behind after an 18-kilometre ascent in my woeful state was a massive pile of vomit. Not exactly a gesture in concert with spiritual rebirth.

We dispensed with the big night post-mortems and began our climb, moving at a canter to generate some warmth. Dave strode along the asphalt road, as if trying to outrun his hangover. I lost him shortly after El Ganso, 5 kilometres west of Santa Catalina, where a thick blanket of frost had covered the fields. The landscape, which invited comparisons with the frozen tundra, was one we were ill-equipped to handle. Up here, I thought, jumpers, beanies and slickers weren't going to cut the mustard. We needed long johns, polar fleeces, gloves and an oxygen bottle.

The path ascended sharply from El Ganso, diverging from the main road into woodland. The boughs of the trees shielded the sun, blocking what little warmth there was. The path grew harder to climb. I recalled thinking in Frómista how eager my feet were to be challenged with a variable gradient or shale or slippery stones, anything to escape the monotony of the Meseta. But after tripping on some loose rock and then crawling on all fours over a boulder, I grew nostalgic for the flat plain.

I hiked for hours along a muddy path that cut through woods and below fallen timber before the path rejoined the main road. I wandered through small villages stolen from another time, passing houses with slate roofs and smoke escaping from crumbling chimneys. All I could hear was the breeze and the solemn clack of my walking pole. Eventually, the path levelled out and the woods receded, leaving me bathed in sunlight. Near the summit, I unlatched my pack, setting it down inches from a precipitous drop and turned around to gauge my progress. I involuntarily gasped at the sight.

From this vantage point, I had the clearest view yet of the wide edges of the Meseta. At one edge, far to the north, the Cantábrican Mountains towered. The sun broke across the cliffs in great spears of light repelled by endless battlements guarding the Bay of Biscay. I looked to the south, where the great plain reached out to the horizon.

My thoughts travelled back in time to El Argar, a place along my line of sight, where people alloyed copper and tin two thousand years before Christ was born. I could almost see them – the ancient metal makers whose bronze brought the Greek and Phoenician traders in open galleys across the Mediterranean. Some of them would settle here, while others converged on parts further north inhabited by the Iberians and Celtic invaders from central Europe.

Eventually, the Romans would take the Peninsula, crushing all but the fiercest tribes. They would name this land 'Hispania'. Centuries later, under the aqueducts and along the roads the Romans built, the long-haired Visigoths would come only to be themselves subdued by Muslim conquerors from Africa. And then across this ancient land – one hemmed in by sea and mountain, flooded in ethnic tides, vitrified in the crucible of centuries of war and conquest – a pilgrim road would be forged.

I looked east from the direction I'd come, bringing myself back to the present. In the foreground the woods spilled down to the base of the mountain before meeting the Meseta. I made out the small villages of El Ganso and Santa Catalina, and further afield I caught sight of the church steeples and towers of Astorga: an island of shimmering light in a straw-coloured sea. I looked further still, picturing in my mind's eye the cities of León and Terradillos and Carrión and Hontanas. I looked beyond them all, through the golden haze to the lonely cross at Punto de Vista, where I had stood over the city of Burgos.

Pilgrims would be there now, trying to fix their gaze on a landmark beyond the city that sprawled below them. Soon enough they would realise that even the keenest eyes couldn't see past a path dissolving into wheatfields. I imagined them turning on that spot, kicking up the dust and joining the other pilgrims hauling their way across the Meseta.

Dave and I had come a long way, but things waited for us further west. I gathered my pack and made my way over the Pass of Foncebadón.

The sun was high in the sky now. The wind cuffed the bushes that sprouted from snowy outcrops. I walked on, following the path as it left the mountain's side and returned to the woods. Presently, the iron cross appeared high above the tree line. As I crested the lip of a hill, a giant pile of stones came fully into view. Dave was at the top of them, leaning against the wooden trunk that propped up the crucifix, a smile across his face. He was talking on his mobile phone, but I was too far away to hear any of his conversation.

I dropped my pack and took a seat on a nearby log, hoping to catch my breath with the assistance of a cigarette. Dave rang off and came down the steep slope of the cairn to join me. He looked to have recovered from his hangover.

'How are you travelling?' I asked.

'It's been one hell of a day,' beamed Dave, plonking himself next to me. 'I woke up with the strangest feeling this morning. I would've waited for you, but I just had to get going. I felt as if I needed to be somewhere urgently, like I had to rush to keep an appointment.' Dave shook his head in disbelief. 'Anyway, after walking like a maniac for three hours, I came to this cairn and looking up at it, I . . .' Dave trailed off, chuckled and shook his head again.

'What happened?' I asked. A pause ensued long enough for us to hear the wind change.

'Did you know it has been ten years since Dad died?'

Somewhere inside me a light switched on. The tetchiness of our conversations, the reprimanding of Boris, the concern for Nikki, even the aggravation with the bedbugs were all put in a different context. Selfishly, I'd assumed this had had something to do with me. But Dave was dealing with far bigger things. My fretting over broken pledges and the moments of melodrama on the Meseta seemed suddenly unimportant.

'Ten years,' he repeated quietly to himself. Dave and I had only rarely discussed his dad's death. He was, from what I'd pieced together, a lot like Dave: a larger-than-life figure, warm-hearted and quick with a joke – the unofficial Mayor of Finley. I'd always figured that Dave viewed his death as a sad, horrible memory, one to be kept confined. I never paused to consider the loss of his old man as something he'd been dealing with all throughout the time I'd known him. Hearing those two words – *ten years* – delivered me from that misapprehension.

I'd never heard Dave indulge in any bitterness or sensed any resentment at having been deprived of a father's encouragement and company. Dave was not one to dwell on such things. Instead, he would speak gratefully of what he did have in his life: his four sisters always ready for a chat and a laugh, a mother as strong and generous and kind as a son could ask for, and a wife who was everything to him. But now I heard something unfamiliar in Dave's voice. It was the sound of a son's yearning to be given the chance to sit opposite his father and talk one more time.

I wanted to convey all these things to Dave, to tell him I was in awe of how he'd made it through those ten years. I wanted to tell him how proud any father would be to have a son like him. Instead, with an open hand, I gave him two giant slaps on his back.

'Relax, mate,' said Dave with a chuckle, sensing that the moment was straying into uncharted, awkward realms. 'This story has a happy ending. So afterwards, I climbed up the cairn to the cross. I can't explain why I bothered. It wasn't anything to do with religion. But as soon as I got to the top, the phone rang. It was my old man's youngest sister, Ros. She gave birth to a boy the other day – Josh – and they asked me to be the godfather.'

At that moment we were surprised to see Nikki frantically wandering past, holding her photograph. She was breathing heavily, moaning loudly each time she exhaled. She was close enough for me to notice that her brilliant blue eyes had turned a watery grey.

'Hey, Nikki,' shouted Dave. She didn't seem to hear him. We watched as she hauled herself up the cairn. Below the cross she let out a sigh and looked skywards. After a few moments she knelt down, gently knocking her head against the wooden stake. Then she stood up, swivelled around and walked carefully back down the stones. She came over and sat between Dave and me.

'How are you going?' asked Dave.

Nikki mumbled something and let her head fall onto Dave's arm. When he brought his arm over her shoulder, she let out a terrible cry and began sobbing. Other pilgrims walked past quickly with nods of acknowledgment. What else could they do? I sat there for a while, feeling stupid as I smoked my cigarette, Nikki's cry echoing over the mountain. I quietly stood up, gathered my pack and made my way to the top of the cairn.

At the base of the cross were scattered pictures, peace messages and love letters. Lying on top of them all was a worn photograph of a younger Nikki. She was being hugged by a woman who looked as Nikki might in twenty years' time. It hardly seemed possible that a photograph could contain all the beaming happiness written into that embrace. I thought about the bravery it must have taken to let that image go.

I trod back down the rock pile, turning towards the iron cross glinting in the sunlight. Something needed to be done here, some gesture made. Everyone else had left something over the Pass of Foncebadón. I bent down, collected a stone and threw it to the top of the pile, watching as it skipped and settled at a point on the cairn's outer crust.

Behind me Nikki continued to cry on Dave's shoulder. My pilgrim companion stared steadfastly ahead, his chin slightly raised. There was nothing undignified or shameful about this moment. His posture seemed to insist on that point. But it must have been hard for him. Sometimes I wonder of what stuff they make Riverina men.

I signalled to him that I would press on. He sent me a wave. As I came down the slope of the highest part of the Camino, I thought of how lucky young Josh was to have Dave McNamara as his godfather.

HIKING-BOOT EPIPHANIES

Dave managed to walk Nikki to the foot of the mountain, where they bumped into Liz. The sight of Nikki's Camino pal precipitated another flood of tears. Liz instructed Dave to walk on. She could take it from here.

I saw Dave strutting over the bridge into the village of Molinaseca like a prize-fighter approaching the ring. I was sitting at a table outside a nearby bar, my beer half full. I knew we were in for a serious night when I went to get out of my chair to buy him a drink only for Dave to push me back into my seat. He walked straight into the bar without dropping his pack and emerged with a San Miguel Grande for each of us.

Dave had come over the Pass of Foncebadón completely rejuvenated. Those things that had been nagging him were now left at the base of the Cruz de Ferro. Now all my mate was searching for was a reason to hit the grog. He found one in the realisation that we were about to enter the final week of the pilgrimage.

That night we conducted sprinting competitions down Molinaseca's main street, placed café tables on top of cars and performed 'Click Go the Shears' to a concierge in a hotel lobby, Dave accompanying our raggedy voices on a piano accordion kept behind the reception desk.

We returned to our albergue well after curfew, the warden graciously letting us in on the proviso that we went directly to bed. We showed our gratitude by smuggling in a dozen cans to the dormitory and singing club songs into the early hours. The warden thundered into the room some time later, delivering the ultimatum of dormitory or pavement. We fell unconscious shortly thereafter. The next morning we left early, hoping to avoid awkward exchanges with any sleep-deprived occupants. With cloudy heads and in near darkness, we squirrelled out the entrance as discreetly as a couple of bison entering a ballet rehearsal.

We were in the Bierzo, a valley between the sun-tinged sparseness of the Meseta and the lush green of Galicia. The first half of our day in the Bierzo would be spent on sealed roads skirted by powerlines, a sharp contrast to yesterday's muddy path up to the Cruz de Ferro and rocky descent down to Molinaseca.

To emphasise this sense of being back in the modern world, giant chimney stacks took up the skyline to the north. You could see a layer of smog sutured across the city of Ponferrada like a yellowy-brown skin graft. It was neverthe-less a pleasant stage and a day of happy reunions.

Like us, many pilgrims were timing their arrival in

Santiago for the last day of October, so as to be among the cathedral's congregation on All Saints' Day. We passed the old firm (Bonjour, Hi Guys, French Pipes), who each greeted us in their respective ways. Irish Michael strode past, whistling the theme to *The Great Escape*, just before the four Argentineans appeared dribbling a soccer ball. Seeing them all put us both in a terrific mood.

We'd skipped breakfast in Molinaseca, fearful that irritated residents might recognise our voices as the drunken yodellers from the night before. We were famished by the time we arrived in Ponferrada 8 kilometres away. The yellow way-markers guided us over busy intersections and past the Castillo de los Templarios, the Castle of the Knights Templar. The castle had all the trimmings – imposing fortifications, drawbridge, crenulated towers and fluttering banners.

The Templars settled here in 1178, responding to a request from Ferdinand II of León, who had seen the benefits of such an alliance. This was the most memorable decision in Ferdinand's short reign (save for having his father-in-law, Afonso I of Portugal, imprisoned in 1169 – a brave move in any era). The Templar presence would provide protection for Ferdinand's people and his interests in the region. The Templars, meanwhile, were gifted an important stretch of path along one of the great pilgrimages.

This castle marked the Templars' most westerly outpost in an unbroken network of safe houses, redoubts, hospices and monasteries throughout Europe and the Near East, all the way to the Order's original base of operations in Jerusalem.

Donations of land and money bequeathed to the Templars in their fight for Christianity helped turn the Order into a multinational organisation. By the end of the twelfth century they could afford to build mighty castles such as this as symbols of power and prestige. Generous papal bulls (Vatican decrees) exempted the Order from local taxes, further consolidating the Templars' strong financial position. Soon the Order was powerful enough to threaten the divine rule of kings. This was a far cry from its humble origins in the ruins of a Jerusalem mosque.

The Knights Templar began as an assembly of nine crusader knights in 1118 who stayed in Jerusalem after the First Crusade. They took vows of poverty and obedience based on the rule of St Benedict inside what they believed to be the Temple of Solomon. They also swore an oath to protect Christians on pilgrimage to the Holy Lands. They called themselves *Pauperes commilitones Christi Templique Solomonici*, The Poor Fellow-Soldiers of Christ and of the Temple of Solomon. The Order's title would be contracted to Knights Templar, the very mention of which continues to excite a sense of intrigue, conspiracy, secrecy and betrayal. Stories of lost Templar treasure and hidden knowledge of the Holy Grail might have something to do with the Order's bloody demise.

The fate of the Order seemed wedded to the fortune of the crusades. While the knights continued to defend the Holy Lands, Templar veneration and power would remain largely uncontested. But the loss of the port city of Acre in 1291, the last Christian stronghold in the Holy Lands after the fall of Jerusalem in 1187 to the mighty Saladin, proved disastrous.

In Europe the Knights Templar had made powerful enemies. Philip IV of France owed vast sums of money to the Order following the war with the English. Philip, an opportunistic and avaricious man, lent his considerable influence to anti-Templar sentiment in the years after the loss of Acre. This was Philip's great chance to eradicate his debt and free his kingdom from Templar influence.

So in 1307 Philip issued a general edict to arrest all Templars across France for blasphemy, sodomy, simony and immorality. Confessions, albeit extracted through torture, lent credence to the idea of Templar heresy. The Vatican was outraged. Pope Clement V issued a papal bull six weeks later instructing Christian monarchs to bring members of the Order before a papal hearing. Freed from the inquisitor's brutal methods of extraction, the knights recanted their confessions. One knight brought a bag of his own foot bones that had been cut off and burnt during his interrogation as proof that his confession was involuntary.

But Philip forced the Pope's hand, threatening military action if the Vatican refused to denounce the Order. Clement was left no choice. He issued his infamous bull, *Vox in excelso*, which enabled the systematic dismantlement of the Order. Templar property was seized and reassigned as knights scattered and fled abroad. Those less fortunate were imprisoned, subjected to cruel tortures and executed.

Jacques de Molay, the twenty-third grand master of the

Knights Templar, a Frenchman like his twenty-two predecessors, recanted his confession, claiming it was extracted under duress. He was found guilty of being a relapsed heretic and sentenced to burn at the stake on the Île de la Cité at the foot of Notre Dame. The grand master requested that his hands be bound in the prayer position and that his execution pyre face the cathedral. Legend has it that as he was led to his death, Jacques de Molay declared that King Philip and Pope Clement would 'face a tribunal with God within a year'.

Philip IV died in a hunting accident before the end of the year while Pope Clement V died one month after the grand master's execution. Lightning struck the church where the Pope's body lay in state, igniting a fire that burnt Clement's body beyond recognition. Philip's three sons would, in turn, pay for the sins of their father. They each ruled France in rapid succession, bringing the House of Capet to an abrupt end in 1328. They were known as 'the accursed kings'. To superstitious medieval Europe, this was the surest sign that Jacques de Molay and the Knights Templar were granted retribution.

The Castillo de los Templarios was confiscated in 1312 after the Order's dissolution. The castle was entrusted to Don Pedro Fernández de Castro and then to a successor with the equally handsome name of Don Fadrique de Castilla. Fernando and Isabel la Católica would eventually claim it by force in 1483 for the Spanish Crown.

We found a pleasant café in which to eat that had a good view back across the Templar castle. The dark clouds that had gathered over the towering sierras to the west were now dumping rain in squally bursts over the city. The weather beyond that mountain chain looked bleak. Tomorrow we'd get our first taste of it. It was better to concentrate on the hot *tortilla* before me than the hard slog to come.

'*God damn!*' snapped a voice in the severe fashion of the affronted American. 'I've been waiting here for *ages*!' I turned around to see a woman rapping her fingers impatiently on the bar. The barman appeared, hands held up apologetically, which the woman perceived as an invitation to complain. After accusing the barman of running a shoddy business, the woman ordered a vegetarian salad and insisted on a complimentary can of Coke for her trouble. The barman begrudgingly acquiesced, grumbling away under his breath.

The woman turned around, considering the most suitable table at which to sit. She looked our way. Dave and I instinctively averted our eyes, sensing a conversation we could do without. She cleared her throat. 'Hey guys, do you mind if I join you?'

'Of course not,' said Dave, friendly as always. He obligingly rearranged the table so she could join us.

'My name is Sonja, and it's *so* wonderful to meet some Australian pilgrims,' she said with well-rehearsed sincerity. Her winning smile and immaculate attire gave the impression of a woman who had tasted enormous success. She had Oakley sunglasses worn headband-style and a bright-red North Face jacket cradled in her arm. She wore a snappy-looking compression suit and her feet were shod in sparkling clean chestnut-coloured boots. This woman meant business. 'You *are* from Australia, right?'

'Yeah, we're from —'

'No, no, no. Let me guess. Sydney?'

'Neither of us come from Sydney,' said Dave. 'Actually, we were brought up in different places. I'm from —'

'I was over in Sydney last year on a business conference.' And away she went, detailing the itinerary of her business trip (Sydney, Beijing, Tokyo), her life (Californian only child, Ivy League–educated), her career (senior business consult-ant at a large Manhattan firm), and her religion (Catholic). It became clear that for as long as we kept company with Sonja, it would be Sonja we talked about.

'Damn it,' she said impatiently, her face screwed into a terrifying ball of contempt. 'Who do I have to murder to get my freaking salad?'

'So have you enjoyed the Camino, Sonja?' asked Dave tentatively, shifting to a more neutral topic.

'Oh my God, it has been *amazing*! Hang on a second.' Sonja stood up, arms crossed, and stared daggers at the bar-tender. 'Excuse me, I have been waiting here for like *fifteen* minutes . . . Well, sorry really isn't good enough.' She sat back down. 'Now where was I? Oh, that's right, the Camino. I've found it hard at times, but I've been blessed to have experi-enced a moment of self-discovery.'

Dave and I had grown accustomed to listening to people's epiphanies. I had no right to be cynical. In hoping to get a sense of what to do with my life, I was peddling the same flighty aspirations. I knew this to be all bollocks now, but I wasn't about to tell Sonja this. Besides, her moment of self-discovery was unlike any other I'd heard about. It was the direct consequence of having purchased new hiking boots in León.

To understand Sonja's epiphany you need to first understand what she wanted to get out of the pilgrimage. Her 'pilgrim objectives', as she called them, read like dot points from a company mission statement – to experience enlightenment through inner growth; to meet benchmark distances at sustainable walking speeds; to undergo spiritual awareness through social engagement with other pilgrims. (She said that having a conversation with us satisfied the last of those objectives.)

'Upgrading my footwear was the best investment I made on the Camino,' she said. 'The boots have a streamlined design that immediately increased walking efficiency, enhanced comfort, and, thus, augmented my pilgrimage experience. From a business perspective, the fashionable design gives the boots a competitive advantage over other labels and that, in turn, has been consolidated with a quality of comfort that far exceeds the standard.'

She expanded on the boot purchase in this fashion, borrowing liberally from the corporate vernacular as she went. 'Moving forward,' she said in conclusion, 'I am going to start a hiking-boot business back in the States, just as a hobby. If I can work out how to make further improvements in terms of shoe design, I think they might take me over some unexplored terrain, in a commercial sense. Ultimately, my dream is to create a hiking experience that is as joyful and wonderful as mine.'

Sonja smiled brilliantly, her teeth sparkling white, then the bartender placed her order on the table. 'What the *Christ* is this?' she shouted. 'Since when has a vegetarian salad come with tuna? And where is my Coke? You've got exactly one minute to get me my proper order.'

She handed the salad back to the bartender. He returned thirty seconds later, breathing heavily and dripping sweat, a fresh bowl of salad *sans* tuna in his one shaking hand, the Coke in the other. Sonja scowled at the browbeaten man, pointedly pushing the salad to the side of the table before resuming her conversation.

I liked the location of Sonja's great moment of realisation. Those of a spiritualist bent seemed to have life-changing moments in the most predictable places – a woodland realm, cresting a summit, below a crucifix. No one had moments of clarity shopping for boots in a hiking store. Despite its originality, I still found Sonja's story implausible.

It was the complete lack of spontaneity in her hiking-boot epiphany and the passages of neatly arranged insight following it that I found galling. It was as if it had been imagined before she'd even left home and then affirmed at some opportune moment along the path. While she crapped on about qualitative and quantitative data for determining the best-practice model for a viable shoe shop business in New York City, she let slip that she had in fact walked the Camino to test the best shoes.

'Hang on,' I said. 'Didn't you say that the idea came to you in the hiking shop in León?'

The smile left her face. She abandoned the charade. 'You're right,' she said, her earnest lilt replaced with something harder. 'What I just told you will be the backstory for the advertising campaign.'

'What do you mean?'

'Every business has to have a good narrative to capture the consumers' imagination. I've been trying out that story on pilgrims for the last few days. Everyone *loves* it. The truth is that I'm really here to find out for myself the best shoes for walking long distances. In business, my number-one rule is that I'm the best diagnostic tool.'

She stood up, her voice back in disingenuous friendly mode. 'Well, it has been *just* wonderful speaking to you guys.' She pulled out a twenty-euro note and dropped it ostentatiously on the table, having not even touched her salad. She glared at the bartender, placed the Coke can in her backpack and left without even asking our names.

HEAVENLY WORK

The day went steadily downhill after the late breakfast with Sonja in Ponferrada. Strong westerlies brought more foul weather over the mountains. It poured all the way to Villafranca del Bierzo. Walking 22 kilometres in the rain almost caused me to hail one of the cabs cruising along the road beside us. Not even a sign marking the 200 kilometres remaining to Santiago could lift the mood.

Villafranca looked pleasant enough. It was snuggled into the base of the mountains, with wisps of chimney smoke snaking through the surrounding pine and oak trees lending the scene an alpine feel. We found the albergue without much trouble. It was one of the first buildings to greet us as we entered the village. The promise of a hot shower and a pilgrim's menu were the brightest thoughts we'd had for hours. The brightness was leached away by the sight of Edward reading Cicero at a table just inside the albergue's entrance. He was dressed in a full-length brown gown and a burgundy fez.

'Well, well, well!' he said, slowly putting the book down on the table, front cover up so we could see what he was reading (*On Government*). 'If it isn't Australia's answer to Bill Bryson and his musical companion.'

'I'm quite fond of Bryson,' I said, not displeased with the comparison.

'I'm sure you are,' he said. It was too wet to keep walking to the next town, although the thought crossed my mind. We brushed straight past Edward to the reception desk, had our passports stamped and went to the showers. The hot water had run out, of course.

We left the albergue before dawn for the second day in a row, this time to avoid a day's hike with Edward. We also had a big stage ahead of us. We were for O'Cebreiro, a solid 30 kilometres away over two massive hills that looked like camel humps on our topographical map. O'Cebreiro would mark our entrance into Galicia, the final province on the Camino. It was also the home of the priest Elías Valiña Sampedro, one of the Camino's great contributors.

In the early 1980s Elías walked the ancient path from Saint-Jean-Pied-de-Port with a bucket of yellow paint. He marked roads, trees, derelict buildings and fence posts along the Way with a simple yellow arrow. He was determined to make the pilgrimage accessible to people unskilled in orientation. His efforts very nearly came unstuck not far west of Pamplona, where the local constabulary mistook him for a Basque vandal scrawling political slogans.

The police did not believe his story and demanded the

names of other members of Elías's terrorist outfit. The priest responded, 'I work on my own, but thousands will follow me.' He was released without charge to complete his work. A bust was commissioned after he died; it is placed outside his old parish in O'Cebreiro. I was eager to lay eyes on that bust without Edward's company.

Everything was going beautifully. We slipped out of the albergue without prompting the slightest stir from the forty or so pilgrims sleeping in the dormitory. With great stealth we eased out the entrance, a couple of Andy Dufresnes escaping Shawshank. As we headed out the albergue door, I was warmly congratulating myself when I spied him. There he was, sitting on a bench not far from the albergue, dressed in his kurta and fedora.

'I thought you two could use my company,' he announced, relaxing into his smirk.

'Morning, Edward,' we sighed, wondering when he'd eavesdropped on last night's discussion about departing early. He lifted his pack onto his back, tightened the straps and clapped his hands together in preparation for an intellectual joust.

'Probably a good move you're out of that smock, Edward,' I said. 'I don't think it would've gone all that well up the muddy slope.' Dave chuckled.

'That "smock" is a ceremonial gown from Morocco, a *djellabah*,' he said aggressively. 'I bought it on my first trip to Casablanca when I was eighteen years old. I would never be so stupid as to wear it on unsealed roads.'

Villafranca's cafés and restaurants were not yet open. Breakfast would have to wait. The day was at least clear and crisp. The company, however, was inclement. On empty stomachs, we walked up the first of the day's vicious ascents, Edward filling us in on his extraordinary life. The first hour of the morning was devoted to his upbringing, 'those formative years when I was subjected to brainwashing at one of Melbourne's most prestigious schools'. He named the school with great disdain, as if his enrolment there undermined his claims to being a champion of the downtrodden. He added that he was on a full scholarship, determined that we not make the mistake of assuming that his education was the consequence of a privileged upbringing.

By hour two, as we scaled a mossy path and the breeze shook the dew from overhanging boughs, we were into his university years – the true making of Edward. Freed from the constraints of a schoolyard crammed with trust-fund babies oozing a sense of entitlement, Edward *learned* about the world. By second year he knew by heart history's most subversive texts – the ones that great leaders used to inspire revolution. He would keep company with likeminded socialists sporting Che berets and Mao caps, dreaming of that day when the worker would inherit the means of production.

Salvation on pilgrimage comes in many forms. Just when Edward was describing his transition from gifted scholar to successful professional, Warren came into sight. When we entered Warren's line of sight, he stood up from the rock he'd been sitting on, grabbed his testicles, saluted and boomed, 'Where the fuck have you pricks been?'

Warren was decked out in his finest outfit – camouflage-patterned singlet, black shorts and Ray-Bans. He was taking a smoko near the top of the ascent. It was the happiest vision of the day. There was no way known that Edward would want to keep company with Warren. Dave and I walked up and warmly shook his hand.

'Christ, it's good to see you blokes,' said Warren. 'I'd give you two a hug if I wasn't afraid they'd think we were pooftas.' I saw Edward shudder.

'How've you been?' asked Dave.

'Never better,' he said, looking over us both. 'I thought you might have lost a few kegs, Tom, but you've still got a fair roof hanging over that tool shed. The haircut's a bloody good improvement, though. You look like you're ready for a tour of Iraq.'

'We'd thought you pulled out of the pilgrimage with Esther,' I said, guiding the topic away from my physical shortcomings.

'Hey, this digger ain't no quitter,' he said, raising his arms into a flex. 'By the way, check out me tatt; the boys at Duntroon are gonna love this.' Warren took off his singlet and turned around. His back was completely covered in a blood-red print of the tapered cross of the Order of Santiago framed by the five stars of the Southern Cross.

I could too easily picture Warren standing over an Iraqi insurgent, smoke billowing from his heated semi-automatic:

a modern-day crusader painting his sword red in Arab blood. I shook the image from my mind.

'Looks great, Waz,' I lied.

'So what happened to Esther?' asked Dave. 'I thought you two might be swinging hands.'

Warren smiled broadly. 'She's still on the scene. She's gone ahead for a bit of a breather. We're meeting up in some town called Triacastela. I think the old Waz was getting a bit much for her, if you know what I mean,' he said, sending us his trademark wink. 'I never got to say thanks to you blokes for all you did.'

'You made the magic happen,' said Dave.

'Speaking of magic, let me give you the tip.' Warren leant in towards us. 'She goes off like an IED in the sack.'

'What's an IED?' I asked.

'Improvised Explosive Device,' he said, his voice now earnest. 'They're causing hell for our boys in Afghanistan.'

'Aren't you two going to introduce me to your . . . friend?' asked Edward. Dave did the honours. Warren was thrilled to meet another Australian, irrespective of his strange dress sense ('You might look like a clown, but you're an Aussie so I won't hold it against you').

The four of us walked on, Warren explaining how he managed to leapfrog us after we'd left him behind with his wounded girlfriend two weeks ago. They'd caught a bus to León and spent a romantic week in a hotel ('A seven-day shagfest'). Unfortunately, Esther's blisters never managed to heal ('The scab kept on getting ripped off in the sack'), so she aborted her pilgrimage and Warren continued on ('I needed some bloke time, so I tried to call the twins'). As yet, he still hadn't made contact ('Those little pricks keep screening me calls').

'Anyway,' Warren went on, 'they were originally planning to arrive in Santiago for All Saints' Day, so I did some calculations, and figured out they should be somewhere in the vicinity.'

Warren conceded it was a bit of gamble, but worst-case scenario was that he wouldn't catch them until in Santiago on the first day of November.

'But who needs those little buggers when I've got you three lads?' shouted Warren. Edward, we noticed, remained silent.

The four of us took a break in Trabadelo, a village on the banks of the River Valcarce. We found a café placed alongside the water and went in for an early lunch. In accordance with his usual practice, Warren went down for one hundred push-ups before chow time. No one bothered to stick around to count them out.

Inside the bar at the far end of the room sat Boris on a stool, talking to two young men whose backs were turned to us. 'For that reason,' said Boris, oblivious to our presence, 'I had to abandon Dave and Tom for the sake of my greater goal. Those two dudes just drove girls the other away.'

'Boys!' shouted Warren, coming through the door, veins popping after his workout. 'Where the hell have you been? Why haven't you been taking my bloody calls?'

The twins turned around blankly and remained silent.

Expressions of reverence had claimed their faces. I imagined Boris outlining his pick-up techniques to two willing apprentices.

'Jack! Steve! Talk to me!'

'We're with Boris now, Warren,' said Jack, trance-like.

'What does that mean?'

'It means we're no longer going to hang around you, mate.'

'Are you telling me that you're breaking up our team for this bearded freak?'

'It was never *our* team, Waz,' said Steve quietly. 'It was your team. You bullied us around like we were pissy soldiers in your platoon.'

'Fine,' said Warren with a defiant pout. 'I've found meself some real mates anyway.' Warren looked around and pulled Edward under his massive arm. 'Carn, Eddie, let's leave these soft-cock fairies to their lunch.' Before Edward could protest, Warren had muscled him out the door. Dave and I looked on in disbelief.

The twins told us where they'd been these last few weeks. I remembered their looks of frustration in their overbearing friend's company in the earlier stages of the pilgrimage. Sure enough, Warren had driven them up the wall. It came down to quitting the Camino or ditching their old mate. They chose the latter, leaving the Estella albergue at three in the morning and hiking a massive 56 kilometres in one go.

After they'd finished the story, Dave walked over towards the Canadian. 'Listen, Boris,' he said. 'I'm sorry I snapped at you the other day. There was a lot going on.'

Boris gave a grunt. He was obviously still feeling sore about the incident back at La Virgen del Camino. Dave's suggestion that we all go for dinner somewhere in O'Cebreiro was met with a half-hearted shrug. So we bought two *boca-dillos* to go and left them to it.

We walked along a wet bitumen road steaming in brilliant sun. Smoke from cottage chimneys gathered in the valley with the morning mist that stubbornly refused to burn away. Sunlight streamed through overhanging pine branches, creating patterns on the road. At Herrerías, 7 kilometres from O'Cebreiro, the road pitched dramatically, rising into a forest of chestnut trees. A yellow arrow pointed us into the woods.

Fatigue gripped my legs, but the sound of Dave's pole regularly striking the stones spirited me along. The path took us deeper into the forest, where the leaves permitted only the skinniest rays of sun to touch the ground. As we went, the woods grew less dense and the path began to level out, leading us to a six-foot-tall stone tablet. It had lately and tackily been converted into a canvas for a thousand pilgrim love messages. The provincial coat of arms stamped into the tablet carried happier connotations than anything stuck to it. We were now in Galicia. The bells of the O'Cebreiro monastery came to our ears.

A crucifix from an adjacent peak caught the afternoon sun and blinked its greeting as we rounded the mountain's crown. We walked slowly along a retaining wall, enjoying the stares of locals. To our left, the sides of the mountain gave way to a valley of autumnal foliage. It was a view worthy of a drink. Before that, though, I attended to other business.

On my behalf, Dave asked a local to direct us to the statue of Don Sampredo. She smiled and pointed through some trees to a bespectacled bust. From a recess along the lichen-covered wall that surrounded his parish, Elías looks out welcomingly to the pilgrims who have followed his yellow arrows. We thanked Elías for the directions and took a seat on the retaining wall. Warren and Edward were nowhere to be seen. The day had turned fair. We greeted the pilgrims walking out of the valley of Valcarce and peered into Castilla y León one last time. It turned orange and red in the gloaming and then was swallowed by the darkness.

ANOTHER NIGHT
OF VICE AND SIN

Galicia immediately felt unlike any other place the Camino had taken us through. This was not a different province; it was a different country. After sunset, we joined a group of pilgrims in a low-ceilinged restaurant with stone walls and an open fire glowing orange from the hearth. In between taking orders, the restaurateur accompanied a *gaiga* (bagpipe) player on his drum. The place evoked the merriment of an Irish pub rather than the passionate exoticism of an Iberian bar. I was left with the impression that a song request for Christy Moore would be met with greater enthusiasm than one suggesting anything by Julio Iglesias.

Our black-haired waitress, with her porcelain skin and green eyes, gave credence to a theory of Irish invasion. She even spoke a different tongue. The Galician language bears only a slight resemblance to Spanish. When Dave ordered vegetarian paella in Spanish he received a blank stare and a plateful of tentacles. Earlier, I had confused the words beer (*cerveza*) and toilet (*servicio*) when ordering drinks. I was hoping the bartender's bewildered expression was the product of his limited Spanish rather than the fact I had just asked for 'two toilets, please'.

The colour of the landscape was different, too. It was as if all that remained on the pallet when it came time to paint this part of Spain was green. O'Cebreiro straddles a ridge that divides two remarkably diverse mountain groups. You can see the olive-and-red-dusted slopes of Castilla y León in the east, and then turn to the west for the vivid green of the Galician hills.

My first proper view of Galicia was shared with Irish Michael on a deck in front of our albergue. He stared across those verdant hills as if he'd just stumbled into his very own Eden.

'This is my favourite place on the Camino,' he said. 'It's like coming home.' He nodded his head absently and began to speak like an old sage wearily drawing his story to a close. 'Beyond these hills stands the cathedral that keeps the bones of the apostle,' he intoned.

'Can we see Santiago from here?' I asked, squinting between gullies shrouded in wisps of threatening grey.

'Oh, I shouldn't have thought so,' said Michael, suppressing a grin. He was right to laugh at me. We still had over 160 kilometres to walk. But the taste of salt on a westerly sent from the Atlantic was a reminder that this journey was coming to an end. Michael set off without a care in the world, leaving me to consider the day ahead.

There was nothing visually ominous in those pleasant green hills spread out before me. Nonetheless, something told me this pilgrimage was far from over. On this rare occasion my instincts proved correct.

I put Edward's willingness to keep company with Warren down to loneliness. Edward had a repellent personality and Dave and I were not the only pilgrims who were trying to avoid him. I felt slightly guilty. If he weren't so mean, I might have found him interesting. At least I could put my conscience at ease. Finally, someone sought his company, albeit for unconventional reasons.

Losing the twins' allegiance to Boris had been a terrible blow for Warren. Their charge, that Warren was difficult and overbearing, seemed reasonable from my perspective. Warren thought it unjust and he was fixed on retribution. In appearing to befriend a perfect stranger, Warren was hoping to stir feelings of jealously in the twins. Edward might not have been a natural companion, but he was better than nobody. They walked up behind us not far out of O'Cebreiro and followed us the whole 22 kilometres down to Triacastela.

'Listen, mate,' said Warren to Edward. 'I don't need to hear about all the awards you won at school. I don't give a shit. I just want the twins to know that I really don't need their company.'

'You're not exactly the type of person I'd befriend,' said Edward. 'The word I would use to describe you, Warren, is "troglodyte".'

'I have no bloody idea what that means.'

'I'd be amazed if you did,' said Edward. 'It means you're like a caveman – an ignoramus and a buffoon rolled into one.'

'Well, that's okay, cos I have a word to describe you, too – "cocksucker".'

They bickered in this manner for kilometres. Eventually, the conversation turned towards our day's destination. We were off to rendezvous with Esther in Triacastela and this gave Warren an idea. 'I'm gonna take a wild stab in the dark and guess that you haven't had a root in a while. Am I right?'

'All I will say is that I haven't found a girl with common interests,' said Edward. By that he meant he hadn't met a girl who appreciated his formidable intellect.

'So, I'm right?' persisted Warren. Edward remained silent. 'Here's the deal: I'm meeting my girlfriend tonight. She's driving from her hometown an hour away. I'll get her to bring some of her mates and I'll try my best to hook you up with one of them.'

'What's in it for you?' asked Edward after a pause. Dave and I looked at each other. Warren actually had the little prig wrapped around his finger.

'If the twins know that I hooked you up with a couple of me girl's friends, then they'll be spewing that they ditched me for that Boris wanker.'

'How do you know they'll be in Triacastela?' continued Edward, looking pensively out across the green valley spread below.

Warren smiled. 'They stayed up there in O'Cebreiro last night, which means they'll have to stay in Triacastela. The next albergue isn't for another 15 kilometres. I checked the map before we left.' We kept walking in silence.

'So, what do you reckon, mate?' said Warren after a while. 'You up for it?'

'I'll think about it,' said Edward. Warren slapped him hard on the shoulders, jolting the fedora from his head.

'Okay,' began the digger excitedly. 'Now, if you're gonna have any chance with the ladies, we need to get you out of that poofy hat and the Pakistani gear and into a singlet. I reckon you might be hiding a well-ripped Aussie rig under that shirt.'

'Do you know what this kurta signifies?' Edward asked rhetorically. 'It signifies that I will not submit to the pressures of wearing Western clothing on a Christian pilgrimage.'

'Mate, all that top signifies is that you're a soft cock.' One way or another, Edward was not going to be wearing that kurta by the end of the night.

By the time we reached Fonfría, rumours of an impromptu party were already circulating. Dave's phone started lighting up with text messages from excited pilgrims as they tossed around ideas for possible venues, eventually choosing a particular bar in Triacastela. Esther rang Warren explaining that she'd told *all* her friends to make the hour's drive from her hometown of Sarria. Warren couldn't believe his luck. Everything was falling beautifully into place.

The side of the road was thick with green foliage growing

from the wet black earth. Warren sang pub tunes as heavy bullets of rain detonated on the bitumen, sending watery shrapnel back up towards the clouds. Water was flowing down the road like a slide. We each fell over at least once. No one minded. Even Edward was pumped.

We found an albergue in Triacastela with a friendly warden who waved off our apologies for leaving puddles in the lobby. We observed the pilgrim rituals (passport stamped, coin donated, bed obtained) and then carried out our own (went to the bar).

Esther needn't have texted the bar's whereabouts. The party was underway early and you could hear muffled music from the albergue a few hundred metres away. We found the bar and peeled back the door. A burst of sound nearly blew us back out onto the street.

The whole room was in motion: bodies contorting in all directions to a pulsating Spanish pop tune. It was as if every twenty-something we'd met to date had found his or her way into that unprepossessing place. Steam from the heaving mass and cigarette smoke mingled near the ceiling. A light with a faulty fuse flickered nervously like a strobe, affecting through the haze the gaudy dazzle of a nightclub. All the while, cackling girls and guys stabbed their limbs into the air.

Dave and I dragged Edward over to the bar and lined up some shots. We were warming to the plan. A girl might do him the world of good.

'I have to tell you,' shouted Edward above the music. 'I haven't imbibed alcohol for a while!' All that holier-than-thou bluster was for the moment a thing of the past. He was looking around nervously as if it were his first time in a serious bar.

'Don't worry!' shouted Dave, clinking shot glasses. 'Neither have we!'

Warren was up on a table searching for his girl. He scanned the room before pointing towards the back of a makeshift dance floor.

'BUENEZ TARDEZ, *SEÑORITA*!' he shouted, flexing his arms.

A scream of joy came up from the dance floor. Warren jumped down from the table just as Esther burst out of the crowd, surging into his arms and smothering him in kisses. She dragged him into that pit of throbbing humanity.

Here was my generation, all orphaned for a time while on pilgrimage but at home in this place, a refuge for those seeking a different kind of spirit. This would be another night of vice and sin happily committed in the knowledge that absolution was less than a week away. I ordered a round of San Miguel Grandes and, with Dave and Edward, assumed the wallflower position. We went shout for shout, the party building in intensity as pilgrims poured into the bar.

A *señorita* sidled up to me. She started talking rapidly, her nasal Spanish exacerbating her general air of desperation. Without translation our affair was destined to fail. Nonetheless, I asked her in my finest Spanish whether she cared for a beer. She looked at me blankly before pointing over my shoulder and storming back to the dance floor. I turned around to see what it was that had hastened her flight. Through the smoke I could just make out a sign on a door that led to the men's toilets.

'I think this venue is in danger of becoming a fire hazard!' Edward yelled into my ear.

'You're right!' I shouted back. 'We better order some grappa to put out the flames.' I headed to the bar and ordered a round to take back to our little gang of wall-huggers, but on my return could not spot Edward. I surveyed the scene.

The night was peaking. In the foreground, a broad-shouldered Scandinavian whom we called 'Eric the Red' beat out rhythms on a table with his empty Grande bottle. His nickname was owed to the ginger tinge of his beard and his indecipherable guttural tongue that we approximated to be a twelfth-century Viking burr. I'd overheard that he was from the Faroe Islands but no one knew for sure.

The four Argentineans, wearing their formal attire (three in Maradona shirts, the other in a Los Pumas rugby top), were jiving with two *señoritas* apiece. Natalia, the dreadlocked Brazilian with the multiple piercings, brandished her staff in a ceremonial fashion. She looked like a voodoo witch casting a spell. The spiritualists were there, too, waving their hands about like Hillsong Church congregants.

And dancing in the middle of them all was Edward, loaded up to his eyeballs. He was cutting up that dance floor with unscholarly abandon. Warren was angling a couple of Esther's friends in his direction. He'd already ripped off Edward's fedora and I could tell he was aiming for the shirt next. I gave Dave a Grande and shouted out a toast for Edward.

Warren worked his way out of the pack of pilgrims and started pushing a table into the middle of the dance floor. With Eric the Red's help, he dragged Edward onto the table. Once he got used to the idea, Edward went crazy. He was kicking his legs like a mule gone rampant.

A chant rose from the dance floor. It was picked up with frightening speed, quickly drowning out the thumping music.

'TAKE – IT – OFF! TAKE – IT – OFF! TAKE – IT – OFF!'

Edward pointed at himself as if to say, *who me?* Then he shrugged his shoulders and ripped off that kurta to thunderous howls of approval. He was jumping on the table now, swinging the garment above his head to the delight of a few ladies who clutched at his ankles below – Edward was a man of the people at last.

As if on cue, Boris entered with a twin on either side. From where I stood at the bar, I could see their eyes goggle before they burst into laughter. But whereas the laughter that had greeted Edward's performance before now had been good-humoured, theirs was mean and derisive. Someone must have told Warren because soaring high above the loud din in that bar I heard his warrior cry.

'THAT'S UN-AUSTRALIAN, YOU FUCKING BASTARDS!'

I'm not sure who threw the first punch. But, boy, was it on. Boris and Warren and the twins were all over each other within seconds, flailing in a hurricane of arms and elbows. Edward didn't help matters. Sensing his mentor was in need of assistance, he tried to crowd-surf his way to the fracas. He only succeeded in landing on an Argentinean's head, who in turn smashed into Eric the Red. That put the Scandinavian on the warpath. With a massive clenched paw, the Red started taking swipes at anything in blue-and-white stripes.

Like an ember attack ahead of a blaze, spot fires started up all over the place. Old international enmities were revived. Brits and Germans squared off at one end of the bar while Russians and Americans shaped up at the other. Peace-loving spiritualists abandoned contemplation and started pulling at each other's hair, while Natalia knocked her staff on people's heads in a way she later claimed was intended to calm things down.

Thankfully, any serious physical damage was mitigated by dint of human density. There was just no way you could properly swing an arm in that place. The scene was nonetheless visually dramatic. We looked like a crowd of street-runners surging through the town square of Pamplona just before the bulls were released.

Dave and I pushed our way over to Boris and Warren. Our attempts to break up the fight were brushed aside. I copped an elbow in the eye that would've hurt had I not been so boozed.

I can't remember exactly how it ended. The bartender had the sense to switch on the lights and turn off the music. The bright silence was enough to bring most people to their senses. Everyone looked around stupidly, as if a hypnotist had just snapped us out of a devilish trance.

I didn't stick around to find out what happened to Boris and Warren. I knew Dave would sort them out. My head was beginning to ache and I really needed to sleep. The bitter chill outside did little to sober me up. I caromed off walls down a poorly lit street, somehow managing to find the albergue. I staggered into the dormitory and fell onto my bunk.

'What the hell!?' came an awful shriek. 'Tom, is that you?' In retrospect, I can see how appalling it must have looked. It nonetheless seemed unjust that of all the beds in that town I could have collapsed onto, I'd found the one occupied by the Texan.

'Ah . . . no . . . no, man,' I said, attempting a Canadian accent while scrambling to my feet. 'Wrong bunk, how *aboot* that, eh?'

'I told you, I have a boyfriend!'

Without responding, I walked into an adjoining dormitory and found a vacant bed. Drunk and humiliated and with an ominous throbbing behind my eye, I couldn't help but let a giggle escape my mouth. Before long I was chuckling loudly enough to make others stir in their sleep. I laughed for many reasons. I laughed for having been involved in a pub fight on a pilgrimage. I laughed for seeing a shirtless smart-arse social-ist ex-lawyer try to crowd-surf. I laughed for having mistaken the Texan's bed for my own. But most of all, I laughed now because tomorrow's hangover would be no laughing matter.

OCTOBER 27

FOUL FEELINGS

The walls shook with greater ferocity than they had in Logroño. Terror was in my veins, sending my heart into a frenzied pulse. I began to fall. Air rushed past my face as I fell into the black nothing, the clothes torn from my back. Instead of the baleful throb that had been in my ears, all I could hear above the wind was the sound of piano music. Something below me came into view, a speck of light growing larger as I barrelled towards it. I braced for impact and landed with a thud.

I looked up into a row of elevated spotlights pointed directly at my face. Using a hand to shield my eyes, I could make out rows of seats in a massive auditorium. Thankfully, it was empty, because I was laid out prostrate without a stitch of clothing on. I stood up and turned around to learn the source of the music. Sitting at an ivory-white grand piano, adorned in his brown cape and felt cap, was —

'Santiago!' The apostle was completely engrossed in the music, something from the Burt Bacharach songbook.

'Hey, man,' murmured a sonorous Canadian voice. 'You

might want to put that cockleshell on.'

'*Boris?*'

'I've been called many things,' he said, modulating into another key. 'The Moor-slayer, the Pilgrim, Son of Thunder, but never Boris.'

'Santiago, where are we?' I asked.

'Onstage,' he said, as if that would clear up any confusion.

'Okay,' I said. 'So what are we doing *onstage*?'

'That's not important, man,' he sang, a flugelhorn suddenly sounding from some unseen place. 'You need to stop hiding and come out of the dark.'

'What —?' I was cut off by a thousand angelic voices singing the refrain.

Out of the dark . . .

'What do you mean, stop hiding?'

'You really need to get over that girl.'

Over that girl . . .

'What do you mean? What girl?'

'That girl,' sang Santiago, nodding towards the auditorium. I slowly turned around. The auditorium was now full of women wearing white angel wings. They were all the spitting image of the Texan and they were all singing.

This girl . . .

I bent down to pick up the cockleshell resting at my feet. The choir of Texan angels giggled and then all at the same time blew me a kiss. Santiago walked over and started shaking me by the shoulder.

'Are you okay?' he said, but he was no longer speaking in

a Canadian accent. He was speaking like Dave.

'Mate, wake up!'

After a reasonable period of time had elapsed, most of which I spent wishing I were dead, I had catalogued the worst of it: I had a black eye; I had bled from my nose all over the pillow; I had lost my wallet; the Texan had asked Dave to text in advance the towns we intended on staying in so she could avoid me; the warden asked for twenty euros to buy a new pillow, which I couldn't pay because I'd *lost my fucking wallet*.

Dave's friendship on that foul morning was unforgettable. Instead of filling up my head with questions he was entitled to ask (*Who gave you the shiner? What happened to you after the brawl? Why is the Texan threatening a lawsuit?*) he paid the warden, packed my gear and helped me look for my wallet.

We found it without difficulty, safely kept behind the bar. The owner had collected several wallets that had spilled out of pockets during the bust-up. Under the circumstances, I thought it good of him not to throw them all out in a fit of rage. The damage done to his establishment was extensive. As it happened, we found the bar owner in high spirits. The party had yielded the best night's takings in the ten-year history of his business, more than compensating for the broken glasses and shattered windows. We even shook hands on the way out.

Last night's revellers were crammed into a nearby café. Mine was not the only black eye in that room. There were a few people in much worse shape. One of the Argentineans had his head bandaged and his arm in a sling.

The room was silent, the atmosphere charged, and people eyed each other suspiciously, making me think of once-warring countries that had just drawn up an armistice. That moment of shared purpose on the dance floor when everyone sang and danced in the universal language of drunken exuberance was long forgotten. The unshackled fists of Boris and Warren, now conspicuous in their absence, had seen to that. National borders had been re-erected. The Argentineans were clustered about their own table as were the Americans, the French, the Danish, the Russians and the Germans. Now we were divided in all but appearance and condition: ashen-faced and hung-over.

As the sole Faroe Islander, or whatever he was, in that room, Eric the Red sat by himself. I took a seat opposite him because I knew he wouldn't want to talk. He held his *café Americana* in a white-knuckled way. I could see his mind turning over, trying to piece together the events of a night that had left his hands blistered and his head sore. He took a pull on his cigarette. His laboured exhale joined the other trails of smoke drifting up from ashtrays to the ceiling. The trails looked like purposeless souls languishing towards Heaven.

Edward appeared at the door, looking as if he had just gone ten rounds with Oscar De La Hoya. His curls were genuinely untamed now and his kurta was ripped and stained with dried blood. He skulked towards a vacant seat next to Eric the Red, collapsing into a chair directly in sight of a television broadcasting the morning news.

America, it said, would vote in eight days and the polls were pointing to Barack Obama in a landslide. This was information that most of us had already heard via murmurs along the Camino. But when footage of John McCain rallying some Midwestern backwater came on screen, Edward's ego demanded that the whole bar hear his insights.

'This man hasn't got a chance,' he scoffed, looking around for someone to defy him. It was hard to disagree. McCain was old: a fading statesman. His fierce-looking wife shunted him about the stage like he was a cardboard cut-out, while his charismatic opponent bounced through crowds exuding class. Obama looked ready for the White House. McCain looked ready for a comfortable chair and a Werther's Original.

Edward saw the sudden intrusion of world events into the Camino as an invitation to pontificate on the perils of neo-conservatism. He blabbered on about the consequences of Obama's win for the conservative elite to the groans of those assembled. It appeared that all of Warren's good work had been undone. The Red shifted uncomfortably, pulling up his sleeve and polishing his elbow, preparing it for a jab across the bridge of Edward's nose.

'Edward, what happened to Warren?' I asked. Dave had told me that he'd managed to push Warren and Boris apart, and that they'd gone in separate directions.

'I can't remember,' he said, slightly embarrassed. 'I think

I over-indulged last night. Things happened that . . . well, frankly, that I am not accustomed to.'

'I'm sure Warren is very proud,' I said. Edward frowned and walked over to the bar to order a coffee. While he was waiting patiently in line, I saw him smile just a tiny bit at the memory of the previous night. Perhaps all was not lost.

I collected my gear, cast an unacknowledged wave across the bar and headed for the road. Dave was out the front, talking on the phone to his wife. He signalled for me to go on ahead, possibly sensing I could do with a stint on my own.

Into the swirling rain I went, sharing the road out of Triacastela with trucks loaded up with felled timber. The water jettisoned from balding tyres nearly blasted me off the street into the river gorge below. My sturdy hiking boots were falling apart. When the Camino cut back into the forest, the flapping sole of my left shoe collected clumps of the muddy path like a scoop. I would have been more comfortable walking barefoot.

The path angled into the Galician wilderness. My appetite had returned but I was some distance away from anywhere serving food. The overhanging branches allowed just enough cover from the rain that I could light up a cigarette. For now it would have to do for sustenance.

How I'd come to accept a fag as a worthy substitute for food is difficult to explain. Smoking had entered my life around the same time as those other inexplicable things.

But why then? And why cigarettes?

I'd hated cigarettes as a kid. Like the rest of my generation, I'd been indoctrinated with the *facts* that *proved* nicotine was the scourge of all humanity. Could acquiring the habit later in life therefore be some expression of a latent inner-rebel? I'd certainly skipped any rebellious stage in my teenage years. You need to be cool to be a rebel and you need to have something to rebel against.

For a while I'd been sure my addiction was the legacy of a happy romance gone sour. I peddled this belief long enough for it to become a means of deflecting concern away from my habit. All of this was misguided. I was indulging a pitiful victim complex, apportioning blame to someone unable to defend herself. Boris (and Santiago) was right. I needed to get over her.

Lately, I'd become favourably disposed to the theory that my smoking was the subliminally constructed sin from which I would be summonsed to grace. This sounded like the ramblings of an Arts graduate who'd taken minors in psychology and theology. It was, therefore, probably nonsense. Maybe I just liked smoking cigarettes.

The curtain of sodden boughs parted to reveal the sixth-century monastery of Samos. Yellowy-green lichen and moss across its slate roof softened its austere edges. A road leading from the monastery followed a river that the rainwater flowing from the hills had whipped into eddies.

'You've come a long way,' came a voice from the wilderness behind me, causing me to nearly slip on the schist surface.

'Is this some kind of joke?' I said in disbelief.

'No,' said Sally, blithely slipping out of the forest. 'You *have* come a long way.'

'I'm not talking about that. What the hell were you doing in that forest?'

'Obviously, I was meditating,' she said. 'Why are you looking at me like I'm some weirdo?'

'It's raining in buckets and it's practically freezing!'

'Yeah, so?'

'Forget it.' I stormed off, wanting to get away from her and all the other freaks. I was not in the mood for any more riddles.

'I was honestly meditating with my boy,' she called after me.

'The *bombero*!' I snapped, turning around. 'Of course, it all makes sense now.'

'You seem upset,' she said, walking over to me.

'Sally, does the *bombero* even exist? I've never seen the guy. I mean, where is he now?'

'He's still meditating, I didn't want to —'

'And what about *you*? What's your story? Clearly, you're from another planet, that's a given. But are you actually real? I mean, what kind of a person meditates in the pissing rain?'

Sally cocked her head in thought and then slapped me hard across the face.

'What in the hell was that for?' I asked, in shock.

'I'm proving to you that I'm real,' she said earnestly. I walked off and again she followed.

'I can't stomach any lectures today,' I said, trying to stay calm. 'Can we do this later on?'

'I told you there'd be disappointments.'

'Disappointments!' I'd already lost my cool. 'Sally, haven't you noticed my black eye? I was elbowed in the head last night in a pub brawl, I'm nursing the worst hangover of my life, which, believe me, is saying something, and I might be facing a lawsuit when I get home.'

'Oh, well,' came her quiet reply. 'It could be worse. I saw that Texan girl everyone tells me you've got a crush on. She's really cute. Any developments on that front?'

There was no use in saying anything. Instead I attempted to focus on my breathing.

'That bad, huh?'

'*Bad* is putting it mildly,' I said. 'Now, listen, I know you're trying to help but, really, I think I'd just like to be left alone.'

'Okay, that's fine. I just wanted to tell you that you're really close now.'

'Big fucking deal,' I said. 'I'm seriously tempted to just catch the bus to the cathedral and then fly home.'

'I'm not talking about Santiago. I'm talking about being close to sorting it all out.'

'Sorting *what* out? Actually, no, don't answer that. I don't care.'

'Okay, then, have it your way. This will be the last time we ever talk. What a shame to end it all on such a note.'

'All right, fine,' I sighed. 'Tell me, what am I close to sorting out?'

Sally smiled. 'Before I tell you, I want you to tell me something, what is it that you're doing here?'

'Not again, we've done this . . .'

'Just tell me!'

'Walking to Santiago.'

'Exactly! That's all you need worry about, just keep walking and you'll sort it out.'

'Okay, so what am I going to sort out?'

'You tell me.' She smiled.

'That's it? That's the hidden secret? Please, I beg of you, tell me you're taking the piss.'

'Haven't you heard the saying —'

'Stop! Don't say another word. I'm warning you, if you reel off one more cliché I'm going to spew. In the last month I've been told a hundred times that "It's not the destination that matters it's the journey" and "Live your dream don't dream your life". It's making me sick in the guts.'

'All I was going to say is that the baggage you're carrying to Santiago you brought yourself,' she said with a frown.

'All right, step aside, I'm going to vomit.'

'I can't tell you what your problem is, and even if I did know, I wouldn't bother telling you. You know already.'

'Sally —'

'Okay, I'm going. You'll know what I mean in a couple of days. Do me a favour, though.' She reached into her bag and pulled out an envelope with my name neatly written on it in cursive script. 'Promise me that you will open this when you arrive in Santiago.'

'What is it?' I said, fingering the envelope suspiciously.

'Just promise me!'

'Okay, I promise. Jeez, what's with all the melodrama?'

'You'll be fine,' she said. Then Sally kissed my cheek and walked back into the woods to find her *bombero*. Before she vanished, she shouted over her shoulder.

'I'd think about giving up those cigarettes!' The cockle-shell around her neck was bouncing over her shoulder. 'It's inhibiting your flow of prana and you only do it because you're bored.'

That was it. Sally had nailed the unglamorous truth of my smoking. I'd taken it up to murder time, to stave off ennui. That was all. Boredom. Who knew if she was right about all the other things? I was determined to keep my promise, though, and not open the envelope before Santiago. I lit up a cigarette and threw the letter unopened onto a cairn. I knew whatever was inside would just make me angry. I walked off as it was washed away by Galician rain.

MEN OF SILENT FAITH

If ever you thought the absolution of sins required an effort beyond physical measurement, then think again. One hundred kilometres of walking ought to do it. That's the distance pilgrims must cover to receive the blessings and indulgences that await them in Santiago. As such, Sarria, the last regional centre with a pilgrim's office, marks the final injection of pilgrims along the path.

I'd expected Sarria to be a real sin city: the last stop before a lifetime of misdemeanours was washed away. In its streets murderers would slink, married men would be plotting adultery, thieves would be eyeing off jewellery through windows and mobsters would be counting out bribes to city officials. I expected Sarria's public houses to be dens of iniquity where undesirables gathered for one last night of criminality before wiping the slate clean. Instead I found the holiest pilgrims I'd yet seen. They were weekend pilgrims, Spaniards mainly, in Galicia for a three- or four-day walk to Santiago. I resented them deeply.

You could spot them a mile away: holding freshly minted

poles, sporting spotless jackets and wearing boots not yet christened by the dust and mud. I couldn't bear their eager chatter as they prepared to join our ranks. I walked straight past a clean-shaven man who shouted 'Buen Camino' right in my face. I remained silent. He hadn't earned the right to deploy the Camino salutation.

I felt a similar hostility towards pilgrim cyclists – those peddling pretenders on their flash bikes who shunted the walkers to the side of the path as they chewed up huge distances in massive gears, assuming aerodynamic positions down hills, allowing gravity to pull them towards Santiago. In a single day a cyclist could make the sort of distance real pilgrims might achieve in four. Yet, just like those starting in Sarria, they were entitled to the same religious and material benefits as we were. And there were material benefits.

The compostela, the document that served as proof of completion of the pilgrimage, was the only thing keeping me from throwing in the towel. I still wanted evidence that I belonged in the confraternity of pilgrims who had travelled to Santiago. The dissemblers could have all the blessings and indulgences they pleased. I'd lost interest in such things. But giving them the compostela was, to put it simply, a bloody outrage.

These phonies would return home with exactly the same document as me and I'd come from France! I bristled at the thought of them fielding questions at dinner parties about the interesting framed parchment hanging above their fireplace. 'Oh, that,' they would say while pouring the organic wine to go with their Peruvian vegan entrée, 'that's my *compostela*. I got that for walking this pilgrimage in Spain. It was an absolute cinch. Now tell me what you think of this track from a Kenyan women's choir that I just downloaded? Isn't it *inspiring*?'

I encountered some of them in a Sarria hiking shop. They were eyeing the latest design in high-performance slickers, waterproof compasses and other overpriced and largely pointless accessories. I recalled in their feverish chatter the excitement I experienced the night before setting off from Saint-Jean-Pied-de-Port. Therein lay the source of my irritation. The Sarria pilgrims were experiencing the same emotions I had and they were getting it for an eighth of the price.

It suddenly occurred to me that I could have walked 100 kilometres and not endured the blistered feet, the sore knee, the vomiting, the trauma of the Meseta, the Texan rejection, the hangovers, the pub brawls, Warren, Boris, Edward and the hollow echo that a bone-jarring walk wakes in the drifting soul. I could have got a *compostela* in three days and then jumped on a plane to Barcelona or Paris or Rome and had a real holiday. Instead I was walking into a hiking shop with a blood nose and black eye, smelling like manure, with my football sock flapping through a giant cavity in my shoe. I bailed up a horrified salesman.

'*Buenos tardes*,' I said gravely. 'Give me four pairs of socks and your cheapest pair of size-1 hiking boots, *por favor*.'

'You walk el Camino?' asked a Spaniard waiting in line, holding an unopened guidebook.

'*Si, señor*,' I said, wincing as my credit card took another tour through the machine. 'It's an absolute jungle out there. *Buen Camino*.'

Rules have been put in place to deter people from fraudulently acquiring the *compostela*. From hereon, Dave and I would have to get our pilgrim passports stamped in two churches for every stage. The theory was that introducing another check in the process would hassle people out of simply driving from Sarria to Santiago. In reality, the two-church policy was no more than a minor inconvenience.

We collected our first stamp in a church 10 kilometres out of Sarria. There were now fleeting bursts of sunshine as we approached midday, but the threat of another downpour was ever present. The hills were layered with outcrops of gorse, pine trees that had been sown in unnatural symmetry and paddocks marked off with stone fences in the fashion of another Celtic land. We stepped inside the church and squelched our way down the nave. A yellow arrow directed us into a tiny chapter house, where a priest busily leafed through some papers. He took our passports, stamped them without inspection and then mumbled a blessing.

On the way out I noticed a pilgrim admiring a statue of Santiago Matamoros prominently placed in the church's retable. The statue itself was a not very remarkable depiction of Santiago at the Battle of Clavijo.

The pilgrim admiring the Moor-slayer was a neatly

groomed man who looked as if he hailed from the subcontinent. He could not have been older than twenty-five and yet he carried himself with the stateliness of someone twice his age. His posture made me think of pictures I'd seen of ceremonially dressed men of Kipling's time. He even pulled back his superbly tailored jacket by hitching his thumbs into his belt buckle as if intending to draw the eye to a sheathed dagger or a scimitar concealed below his robes. He turned to face us when we walked past.

'Excuse me, gentlemen,' he said in an accent a Pakistani might pick up after graduating *summa cum laude* from Oxford, 'may I walk along the path with you for a short duration?'

The formality of his request stunned us both into silence, before one of us drooled out, 'Yeah, no worries, mate.'

'Ah, I see you are not only men of faith, you are also men from Australia. This is most excellent, indeed.' The man courteously stood back, holding open the church door that led us back outside. We hit the road together within metres of a bollard that marked 100 kilometres to Santiago. The morning mist had lifted into low grey cloud that was tipping a fine drizzle over the landscape. With the rolling green hills, it was a scene out of Tolkien. I stole a glance at our newest companion, wondering what to make of him, before resuming the conversation.

'I'm not sure about being men of faith,' I said, 'but we're definitely Australian.'

'If you are not men of faith, then why did you venture inside this place of worship? And why do you walk the

Camino de Santiago?' His words were beautifully arranged as if they'd been scripted.

'We have to get our pilgrim passports stamped at two churches as proof we walked the Camino,' explained Dave. 'If we don't, we won't get the *compostela*.'

'Ah, yes, the *compostela*. But the question remains: why do you need proof of walking this pilgrimage if you are not men of faith? Surely you are walking this pilgrimage for more than just a holy document?'

'You ask a lot of questions . . . sorry, I didn't catch your name,' said Dave, offering his hand.

'Forgive me, my name is Abdul,' he said, shaking Dave's hand and then mine. 'I apologise for prying. This is a habit I have not as yet learnt to curb.'

I remained silent. There seemed little point in dragging down Abdul's curiosity with the miserable truth that I no longer had any idea why I walked so far. So Dave explained for us both that our reasons for walking were not what you'd describe as 'traditional', but that we were still interested in some of the ritual.

'It'll be nice to have something to show for the distance we've covered,' he said.

'I understand,' said Abdul. 'The stamping of your pilgrim passport is not unlike the rituals the Muslim observes on the Hajj to Mecca. We were required to circumambulate the Kaaba —'

'Sorry, did you say *we*?' I asked.

'Yes. The Hajj is the fifth pillar of Islam. It is the obligation of every able-bodied Muslim to perform the sacred rituals in Mecca during the week of the Hajj at least once in his lifetime.'

'That's amazing!'

'Thank you, but tell me, please, how is a pilgrimage to Mecca any more amazing than a pilgrimage to Santiago? I grant you that the rituals are somewhat different, but I think in purpose they are the same.'

Abdul had misunderstood me. I wasn't amazed to meet a man who had completed a pilgrimage to Mecca. I was amazed to meet a Muslim about to finish a Christian one.

'It seems to me,' continued Abdul, 'that even though they may differ in practice and expression, these rituals drive towards the same concepts. They are demonstrations of faith, humility and chastity. In this way, the pilgrimages and the pilgrims are identical. Would you not agree?'

I couldn't help but wonder whether Abdul would have arrived at the same conclusion if he'd spent an afternoon with Boris or Warren.

'You're right, Abdul. I really meant . . .' and then I stopped, feeling myself go red. Explaining that my amazement was born of having met a Muslim on the Camino might be seen as prejudice.

'You meant it is amazing to meet a Muslim out here, didn't you?'

Dave shot me a look. I was on my own on this one.

'I suppose I was thinking that,' I said slowly. 'I'm sorry if . . .'

'Not at all,' Abdul laughed. 'I completely understand your

meaning. If I were to happen on you two kind gentlemen at the Kaaba I would be no less amazed than you were to see me in that church. But let me tell you something I learnt in my studies of this pilgrimage. It is true that I am a Muslim man walking to these holy places for Christians. But the fact that a Muslim is walking this ancient path bound for Santiago de Compostela is not without precedent. Allow me to offer the example of Emir Ali ben Yusuf.' Abdul allowed a lengthy pause to gather his thoughts.

'The emir came to Santiago in the early twelfth century to meet with Queen Doña Urraca. So impressed was he by the size of the crowds assembled before the cathedral that he asked his guide the name of this character so great and famous that Christians came to pray to him from beyond the Pyrenees. Not easily would the emir forget the name of Santiago the apostle. If a Muslim went to Santiago de Compostela during those endless years of religious conflict across this land, then I do not think it is so remarkable that I come here today when this land is at peace.'

'Is this why you are walking to Santiago,' I asked, 'to see for yourself what the emir saw?'

'Not entirely,' said Abdul. 'A friend with whom I travelled to Mecca and studied at the London School of Economics returned recently from a month's tour in Spain. He was interested in visiting the Alhambra, the great red fortress in —'

'Granada,' said Dave. 'I'm living there at the moment with my wife.'

'Then you would know that the Alhambra is a building of great importance to Muslims,' Abdul said, looking at Dave with admiration. 'Long has my friend been fascinated with the Alhambra and the tragic figure of its last Muslim ruler, Boabdil, who surrendered it to Isabel and Fernando the Catholics. Many of us grew up with the story of Boabdil's retreat. It is said that as he walked over the pass south of Granada, he turned towards the red citadel and sighed.'

'*Suspiro del Moro*,' said Dave, before turning to me, 'the Moor's last sigh.'

'Right you are, my learned friend,' beamed Adbul. 'It is also said that Boabdil's mother, Aisha, accompanied her son during that sad retreat and on hearing his heartfelt sigh said to him, "Do not cry like a woman over this kingdom that you could not defend like a man." Those are the words of a strong woman –' a smile came into his voice – 'but one you would not care to have as a mother-in-law, if you understand my meaning.'

'You're not wrong there,' we agreed.

'In his attempts to persuade me to accompany him on this journey to Granada, my friend lent me a number of books on the Alhambra. The problem was that his books only suc-ceeded in piquing my curiosity in another great story of the Iberian Peninsula: the story of the Camino de Santiago de Compostela.'

Abdul allowed us to absorb the reverence he clearly held for the Santiago pilgrimage.

'I felt some level of shame that I knew so little about the Camino, having regarded myself a student of pilgrimages.

5

I felt an even greater level of shame that I did not know of the fierce battles that were waged between Muslims and Christians around this path.'

Abdul looked about wistfully, his eyes scouring the landscape, looking back to a time when these green hills were theatres of war. The drizzle developed into something harder. Dave and I dropped our packs and fished out our jackets. Abdul smiled softly, the rain seeming not to bother him. We walked on.

'I felt duty-bound to walk part of this pilgrimage, so I organised a flight to Valladolid and then travelled by bus to León. I plan to raise my arms before the cathedral of Santiago, give praise and thanks to Allah for granting me safe passage, and then return to London.'

'Are you walking as a pilgrim, Abdul?' I asked.

'No, no. I am just a humble observer. I am not sure whether it is possible to be a pilgrim of two faiths. Although I must confess that I obtained a pilgrim passport in León so that I might observe at close quarters the behaviour of Christian pilgrims in their accommodation.'

'And to sensibly take advantage of the Camino's subsidised accommodation,' I said.

'Indeed,' laughed Abdul, 'but now I will recall the words written in another twelfth-century document kept in a pilgrim's shelter along the Camino de Santiago. I committed these words to memory should I ever be called on to morally defend obtaining a pilgrim passport. This, I believe, is such an occasion.'

Abdul cleared his throat, narrowed his eyes and intoned, '"Its doors are open to all, well and ill, not only to Catholics, but to pagans, Jews and heretics, the idler and the vagabond and, to put it shortly, the good and the wicked." I believe, in a moral sense, that any ill-behaviour on my part with respect to my carrying a pilgrim passport may be waived on account of these words.' Abdul smiled brilliantly. 'This document is kept in —'

'Roncesvalles,' I said. 'I read about the document. I actually went looking for it when we were there, but no one seemed to know what I was talking about.'

'*You* were there, in Roncesvalles?' It was Abdul's turn to be surprised. 'Are you saying you began your pilgrimage at the border of Spain and France?'

'We actually started inside the French border at Saint-Jean-Pied-de-Port,' I said.

'You are very strange men, indeed,' said Abdul, 'for what kind of men would walk such a distance but men of faith? You will forgive me, if, when I am relating the stories of the Camino to my friend, I refer to you two kind gentlemen as the men of silent faith?'

'Sounds good,' chuckled Dave.

'Seeing as you two have travelled for so long along this path, could you tell me one more thing before I leave you to complete your journey?'

'Sure thing,' one of us said.

'There was a statue of a bearded man in the church we just visited. He was riding on horseback and brandishing a sword in triumph. Have you seen this image before?'

'Many times,' we said cautiously.

'So this is an important symbol of the Camino,' Abdul muttered to himself. 'Forgive me, but who is this rider that wields the sword?'

'It's the man whose bones we are walking towards,' said Dave.

'Curious. I thought that St James was a fisherman. I did not realise he was also a great warrior,' said Abdul. 'Do you know what moment it commemorates?'

Explaining that one of Santiago's miracles was his annihilation of an army of Muslims was, in the circumstances, no easy task. In the end we both shared the burden, delicately walking Abdul through the miracle at the Battle of Clavijo.

'Santiago was a great warrior, indeed,' said Abdul solemnly.

'You're not telling me you believe any of that stuff, Abdul?' asked Dave. 'I mean the Battle of Clavijo, if there was such a battle, happened about 800 years after Santiago was beheaded.'

'As a Muslim man, I am not sure whether I am permitted to believe the miracles of Christian saints. But I do know that my religion is defined by such giant leaps of faith, so why should not yours be, too?'

'Yes, but there is no proof,' I said, picking up Dave's point. 'These stories were the creation of wild imagination. I mean, where are the facts?'

Abdul pondered this for a moment and then said, 'Please do not take this personally, but I believe there is something

vulgar about proving one's faith with empirical facts and data.
Such an activity entirely misses the point. My professional
life is spent with numbers, patterns, formulas and logarithms.
My studies were defined by pure logic. I have been trained to
believe in only what I can see and prove. So my mind strug-
gles with much of what I have been taught of Islam.

'The fact that God can hardly bear the mathematician
and logician's scrutinising eye is unsurprising,' he continued.
'In all probability, God cannot exist. Saying such things does
not make me a very good Muslim, I am afraid. But I *am* a
Muslim and I *do* believe. To me, what is not known is the
essence of my religion. God cannot be found in the museum,
or in a mausoleum, or inside the calculator. The intangibility
of the matter is, I think, part of the point. Believing is supposed to be a gigantic leap of faith. Now, you must excuse
me. Just as you have observed the rituals of your faith by
stamping your passports, it is time for me to observe those
of mine.' Abdul offered us his hand.

'Before you go, Abdul,' I said, shaking his hand, 'what is
it that you gained when you went to Mecca?'

'*Gained*, you ask? What is it that I *gained*?' Abdul spat
the word out. 'Forgive me, but you sound like some of my
colleagues. They work for nothing but money and they most
certainly will make plenty. But few of them will ever experience the beauty of economics. My only advice to you is that
you let go of the idea that you are here to *gain* something.'

'But you sound like someone who sees great value in
walking a pilgrimage.'

'You are right. But such things must be viewed as incidental. A pilgrimage is, after all, not to be undertaken for individual glory but the glory of God. Those who embark on a pilgrimage for self-gain will find nothing but disappointment at their destination.'

'But self-gain is precisely what the Christian pilgrimage offers: absolution of sins and a free pass into Heaven,' I said. 'I'm not sure I understand your meaning.'

'Do not trouble yourself with such things. Just keep heading west to Santiago. Now I must go. *As-Sal ámu `Alaykum.*' Abdul nodded. He stepped over a stone fence, pulled a rug from his pack and laid it out, facing east towards Mecca.

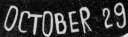

BLIND INSIGHT

There was a good reason that Hospital de la Cruz was not featured in my guidebook. There was nothing there. This was a town of ten horses, a newly renovated albergue and an eatery called *El Labrador*. We dined in the empty bistro, chewing our way through the sort of stringy food you might expect to be served up at a restaurant named after a dog. The albergue was practically deserted, too. Dave and I shared a building equipped to accommodate fifty-five pilgrims with Liz, Nikki and Natalia. At about 9 p.m., the warden chucked the keys our way and asked us to lock up.

The next morning Dave left the albergue an hour before I surfaced. He was no longer just a pilgrim making his way to Santiago. He was a husband walking towards his wife. I had noticed the change after we'd left Abdul to his prayers the previous day. There was an even brighter than normal glint in his eye. He was ready to go home.

I searched for somewhere to eat while Dave went to rendezvous with Rachel at Palas de Rei, 15 kilometres out of Hospital. Not for the first time, the disparity of our lives was thrown into relief. There was Dave, charging across Galicia contemplating a romantic reunion, and here I was in a forgotten town contemplating another meal at The Dog. I left on an empty stomach in favour of an early lunch in the next town.

The land around Hospital de la Cruz is covered with eucalyptus trees. They looked spindly compared to those of the Australian bush. Despite these particular gums looking slightly malnourished, eucalypt colonies were thriving right across Galicia. The familiar perfume of wet gum leaves brought on a sort of pride; it was like seeing a countryman make it good in a faraway land. The feeling in Galicia is not mutual. In 1865 several eucalyptus species were introduced as a cheap alternative to native timber used for the construction industry. The quality of eucalyptus wood, however, proved not to be up to scratch and so the plantations were largely abandoned. Plantation owners figured that if left untouched, the eucalypts would simply die out. This strikes me as an odd conclusion to draw. I would have thought that for most trees, being sown in Galicia's nutrient-rich soil and soaking up its plentiful rain would be like taking root in the Garden of Eden. So it proved to be.

In the familiar tale of introduced species with no natural controls, the steady march of the eucalypt was inevitable. It drove out local species, poisoned the native soil with its litter of bark and leaves and damaged Galicia's ecosystem. Eucalyptus trees are Galicia's equivalent of the cane toad.

These days, the eucalyptus forests are logged and made into cheap furniture and paper.

Sunlight streamed through a crack in the blanket of grey cloud above, transforming puddles along the path into shimmering pools. The sun was high with the approach of midday. The momentary burst of light vanished and a fresh charcoal-coloured ceiling formed, unleashing another downpour.

As mud covered my new boots, my mind turned to Rachel. I was excited about meeting up with her, but it would be of more significance than just seeing a familiar face. It would be a dress rehearsal for what awaited me back in Melbourne – reuniting with family and friends and old work colleagues. Rachel would be the first person I knew from home to hear the tales of my pilgrimage to Santiago. But what could I tell her?

Rearranging the experiences of the last four weeks into a deeply spiritual quest was a feat of narrative sorcery beyond my means. My story was hardly the stuff of admirable stoicism in the face of hardship. The Camino had only proved that I was too old for this journey to be a coming-of-age story, and too young for it to be a lamentation of a long-expired childhood. Herein lay the problem. I couldn't tell her what it all meant, because I didn't know myself.

'*Eh! Peregrino!* Pilgrim!' a raspy voice called from the road's edge.

I hadn't noticed him earlier, the peak of my cap having been brought low to shield the heavy rain from my eyes. I looked up to see a man whose face was concealed behind a woollen hat. He was crouched on a crate below the awning of a barn at the side of the path. A waterlogged blanket was draped over his shoulders, heavy enough to thrust him into a lean. All that seemed to be keeping him from falling forward was a long wooden stick, thin and straight like bamboo, wedged into his armpit like a crutch.

'*Eh! Concheiro*,' he croaked again, invoking the name used for my pilgrim forebears. He beckoned me towards his shelter with an open hand. I was near the town of Casanova, 10 kilometres shy of the arranged meeting spot in Melide.

'*Yo no entiendo*,' I said. '*Habla Inglés?*'

'*Eh! Peregrino!* Come here! I have something to say to you.'

I walked towards him cautiously. He removed his woollen hat and craned his neck towards me. His face looked like a fissured cliff and his eyes sat well back in their sockets. The long wooden stick was no crutch. It was a blind man's cane.

Here I was in a remote corner of Galicia, an obscure pocket of the world, and before me, sitting at the edge of the path like a cairn, was this wise old blind man calling me by an ancient title – *concheiro*. It seemed fated. This man was a man who knew things, not like that false prophet in pink leggings. Here at last was a character of Chaucerian calibre.

The poetry of it was sublime. A sage in the evening of his days had selected me as the recipient of his wisdom. That he was blind only intensified his enigmatic quality: here was a man deprived of sight but conferred with greater insight. Forget about looking for advice about getting a job when I returned home. His would be the sort of knowledge profound enough to carry me through what remained of my three score and ten.

'*Eh! Peregrino!*' he said again, lubricating his lips so that he could speak easier.

'*Si, señor?*' I said slowly, leaning in close to catch every syllable.

'*Concheiro,*' he said, 'give me euro.' The man extended his hand.

This was to be expected. Everything material costs money, so why should knowledge be free? I placed a coin in his hand. He put it in his pocket while pulling his hat back over his dead eyes. I waited as he shuffled on his crate, searching for a satisfactory position. His jaw stopped moving, his back stiffened. I waited.

'*Peregrino,*' he said finally.

'*Si, señor?*'

'*Buen Camino.*' And that was all.

I saw my friends, the couple, outside the municipal albergue, beaming in each other's company. I quickly checked in and then joined them outside. After an exchange of hugs and observations about our appearance (Rachel looked great; I had a beard, a shaved head and a black eye) we found a sleepy bar alongside a restaurant off the plaza. Thankfully, we avoided the topic of the pilgrimage altogether.

Nikki and Liz joined us, delighted to meet Dave's wife.

After an excellent meal of octopus relearning to swim in a pool of garlic-flavoured oil, we all decided to turn in early. Dave and Rachel had booked a room in a hotel and I made for the albergue.

In two days, this walk would be over.

GALICIAN MUD

My evening at the Melide albergue began in a flurry of sulphurous farts let off by a warden who looked like an ancient missionary returned from evangelising a Central American tribe. He wore black pants and a long black shirt that could have passed for a cassock. Around his neck hung a wooden crucifix big enough to pull his shoulders into a hunch.

'*Credencial, por favor*,' came an ill-sounding rasp.

His request released a smell of chorizo and putrefied gums. Holding my breath, I quickly handed over my pilgrim passport. He stamped it and then went outside for a cigarette.

The look of the warden was not the only sign that I was in for a rough night. My mattress was decorated with fur-covered stains and my pillow was the colour of weak coffee. French Pipes had selected a bed directly adjacent to mine, and our heads were inches apart. Boris had taken the bunk below but refused to talk to me because of my 'betrayal in Triacastela' (I assumed he was talking about the pub brawl and not my attempt to pin the blame for the incident with the Texan on him).

Ian, a stoutly built Scot we'd renamed 'William Wallace', was laying out his gear on a bed at the far end of the dormitory. Dave and I had tried to avoid staying in the same albergue as him after he'd threatened to slit the throats of everyone in his dorm back in Frómista. He had no memory of his comments the next day but mentioned mildly that he'd been known to occasionally talk in his sleep.

Werner, an eccentric middled-aged German, was there, too. He was getting around in nothing but sandals and a very brief pair of underpants, which were black with the word '*WUNDERBAR*' charged in pink across the behind. It was as if all the freaks had come out to play and I was stuck squarely in the middle of them.

As I made my way to the showers, Werner grabbed my arm and with great terror in his voice told me to 'bevare of ze pilgrim turds'. Sure enough, bobbing defiantly on the toilet water's surface was a menacing-looking stool. The fraying pieces of faecal matter pointed to a number of unsuccessful attempts to flush it away. I had a shot at getting rid of it, pressing down the button. There was a whine from the cistern and a groan from the ancient pipes, but the beast went down. I hit the showers. The pressure was weak, but the water was hot and that was as much as you could hope for in a public albergue.

French Pipes paid a visit to the latrine. I knew it was him because of the cigarette smoke that floated from the cubicle. He finished up and hit the flush, sending the pipes into a fit of vibrations. These were much louder than before. The bathroom walls began to shake. I could hear rusted screws unfastening from corroded pipes and plumbing falling apart beneath me. The focus of the sound shifted from the toilets to below my shower just before a calamitous *bang* brought everything to a halt. It was like the sound of an erupting volcano and sure enough the lava soon followed.

I leapt out of the shower as French Pipes' refuse oozed through the drainpipe. He emerged alongside me and extracted a fresh cigarette from his pocket, watching as the shower floor transformed into a pan of raw sewage. There we were, the mute Frenchman and the naked Australian, watching in horror as the poo-nami threatened to burst the levy. In keeping with European etiquette he offered me a smoke before muttering the only word I ever heard him speak on pilgrimage – *'Merde'*.

French Pipes' poo eventually went down the shower drain. I could hear his shit trickling from the fractured plumbing while I washed my feet in the hand basin. The smell in that bathroom was atrocious, an odour that would outlast Christendom. I stumbled back into the dormitory gasping for fresh air. A group of pilgrims were huddled outside with chairs and bags, preparing to barricade the door. It was a futile exercise. Before long, the reek of pilgrim waste had seeped through every room and across every bunk in the albergue. The smell did not, however, prevent the early snorers from getting underway before lights out.

The snores were not intolerably loud. I sensed, though, that these snores were the opening bars of a great symphony, the woodwind section establishing the theme in the first movement. At this early stage I could not be sure of the standard of the strings, but I knew from experience that in French Pipes we had a quality brass section in the house. I had discarded my earplugs, normally preferring to bury my head inside my sleeping bag. But the warden must have turned the heaters right up. I couldn't even sleep with a shirt on, much less a sleeping bag over my head.

An hour after lights out it seemed everyone was asleep except me. The hideous coughing and snorting of French Pipes' sleep apnoea seemed to jolt my bed to life. My bed rattled violently to the gasps and wheezes of the night. Either the pilgrim sewage had seeped into the building's foundations or Galicia was experiencing seismic activity. A third explanation dawned on me when I heard whimpering from below. I stole a glance over the bunk to confirm my suspicions.

The moonlight from the window cast a pale luminosity over Boris and a female pilgrim, who were tangled up in an impossibility of naked limbs. Boris had transformed his sleeping quarters into a boudoir. I pulled my sleeping bag over my sweaty head, shuddering at each thrust before I noticed that my nose was bleeding again. The ache behind my eye got worse. As the snoring got louder, the gyrations below became more feverish, causing the bed to bang against the wall and tap out an ever-quickening rhythm. Fittingly, the orchestra had acquired a percussion section just as the symphony was reaching its climax. The panting, the banging and the snoring became extravagantly loud until finally, in a bloodcurdling moan, the stout Glaswegian wailed from across the room.

'AHHHH! I'LL SLIT YA THROAT AND CHIP YA FUCKING WINDOWS, YA BASTARD!'

The room fell silent, but only temporarily. The snoring was back at full throttle within minutes. I turned over to face the window and caught the reflection of a small statuette hanging on the opposite wall. It was a depiction of the Madonna with arms outstretched. The moonlight illuminated a glistening stream of dew leaking behind her opened palms from the ceiling. In this godless place even the Blessed Virgin was leaving a trail of tears.

Dave found me sitting on a crumbling stoop leading up to the albergue early the next morning. I had been there for a while, smoking a cigarette, preferring the freezing conditions at first light to the warmth of that vile place.

'You've got Scottish heritage, don't you?' I asked as Dave approached.

'McNamara ain't French.'

'Do you know what "chip ya windows" means?'

'It means knock your teeth out. Where did you hear that?'

'William Wallace was playing up again last night.'

'Are you okay, mate? You're looking a little weary.'

'I'm fine,' I said. I was tiring of that question. 'Where's Rachel?'

'She's waiting for us in the café.'

'I'm going to skip breakfast. Let's meet up further along.'

'Okay,' said Dave warily.

'Where are we headed tonight?'

'Arco do Pino. You're sure you're right?'

'I'm fine. I'll see you later on.' And with that, I brushed past Dave and returned to the path.

I was three hours out of Melide when I experienced the panic attack. This was not the first time. I'd been suffering from them for the last six years. I'd even experienced them along the Camino. In the past they tended not to happen in dreams distinguished by visitations from Santiago look-alikes; that was a strange new development. But the attack I'd had that day on the Meseta was particularly nasty, when the matter was compounded by genuine illness. Regardless of how protracted they were, I could always depend on the same set of themes: dizziness, shortness of breath, throbbing in the ears, disorientation and fear.

The surge of terror that I felt now had caught me unawares. I was walking along a narrow stretch of path with paddocks either side, contemplating my future beyond Santiago. I suppose my thoughts were dismal enough to trip me into panic. When the horrible rush came, I lost my balance, catching a rock with my boot and landing squarely in a puddle of mud.

Six years of experience had equipped me with techniques to calm things down. I needed to be seated, to focus on something, blank out my mind, slow my breathing. I picked myself up, gritted my teeth and started to breathe slowly. Being outside presented some challenges. I was terrified that a stranger would encounter me at my most vulnerable. Thinking along those lines was a sure way of quickening my breathing and prolonging the fear. But unlike being inside – contending with confined spaces and shaking walls – out here I could find a spot on the horizon on which to focus. In this case I picked a particularly large cow a few hundred metres away.

Before focusing on the cow, I'd stolen a glance down the road. There was nobody around. I was safe. The fear would pass in a few minutes. I usually knew the attack was nearing its end when I felt a desire for tobacco. Already I could feel the taste for it returning. My jaw loosening up. I was beyond the worst of it now. As attacks go, this was a good one. They weren't always this easy.

Some moments are so full of stuff they cannot be properly lived at the time. They pass unremarked upon, but are engraved in memory where they wait to be processed and understood further along the track. My first panic attack was one such moment. That it happened in the toilet of an Amsterdam 'coffee shop' gave the whole event an even greater flavour of dejection. I was high, of course, in the middle of touring Europe with a friend, and we'd dived into one of those sticky dens for a joint. Very quickly, I could feel myself slipping under the warm blanket of ease and wellbeing. But something was going wrong. The television was too bright, the young backpackers were too loud, the walls were bending.

I stood up and went to the bathroom. Nothing mattered more than being on my own at that moment. My breathing was all over the place and there was a terrible buzzing in my ears. Sometime later, I don't know how much later, I managed to calm myself down and go outside. The change was instantaneous. It felt like I'd emerged the next morning after a night of not sleeping. Certain colours I normally wouldn't have noticed were intense and particular noises now seemed unnaturally loud. There was an internal shift, too. A happier part of me felt like it had been exhaled out along with the smoke in that coffee shop. In its place was a magnetic ball in my head that drew negative thoughts to it as it bounced.

I'd had other moments like these, more intimate in their loneliness. But this was the first time the pendulum had swung the other way. I was fundamentally changed somehow. I barrelled through life for a while after that, using the drink and the cigarettes to ward off dark thoughts, ignoring the attacks as best I could. They always passed eventually. I became an expert at hiding it all, and that for me was the priority. After all, what fucking business did I have being sad? What trauma or calamity permitted such grief? I was the author of my own demise. The shame of it was terrible. But the attacks were becoming more difficult to bear.

So I told my parents. They had known there was a problem, but I'd insisted things were fine so they kept their own counsel. Breaking it to them that their son was desperately sad should have been much harder than it was. They made me feel liberated. Like I had as a child, I slipped in behind their wake and let them guide me to where I needed to go. It was the most mature thing I'd done in ages.

Eventually, I would sit down on a chair too comfortable to be enjoyed, confessing to a stranger wearing a brown tie and a sober expression. I had a panic disorder, he would say, which led to an incapacity to still the mind. This all seemed shockingly trivial. He assured me it was not. I was prone to entering an unbroken cycle of intense introspection, dwelling on usually the most miserable of things, incapable of focusing on the present or what was real. At any moment, if the fantasy was over-indulged, the mind could trip the body into a physical response – a panic attack.

With his help, the attacks would subside, although they'd never fully leave me. The joint in Amsterdam may or may not have been a trigger, he would say. It didn't matter. I needed to focus on the now. What was done could not be undone. But it mattered to me. I could never submit to his line of reasoning that this was something that just needed to be managed.

This thing inside of me was *my* own doing. The years the old-timers look back on wistfully as the best of their lives had been washed away in booze, nicotine and boredom. I'd spent them mourning that part of me that was lost in a coffee house, waiting for it to come back, a prisoner of my own nostalgia. I wanted to be that person again. But the pendulum never swung back the other way. This is the baggage I took to Compostela.

I turned over my pack, which was now caked in black mud, and pulled out a cigarette from its packet, miraculously the only dry item left among my saturated gear. I thanked Santiago for small blessings and successfully retrieved my lighter. As I looked over the green fields of Galicia, my mind wandered over the events of the last month.

It was hard to believe I was on the same path that had threaded through the summits of the Pyrenees, through Pamplona and Burgos and León, through lush vineyards, across an endless tableland and before mighty cathedrals. The Camino was now slicing through paddocks where stone cottages and slate-roofed barns clung to the path like barnacles.

Dave and Rachel came striding around the corner shortly afterwards. I suppose it was reasonable for them to be worried. What would I have thought, rounding a bend in torrential rain to see my friend sitting between a puddle and a cowpat, his right side painted in mud, a bent cigarette drooping from his mouth?

'You right down there, mate?' asked Dave.

'Don't mind me,' I said, flicking a salamander off my leg, 'just stopping for a quick smoko.' I was still an expert at hiding things. My friend helped me up and we made for Arco do Pino.

We were closing in on Santiago. We'd met our 30-kilometre average over the last week and would arrive as planned on the last day of October. Bollards appeared at the side of the road in 500-metre intervals with the distance remaining to Santiago embossed on each face. The cockleshells pointed us through more paddocks and copses of trees. Farmers with prods urged cows through gates and along paths. One old man was leading giant oxen whose heads swung in unison as they drew their two-wheeled cart. Locals doffed their hats and retreated courteously to the side of the path as we converged on the apostle's remains, shouting the Camino salutation as we went.

To dress up that day as a sort of spiritual rebirth would be too much: the troubled pilgrim baptised in the rain. But something very small had happened. A wall inside me was crumbling away. I like to think something foul got stuck in that puddle and was left in the Galician mud.

As we crested a small rise, I looked at my friends and then the interminable rain and then to the asphalt road where a pilgrim had written *casi!* (almost!) in yellow chalk. These were the most humble moments of the Camino and they were the most beautiful.

THE HOLY DOCUMENT

Goethe said, 'Europe was made on the pilgrim road to Compostela.' He's speaking figuratively, of course, and referring to the staggering reach of all the routes that comprise the Camino de Santiago de Compostela. They spread like capillaries across the Continent, drawing the faithful to its life source in a city in the wild hills of Galicia.

The routes have carried pilgrims from the east across the Slavic states since before the age of the Tsars, and pilgrims from the north since the Danish king Gorm the Old raised the Jelling stones whose runic inscriptions marked that land's transition from paganism to Christianity ten centuries after Christ. It is a reach that goes beyond the dust and the dirt; the routes are written into the night sky, too. When the sun sets, stars and planets light a path. They are the Heavenly way-markers known to sailors who went to Compostela in open barges along the Camino Inglés, the Way from England.

These Ways have outlived dynastic wars, kingdoms, military orders, the vanquished Moors, the Christian conquerors and autocrats: all the kings, queens and despots long committed to the earth. The routes are a part of the European landscape – as timeless as the sea and as steadfast as the mountain. But unlike the sea that separates and the mountain that divides and the expanse that isolates, the paths unite to a single purpose. But the Camino also has a dark side.

The paths to Compostela have also carried the rapacious armies of Christ, which felled the Moorish warriors across the Peninsula, invoking the name of Santiago Matamoros as they went. But for the network of paths – sometimes no more than a worn scar of earth through a mountain range or across a floodplain – the march of the Moors may not have stopped at the Pyrenees. So perhaps the pilgrim road to Compostela did make Europe. But the reverse is surely true. This road was made by Europeans and made by many across the ages.

Pagans and Christians built their temples and cities along the holy passage. They also shaped and maintained that road. Listen closely and you hear the whispers of ghostly potentates and long-dead pilgrims and pagan shades. They guard the pilgrim's passage alongside the ruin, the cathedral, the hospice and the cairn. In time, when the record is lost, these things will be all that keep the memory of the journeys they once undertook.

This is what the road to Santiago means – different things to different people.

From Monte del Gozo, the Mountain of Joy, the pilgrim views for the first time the great city of Santiago de Compostela. The proper way to arrive in the city of the Field of Stars is to fall to your knees, burst into tears and recite the '*Te Deum*'. This is the way of the devout. Dave, Rachel and I preferred to crest the hill in silence.

We walked past a monument commemorating Pope John Paul II's 1989 pilgrimage to Compostela. The view was unexceptional from here, a skyline dominated by a sports stadium, a few old towers and some forgettable public buildings. In the foreground was the 800-pilgrim-capacity Monte del Gozo albergue, its dormitories arranged in rows.

As we walked on, the Way became a footpath stitched alongside a busy street that crossed frantic thoroughfares and intersections. The cockleshells pointed us through the Porta do Camino, the entrance to the old town. Into the city we went, Dave's staff keeping the same beat as it had when we passed through the Porte Saint Jacques back in Saint-Jean-Pied-de-Port.

We ambled along narrow streets and byways that led to ancient monuments, the city growing older the further we progressed. I peered around the austere structures and statues that impeded the view, hoping to catch sight of the cathedral that kept the holy relics. We were close now.

Dave's phone beeped its receipt of a text message. He read it out: 'Congratulations boys, look to the noticeboard in the pilgrim's office for your message, Warren.' It seemed prudent to go to collect our *compostelas* from the pilgrim's office before looking over the cathedral. Who could possibly know what sort of profanity awaited us on that noticeboard. It needed to be discarded.

Until relatively recently, those identifying themselves as pilgrims were subjected to rigorous interrogation in the cathedral sacristy to prove their claims. The booming popularity of the Camino forced the staging area for this inquisition to be moved to the slightly less grand Oficina de Acogida de Peregrinos.

The noticeboard was prominently displayed in the waiting room of the pilgrim's office. It carried messages of Christ ('God is peace'), messages of contrition and redemption ('I drank too much in Burgos, but sobered up on the Meseta'), messages of philosophy ('What a journey this was, or was it but a dream?'), and, of course, messages of slithering cliché ('Remember, pilgrim, it is the journey that matters').

In terms of impact, however, none bested Warren's message. It was written on a page torn from a large exercise book. Other notes in its immediate vicinity were scrawled on discreet pieces of paper and seemed to recoil from Warren's message in horror. It read, 'Well done ya fucking pooftas! Wazza '08'. Dave quickly peeled it from the board and threw it in a dustbin. We lingered there for a while before heading for the sacred room to be issued our *compostelas*.

Two neatly dressed women of undergraduate age sat on stools behind a fixed bench. We were on the cusp of taking part in an old ritual, poised to receive the holy document that would place us officially in the company of our long-dead kin. Dave and I gave each other a pat on the back and then we turned towards our respective inquisitors. The last step had to be taken alone.

'*Hola*,' said the young lady.

'*Buenos tardes*,' I said gallantly, '*habla Inglés?*'

'Yes,' she said. 'Do you have your documentation, *por favor?*'

I placed my pilgrim passport alongside my Australian equivalent and waited nervously as she checked my name. She was fiddling around with something under a bench, another unseen document. A sudden stab of dread plunged into me. What if this other document was some sort of personal profile of my time on the Camino? What if the wardens were actually on the church payroll reporting on the behaviour and worthiness of each pilgrim who had lodged in their albergue? I bit down on my fear and raked over the depraved and un-Christian acts that had punctuated my journey to Santiago. There were the countless nights on the booze, the repeated breaking of curfew, that outdoor setting I placed on the roof of a car, the pub brawl, the sacrilegious compositions of the Moor-slayers, and the abuse hurled at wardens. These were the acts of an unholy pilgrim. She scribbled something down on a document below my line of sight.

'Your name is Tom?' she asked.

'Yes,' I said nervously.

'I have written here, on this *compostela*, your Latin name – Thomasum.'

I gazed down at my *compostela*, admiring the decorative cursive swish of the young lady's hand.

'*Muchas gracias*,' I said to the lady.

'*De nada*.'

'Before I go,' I said, 'you wouldn't happen to have any suggestions for some cheap hotel accommodation?'

The young lady fossicked about her desk, searching for a piece of paper to scribble on. After a minute or so, she grabbed another *compostela* from its adhesive pad, tearing it away as carelessly as one might rip off a Post-it note. She folded the very holy document crudely in half, tore it cleanly down the middle and then jotted down a hotel name and an address on the back.

'Here, this one is good. *Buenos tardes*.'

I took the torn scrap of holy *compostela* and went to fulfil our quest. Dave, Rachel and I glided through annexes and along ancient streets, revelling in the deferential smiles of locals and basking in our pilgrim celebrity. We passed through an emporium of merchandise shops where stunned pilgrims, most likely returned from the cathedral, searched the streets for a new purpose. We rounded a bend that opened up into a larger annexe. A rushing tide of pilgrims hurried towards a narrow set of stairs that led below an archway. At the base of the stairs, a man dressed like a monk filled the air with the sound of his Galician bagpipes, his reptilian fingers dancing over the chanter. We dropped a euro into his hat and passed below the arch.

And there it was, the Catedral del Apóstol, lichen clinging to the baroque facade. Having seen the cathedral in countless pictures in albergues along the Camino had made it familiar. It was like returning to a place I'd been before.

Dave and I shook hands and went in briefly for a man hug that ended before it started.

Rachel went inside while we swung around to see the pilgrims gathered about the plaza. There must have been hundreds. But they seemed to fade into insignificance at the sight of an unexpected vision. Seated in the very heart of the plaza were Edward, Boris and Warren. That very strange trinity were looking in awe at the formidable building before them. We went to join them.

'You don't see this every day,' I said.

They all looked up.

'Where the fuck have you blokes —'

'Warren,' interrupted Edward very quietly. 'No need for any of that.'

'Yeah, righto, Edward.' Dave and I laughed in disbelief. Could it be that Edward had subdued the digger?

'Hey, man,' said Boris to me. 'I'm sorry I didn't talk to you back in the Melide albergue.'

'You looked like you had your hands full.'

'Anyway,' he said, ignoring me, 'I was still a bit tender over that fight we all had in Triacastela.'

'What is going on here? Don't tell me the sight of the cathedral has turned you all into peace-loving hippies.'

'I wouldn't say that,' said Edward. 'I convinced Warren that his behaviour towards Boris in Triacastela was most un-Australian. I only needed to give as an example the numerous occasions Australian soldiers and Canadian soldiers fought side by side for him to see the error of his ways.'

'I acted a little hastily,' conceded Warren with a wince. 'Turns out old big beard here isn't such a bad bloke after all. He loves a beer and a root, which makes him all right by me.'

As a peace offering, Warren had introduced Boris to a couple of Esther's friends. This was suitable compensation for the Canadian.

'What happened to the twins?' asked Dave. None of them knew. They hadn't been seen since the fight and neither of them was responding to phone calls.

We sat down alongside them and watched all the pilgrims flood into the plaza. In came Bonjour, Hi Guys and French Pipes. Bonjour rushed over to Dave and me and planted kisses on our cheeks, Hi Guys gave us both a high five and French Pipes waltzed over with cigarette in mouth. I gave him a standing ovation. To smoke non-stop for 800 kilometres was a towering achievement. I presented him with one of my Malboro Lights as acknowledgment. He exhaled in gratitude.

Then came some of the Pamplona gang: Constanza and Lorenzo holding hands, Jacob and Liz laughing madly together, and Nikki a little behind. Her eyes looked swollen and sad, but the smile across her face was for real this time. The four Argentineans were there, kicking the soccer ball with Eric the Red. Esther jogged over and hugged Warren about the neck. Even Zoe the Zealot and her boyfriend Joey were there, kneeling before the cathedral in tears. The Texan was there with her Harvard-graduate MSF-volunteering superstar. As if sensing that his intellectual status was threatened, Edward flashed his teeth and mumbled something rude under his breath. Dave, of course, had smoothed things over with the Texan in regards to the unfortunate event in Triacastela.

I walked away from them all and drank in the scene around me. Four mighty structures framed the square. To the north stood the former royal hospital the Catholic kings had built to heal the sick, lately transformed into a *parador*. Rising in the south, the great halls of Colegio Mayor de Fonseca hovered grandly. I recognised the decorative five-pointed star of the Fonseca coat of arms above the great columns that bordered its door.

Looming larger still in the west was the Palace of Rajoy, crowned with the mightiest depiction of Santiago Matamoros seen yet; his horse rampant, the apostle's face paused in an attitude of piety and his merciless sword stayed high for eternity above the cowering Moors. The Moor-slayer's eyes looked east, across the plaza to the cathedral façade, fixed on a statue carved in the centre of the gable. It was Santiago Peregrino, our patron; his staff in his hand, his granite cape captured fluttering in the Galician wind, his benevolent face shining down on the pilgrims who bore his attributes below.

I wandered back to the group and sat alongside them quietly. We each looked in awe at that cathedral, the moment meaning different things to us all. Then we emulated the most solemn ritual observed through the ages by Santiago pilgrims recently arrived in the city of the Field of Stars. We went and celebrated hard.

ALL SAINTS' DAY – RITES OF PILGRIMAGE

We returned to the Catedral del Apóstol the next day, All Saints' Day. As promised, the *botafumeiro*, the world's largest thurible, was in action, belching smoke over the north and south transepts. This was the cathedral's third *botafumeiro*. The first was replaced with a larger model donated by King Louis XI in the fifteenth century. Napoleon took that thurible back to France and it was replaced in 1851 with a silver-plated brass beauty still in use today. The giant thurible is attached to a rope fed through a pulley system from the cupola. I had read that when in motion, the *botafumeiro* describes a perfect pendulum, swinging to within centimetres of the transept vaults.

From my seat in the southern arm of the church, I noticed the 53-kilogram censer regularly breaking from its axis. At times the mighty vessel kicked out so violently that the flames that heat the incense could be seen licking up the censer's silver sides. I found out subsequently that in 1499 and 1622 the *botafumeiro* had come crashing down atop the hapless congregants below. No record was kept of any casualties.

The five men it took to heave the thurible aloft and send it on its merry swing slowly paid out the rope and brought it back to rest. The sound of court music suddenly filled the nave and a procession of musicians playing flutes, whistles, recorders and drums appeared in medieval costume leading a sarcophagus. Inside were the relics of St James. We peered around the congregation to behold the bones that set so many million pairs of feet moving across Europe. A priest slowly hauled himself up to the pulpit. The lingering incense from the *botafumeiro* shrouded him from view. I could only just make out his hand diving into his vestments, retrieving a piece of paper. He muttered a short blessing and then, from those pages, began reading yesterday's pilgrim arrivals and their nationalities.

The priest began with the pilgrims who had taken the Camino Francés, the path that has carried the faithful for the longest time. Naturally, those pilgrims who had travelled the furthest would be accorded the honour of being read out first.

'*Dos Australianos de Saint-Jean-Pied-de-Port,*' he said mellifluously. I shook Dave's hand. In all likelihood, there were other Australians in that church who had departed from the same place and arrived here on the same day. Evidently, though, only Dave and I had registered our arrival at the pilgrim's office.

After the pilgrim arrivals had been read out, Rachel and Dave quietly absented themselves. Rachel was heading back to Granada in a couple of hours, leaving Dave and me to our own devices for five more days. I gave her a hug goodbye, agreed on a bar in which to meet Dave and then listened to a soprano perform 'Ave Maria'.

There was not much more to do. In keeping with tradition, Dave and I had observed most of the rites of pilgrimage the previous day. We had kept a short vigil in front of the cathedral; through song we had given thanks to the apostle for granting us safe passage (a Moor-slayers concert was held at the bar the previous night); we had hugged the St James statue behind the altar, attended mass the following day and presumably received the blessings and indulgences.

At close quarters, we admired the work of the cathedral's architect Master Mateo, noting all the artistry and allegory woven into the Portico of Glory. We even observed the local custom of bumping heads with a carving of Mateo depicted on his knees in the cathedral, on the understanding that doing so boosts your chances of acquiring his genius. Edward had told us that he didn't believe in all this twaddle, but I did observe him knocking heads with the Master. There were other quaint rituals – placing hands on holy places and praying in certain spots – that I had intended on observing. But I was all churched out.

I slipped outside into a steady drizzle and onto the soggy streets. The final transition from pilgrim to tourist had been made. That itch that had driven my legs across Spain had been scratched. I walked around the plaza in imperfect circles, like a rudderless ship that has forgotten her purpose. All that kept the encroaching disquiet of an uncertain future at bay was an appointment I had to keep with an old friend. So I made for the rendezvous point to get a head start on Dave before he returned from the airport.

The bar was almost empty. I ordered a San Miguel and sat at a table with a good view back out onto the street. Through the window I could see others bearing down on the cathedral. Those who had performed the rites looked vaguely lost as they rummaged through merchandise shops. They all had faintly disappointed expressions, as if discovering no trinket existed that could properly capture their time on the ancient path. My walk was already slipping into memory. Soon I would be just another anonymous pilgrim among the forgotten millions.

Before the worry kicked in, something familiar caught my eye, a flash of pink wandering past the window. I could see the fire in her eyes and the cockleshell about her neck. Sally peered inside the bar and caught my gaze with a smile. With backpack on and staff in hand, she kept on walking. I raced outside and called after her, but she was already hemmed in among the tourists and pilgrims walking to the cathedral.

I quickly grabbed my gear and went searching for Sally. I walked through that old town for what seemed like hours, skating my way over rain-drenched cobblestones and peering through the mist. I went to the cathedral, the pilgrim's office, the pilgrim's museum and every other place I could think of. It was no use. Sally had been right back in Samos when she said we'd never talk again.

I laughed to myself on the way back to the bar. I was

laughing at the thought of me chasing a spiritualist through Compostela for a chat. What a change had come over me. Maybe I wanted a diagnosis for my fourth dimension after all. Maybe I wanted her to tell me the flow of prana had resumed and my chakras had healed. Maybe I wanted another dose of spiritual guidance. To be honest, I'd never gone for any of that stuff. Really I just wanted to say thanks.

The bar was filling up with pilgrims when I walked back inside. The bartender eyed me when I walked in and waved his hand around.

'*Eh, peregrino!*' Fifteen heads turned around, but he was talking to me.

'*Habla Inglés?*' I asked, walking over, thinking he was going to demand I fix up the bill for my unpaid beer.

'Your pretty friend in pink came here looking for you.' I'd missed her.

'What did she say?'

He reached under the bar and pulled out a damp and damaged envelope.

'She told me to give you this. But you don't get it until you pay for your San Miguel.' I paid for the beer and ordered another and took the envelope that I'd discarded on the cairn near Samos.

I could just make out my name, nearly smudged off by the water. I gently prised it open and pulled out the card inside just as Dave entered. As he walked through the throng of drinkers, he threw me a wave and signalled his need of a beer. I returned the card to the envelope and pushed it into my bag.

'I was thinking,' he said, gratefully taking the Grande from me, 'we've got five days to kill before you head home.'

'Got any ideas?'

'There's this pilgrimage to a place further west that the locals call the end of the world.'

'Really? That sounds like a nice little stroll. I wonder, how long does it take to walk to the end of the world?'

'Three days, apparently.'

'Sounds terrific,' I said. 'When do we leave?'

We chinked glasses, arranged a departure time, replaced the cockleshells on our packs, set our minds to this new purpose, and on the next day, we went to walk to Finisterre.

EPILOGUE

The twins joined us for the last couple of days to Finisterre. They'd discovered that Boris wasn't remarkably different to Warren and decided it was time to go it alone. They were out here with us at the Cape now, watching the fishing trawlers chug back into port.

I stared out to the offing, here at last at the end of the world, swinging like a pendulum on the fulcrum of old world and new. A firm westerly pressed my shirt against my chest like a mainsail setting fast before the wind. The Atlantic was in a lively mood, an unending broth of grey turbulence with white and orange caps. The Celts, who brought many of their customs to this part of Spain, used to call the place beyond this sea Tír na nÓg – the land of eternal youth.

With the lighthouse at my back, I stared out to that place with hopeful eyes. If you stared for long enough, you could almost make out something in the distance. But it was beyond reach, like something lived long ago. Soon enough, what I thought I saw vanished from sight, and it was all I could do to try to bring it back into my mind's eye.

It would never return. A person could become lost staring back in such a way. Better to just keep moving, just keep walking.

Other pilgrims had left us a bottle of kerosene, having completed the ritualistic burning of a piece of their own clothing. They were observing a tradition inaugurated by unknown ancients in unrecorded times. My *compadre* had doused his sweat-stained baseball cap in kerosene and set a match to the peak. He placed the burning hat in the shadow of a large stone to protect the flame from the wind.

Dave looked at me expectantly as the flame began to dwindle. This was a place of grand gestures. I extracted the last cigarette from its packet and lit up. Then I reached into my bag and pulled out my *compostela*. With one last look at my holy paper and one last pull of the smoke, I rolled the cigarette into the heart of the document and threw it onto the fire. A thin line of smoke snaked out of the flame like a warm breath exhaled into a cool night. I watched its progress as it fought bravely against the wind and then vanished across the open sea.

'What do we do now?' asked Steve of Jack.

'No idea.'

Dave stood up and slapped them both on their shoulders and then made a gesture towards the town. I pulled the card out of the envelope and tossed it at the twins' feet and went to join Dave.

'What does it say?' I heard Jack ask Steve.

'Just keep walking,' was the response.

'Where?'
'It doesn't say.'
'Bloody spiritualists. C'mon, let's go and get a beer.'

ACKNOWLEDGEMENTS

The Camino took one month to walk and two years to write about. The writing proved no less challenging than the pilgrimage itself. It could not have been done without the help and inspiration of a great many people.

Throughout my life, my parents, Mary Ann and Simon, have fulfilled many roles. At various times they have been my providers, protectors, role models, counsellors and, on occasion, my patrons. Above all else, they have been my most trusted friends. I can't thank them enough. To my sisters, Lucy and Sophie, and brothers-in-law, Damian and Paul, and niece, Patti, thanks for your love and support.

My grandmothers, Helen Trumble and Patricia Rofe, died during the editing of this book. Both were extraordinary women who stood as inspirational figureheads on either side of my family. On my part, they nurtured a love of words and music. I miss them both. To this list I include my late aunt, Sister Deirdre Rofe IBVM. My sisters and I were blessed to have had all three of these women in our lives.

I would like to acknowledge those people whose

encouragement and assistance kept me going during that period when this book seemed unlikely to see the light of day. My indomitable godfather, Angus Trumble, and my friend Tony Sidebottom gave me helpful advice and, in the case of the latter, provided me with gainful employment. Special thanks to Jaclyn Bond, who, for next to nothing, line-edited the first manuscript, turning it from an incoherent jumble into something a publisher might consider.

I am forever grateful to Andrea McNamara (no relation to Dave) for seeing something in this story and relaying to me the most superbly arranged six words I have ever heard – we want to publish your book. I thank Andrea (and hold her responsible) for making me a published author, and for assigning Bridget Maidment as my editor. Without Bridget's compassion, skill and guidance, this story would not have gone to the place it had to go.

I am deeply indebted to the pilgrims I encountered along the way to Santiago. Their identities have been disguised, with the exception of my pilgrim companion Dave and his wife, Rachel. In every way, this story depended on them all.

And so, finally, to my great mate Dave McNamara. For convincing me to walk across Spain and for holding me to a promise made at a lighthouse at the end of the world, you have my eternal thanks.